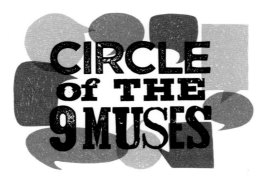

Other Books by David Hutchens

A Slice of Trust: The Leadership Secret with the Hot & Fruity Filling (with Barry Rellaford)

The Learning Fables Series

Outlearning the Wolves: Surviving and Thriving in a Learning Organization

Shadows of the Neanderthal: Illuminating the Beliefs That Limit Our Organizations

The Lemming Dilemma: Living with Purpose, Leading with Vision

The Tip of the Iceberg: Managing the Hidden Forces That Can Make or Break Your Organization

Listening to the Volcano: Conversations That Open Our Minds to New Possibilities

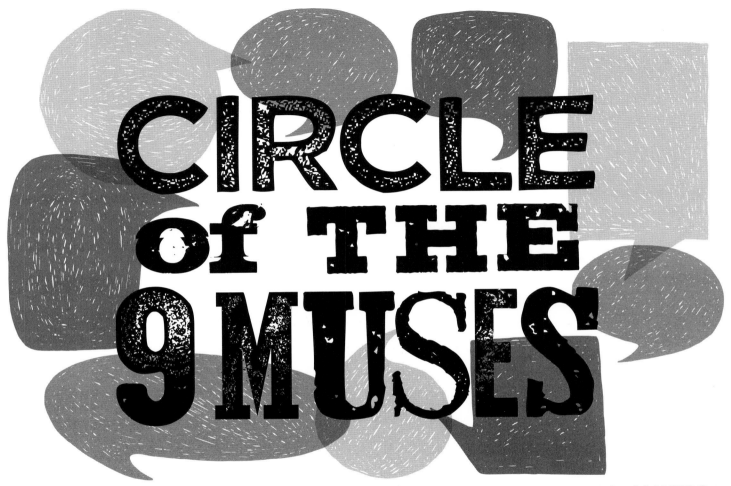

CIRCLE of THE 9MUSES

A STORYTELLING FIELD GUIDE FOR INNOVATORS AND MEANING MAKERS

DAVID HUTCHENS

WILEY

For my mother, Pat Hutchens,

story maker, author of family legacy, weaver of a narrative that extends into the future

Contents

Contents

Contents

If you are a leader, you are the

NARRATOR

Think about the role of the narrator in movies you've seen. You know, "After that magical summer, nothing was ever the same again . . ." The narrator is the voice that comments on the story and draws meaning from it.

What is the story your team is living?

Which parts of the story will you direct their attention to?

What will you say to help them draw meaning from it?

If you are a leader, you are a

CURATOR

In museums, the curator makes decisions about which pieces of art to display, and how to sequence them to tell a bigger story. "Women in the Renaissance" is a curator decision.

What is the bigger story that you want to create for your career, your team, and your organization?

What individual stories do you need to purposefully find and tell—curate—so that you can begin creating that bigger story?

Where will you find those stories? Who has them? How will you put them on display for others?

If you are a leader, you are a Storyteller

Storytelling is influence. And when you tell stories purposefully, you establish identity. Build culture. Speed the change process. Enrich the brand. Align people to the strategy. Attract talent. Engage the marketplace. Capture knowledge. Lead. Grow. Connect.

Are you telling stories?

Are you telling the right stories?

Are you telling them in ways that engage, connect, and move people?

Ready to get started?

Dispatches from a World of Stories

Scene I: A Small Club in Nashville, Tennessee

"Are you sure this is the place?"

As I pull into the cramped parking lot, my wife Robbie isn't confident.

"This is the place," I assure her as I seize upon the last parking space, and it's not hard to imagine every first-timer asking the same question. Seeing it situated in a generic strip mall between a dry cleaner and a furniture store, one would never guess that this suburban Tennessee retail space would be home to one of the most influential venues of the modern music industry.

This is the legendary Bluebird Cafe, and in Nashville where songwriting is a sacrament, the Bluebird is the high temple. This cramped 90-seat club has launched the careers of country music stars like Pam Tillis and Garth Brooks while also supplying them with many of their greatest songs. It is a nest where stories are nurtured and then released into the wild.

I lead Robbie past the locals and tourists who line the sidewalk, bundled against the cold and hoping to score a seat inside. We head straight to the VIP entrance. Tonight, we're here at the invitation of my friend Billy Kirsch, who has written songs for Wynonna Judd, Faith Hill, and many others. His songs are rich in storytelling, and one of them—titled "Holes in the Floor of Heaven"—was named the *Song of the Year* by the Country Music Association a

few years ago. As we find our way to our cramped table, we wave to Billy, who is just a few feet away from us, along with three other songwriters who are tuning their instruments and sitting in a circle facing one another. *In the round*, they call it.

As people find their seats and the show begins, there is no rowdy laughter like one hears in other clubs. The audience at the Bluebird Cafe is respectful and hushed, like parishioners waiting for church to start. With only minimal instrumentation—often just an acoustic guitar or a keyboard—these accomplished songwriters will take turns sipping their beers, singing songs, and telling stories.

Billy begins the evening by picking out just a few chords on his keyboard. The crowd immediately applauds in recognition and, as Billy starts to sing, people quietly mouth the familiar words:

> *One day shy of 8 years old*
>
> *When grandma passed away*
>
> *I was a broken-hearted little boy*
>
> *Blowing out that birthday cake . . .*

It is spellbinding. The audience members bob their heads in unison, creating an effect of waves rippling through the room. And when Billy sings the chorus—*there's holes in the floor of heaven, and her tears are pouring down—*

some people cry, some people merely close their eyes, but everyone is moved simultaneously. I watch this room full of strangers who have become an instant community through shared experience, and I am overcome by the strong sensation that we are a single organism.

It is a sacred experience—one that many here in *Music City* fear may be in danger of getting lost.

Marcus Hummon is another one of the great modern songwriters; a Grammy-winner who has penned chart-topping hits for the Dixie Chicks, Rascal Flatts, and many others. It's just a few days after my Bluebird epiphany, and we are seated in a hip coffee house frequented by health-care executives and students at nearby Vanderbilt University. Marcus and I have been talking about the unique role that story plays in classic Nashville songwriting. We talk about some of the great story-driven songs: Johnny Cash's "A Boy Named Sue" and Kenny Rogers' "The Gambler." Sipping lattes and talking about our favorite music is fun, but then Marcus' tone turns serious.

"You don't hear as many story songs as you used to," he says.

I ask why that is.

"People have a different relationship with music today," he says. "With the Internet and streaming, music is so available. It's everywhere, and now it is disposable. So today's writers are all chasing the pop hook; something

that can grab listeners immediately. I don't think this will be permanent. I hope it isn't. But it is certainly the age we are in."

"So, you're saying that people are less engaged with their music today," I say, trying to process the implications.

"Generally, yes."

"And songs that tell stories require more engagement."

"That's right. Stories demand a bigger investment and more participation from the listener."

The implications of this are fascinating. After all, my work is to advocate for stories in organizations and this is a contrarian perspective that has simply never occurred to me: If people *don't* value engagement, don't tell stories! The idea seems alien, and yet it is echoed by screenwriting legend Robert McKee. In his classic text *Story*, he suggests that Hollywood, too, has entered an age of impoverished storytelling because the public has lost its appetite for wrestling with life's biggest questions.

And yet this is precisely the opposite of what I keep encountering in my organizational world, where *everyone* is seeking greater engagement. Leaders want it. Employees want it. And although I suppose there will always exist corners of the marketplace where people demand disposable transactions, consumers are asking for greater engagement, too.

Indeed, the continued success of Marcus' and Billy's art in this chaotic music industry offers hope. It suggests that a market still exists for music that meets its listeners in a place of deep humanity. Storytelling may be vulnerable in today's entertainment industries, but story never truly goes away. And sometimes it just finds new homes, where it can find new ways to exercise its mysterious capacity to connect, engage, and bring people together.

Today, that new home is in the world of organizations. I've told Billy and Marcus, "Leaders are all looking for what you have." Billy has made precisely this shift by developing a storytelling and songwriting experience that he now brings to organizational teams all around the world.[1]

Story never goes away. It is always here. And today in the organizational world, storytelling has become the hot, new idea that isn't new at all.

Scene II: A Cave in the South of France, 1994

A wall of ancient stone gives way, raising a cloud of dust in the cold December air. Three explorers lift their lights, throwing yellow beams into a cavern that hasn't been disturbed by light in more than 30,000 years. Through the fog of their frozen breaths, the three astonished explorers first spy tiny footprints in the sand, left by some

1. Explore Billy's program at www.kidbillymusic.com

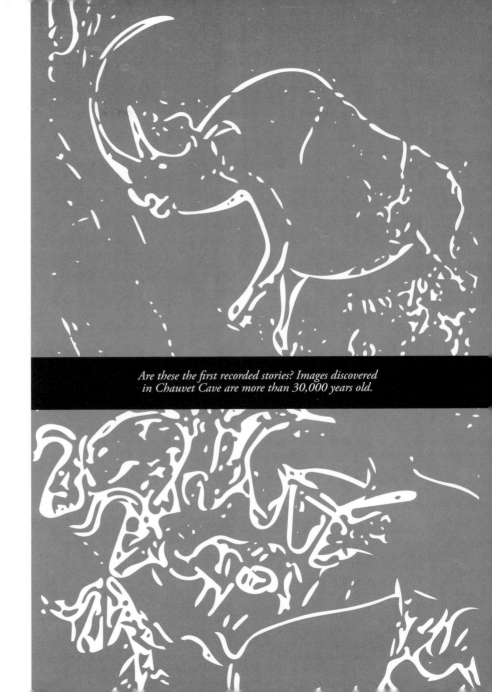

Are these the first recorded stories? Images discovered in Chauvet Cave are more than 30,000 years old.

Paleolithic child who could never have dreamed they would become a source of wonder to these future members of the race.

Then they point their lights to the walls . . . and are immediately transported into a world of stories. Marvelous stories; stories that require no special skills for translation, depicting narratives of hunting and survival, animal mating cycles, and shamanic rituals; all presented in movements that a novelist or screenwriter would now refer to as *scenes*.

Chauvet Cave, now a designated World Heritage Site, gives us our very earliest glimpses of the human capacity for storytelling. What is remarkable is how well-formed the ancient capability appears to be.

When the Epic of Gilgamesh was discovered in 1853 on clay tablets that were merely a few thousand years old, we found that the ancient practice of what we might now call *story theory* had made astonishing advances. There are sophisticated narrative arcs with themes; heroes and villains; drama and intrigue; sexual betrayal; surprise twists.

If we were to time-travel across the ages, wherever we landed we would find communities of human beings: in circles, gathered around scrolls, around cave paintings, around campfires. And they would be telling stories. I imagine the child who left those footprints in Chauvet Cave, sitting in the circle as the tribal elders narrate the cave paintings, listening with rapt attention, her upturned face illuminated by flickering light, her imagination ablaze.

This is how it's always been. Across the ages, across cultures, across contexts, stories are our first path to community, to connection, to survival, to the collective act of meaning making.

And today's tribes are asking if stories are capable of doing even more.

Scene III: A Conference Room Somewhere in Paris

Jump forward 30,000 years. I'm in a brightly lit conference room where an iPad is connected to a digital projector that allows participants in the audience to stream images to the wall, bringing spontaneous, crowd-sourced meaning to our storytelling.

But, at its core, nothing has changed.

This international group of executives is sitting in a semicircle, their faces all relaxed in universal expressions of unselfconscious wonder that are common to all cultures. They are listening to one of their own—a soft-spoken woman who doesn't like speaking before a group and who earlier told me she wasn't a storyteller.

Oh, but she is! She is here from the Asia-Pacific affiliate of this global consumer products corporation, and she struggles with her English, but the executives are spellbound.

She is telling the group a story about innovation, which is the topic we are all here to explore at this leadership summit; but her story is about much more. Speaking barely above a whisper, hers is a story about her team's bravery, fear, resilience, and dignity in the wake of her manufacturing site's biggest setback. Her story speaks to the deepest aspirations of everyone in the room. She has no idea how good she is or how much power she has at this moment.

I see the Director of Finance in the audience, and he is biting his lip because he doesn't want to be seen getting teary-eyed at this corporate event. He's not the only one. Everyone was aware of the manufacturing setback in terms of the financial implications, but they've never heard this side of the story; not told like this. For everyone in this executive audience, the values of the organization have never felt so urgent or personal or alive. Later I hear one leader say, "This demands action," and he's exactly right because that is what the best stories do.

"Why does this work?" one of the executives asks later, trying to understand the implications of this moving experience to the work of his organization. "What are we supposed to do with this?"

Those are the questions everyone is asking. This is where the modern discourse around story offers new lenses and

insights that were unavailable to the storytellers in Chauvet Cave.

I explain how the still-new lens of neuroscience demonstrates that our brains are doing all kinds of acrobatics every time we tell or hear a story. For example, we know now that when you hear a story, the neurons in your brain will activate in the very same patterns as the neurons in my brain when I'm telling it in a phenomenon called *neural coupling*. (One theory suggests that our brains have *mirror neurons* that join peoples' minds in these parallel mental states.)

And we also know that the more dramatic elements of the story will flood your body and elevate your heart rate with the flight-or-fight hormone *cortisol,* and that the satisfying or redemptive resolution to the story will flush your nervous system with pleasing *oxytocin.* (Recent studies even suggest that this specific cortisol/oxytocin two-step is much more likely to move people to open their checkbooks and give—a tantalizing prospect for those in nonprofits who seek to connect storytelling to their fundraising.[2])

My group of executives digs these geeky neuroscience explanations because it gives them a chance to dry their eyes and regain their composure. The data gives credibility and validation to what the authors of Gilgamesh or the writers of Nashville's hit songs have known all along, which is

2 Paul Zak, *The Moral Molecule: The Source of Love and Prosperity* (Dutton Adult, 2012).

that story is almost magical for its ability to move people to do something.

Another executive, sipping her coffee, asks: "Why is this old idea coming back now?"

Ours is a crazy world. You may have noticed this. Much has been said about today's *volatile, uncertain, complex, ambiguous* (VUCA) environment. Change is happening fast—too fast—and people in organizations are exhausted. It's all whitewater rapids, all the time, and for a workforce barely able to keep up, anything that offers continuity of identity and meaning is a life raft. And story is all about continuity, an answer to the question, "What does it mean to be us?" It is the mind's most effortlessly efficient technology for creating persistent threads of meaning, purpose, and identity in worlds gone crazy. It is more than entertainment and more than a social experience. It

is a survival capability. McKee calls story "equipment for living."

A lot of the most fascinating work in storytelling is currently emerging from the growing discipline of *knowledge management*. The idea goes like this. We are living in the age of information, and there are some kinds of information that are easy to capture. Data points, outputs, events, and processes can all be jotted down and documented in an Excel spreadsheet. All good. But then there's that *other* kind of information—you know, the deeper stuff, the good stuff, like *knowledge* and *wisdom*—that behaves differently. It's rich and robust and you can't put it in a spreadsheet. Leaders need a different kind of container in order to capture, understand, and draw meaning from that kind of complex information. It turns out that story is the most efficient container for wisdom.

Types of knowledge in organizations. As you move to the right, the knowledge becomes increasingly difficult to capture. It's the hard stuff, where story becomes increasingly important.

Modified from Harold Jarche's framework, "Codifying Knowledge Artifacts."

 Outputs

 Events

 Processes

 Decisions

 Meaning / connections

 Wisdom / Knowledge / Expertise

need for storytelling increases

This is especially urgent because the generation known as the Baby Boomers are about to create a mass knowledge crisis by retiring from their organizations all at once. Decades of priceless knowledge will exit with them. Before they go, we'd better ask them to tell us their stories.

If the modern need for story is being driven from inside organizations, it is also being pulled from the outside. The marketplace is demanding more humanism from companies. Customers want to see authenticity, motive, and purpose. They want to know how the ingredients in their food were grown, where the materials in their cars come from, how the product or offering got there, who the people are who made it, what motivated them to make it, and more. They want to know your story, and if you've got an authentic one that connects to their deep aspirations, they're buying.

Likewise, the *war for talent* will hinge on your firm's ability to articulate a story. Those talented young knowledge workers that you want to hire don't have salary at the top of their list of motivational drivers, and they aren't all that impressed by the corporate sushi bar or the pool table in the break room. No, they want to do something meaningful. They want to be part of a story that is worthy of their belief, and they will bring their gifts to the company that provides it.

People in the organization want continuity. Customers want engagement. The new generational worker wants meaning. A storm is brewing, and today's leaders are going back to their toolboxes looking for new paths to influence and sense making, and *hey!* there's story, gathering dust at the bottom, ready for rediscovery. It helps that it is an innate capability and the brain's most effortless path for parsing information. You will exercise this capability over dinner tonight, and you probably won't even pause to recognize that's what you're doing. Perhaps there is a place for this most-human capability in the C-suite, if only we can figure out how to connect it to the work.

In the corporate boardroom, however, this *soft* and *slow* capability has been viewed with suspicion for such a long time that some now find it difficult to reawaken; difficult, but not overly so. All you need is a little bit of purposeful intent and a touch of imagination.

It All Began with a Sheep

I fell into this work by accident. In 1998, I was living in Atlanta, Georgia, where I began my career as an advertising copywriter ("brand is a story") and then as a communications consultant and learning designer. It was at about that time my colleagues at The Coca-Cola Company asked me to develop a communication tool to introduce an idea that people in that organization were struggling to understand. It was Peter Senge's idea of a "learning organization," which was still a relatively new body of

My journey into the world of leadership storytelling began with a sheep named Otto.

Outlearning the Wolves *suggests that the antidote to organizational fear and reactivity is learning. Although the fable is short and playful, the story yields rich conversations.*

theory. The promise of the learning organization represented a vision that many people found to be challenging and abstract.

So I wrote a story for Coke. It told the story of a flock of sheep that outwits a pack of hungry wolves and, in the process, they become a learning organization. Illustrated by my buddy, talented illustrator Bobby Gombert, I titled the manuscript *Outlearning the Wolves*.

When Coca-Cola didn't pick up the unconventional little project, a forward-thinking New England publisher with ties to the organizational learning community did. *Outlearning the Wolves* ultimately became the lead title in a series of books that today are known around the world as the *Learning Fables*. The books have been translated into more than a dozen languages and have found audiences in MBA programs, executive C-suites, and fourth grade classrooms. I continue to hear stories from organizations

of all kinds about how they have used the *Learning Fables* to drive organizational dialogue—and action—around learning, mental models, systems thinking, and more.

Why did that work? At the time I didn't know. I also didn't quite appreciate (at least, not consciously) that I was stumbling into one of the most potent forces for engagement and transformation for knowledge-era organizations.

In many ways my career since 1998 has been an attempt to extend the applications of that discovery. The timing was good because the all-whitewater-all-the-time age of the Internet was just around the corner, and all of a sudden everyone was asking questions:

Why stories, and why now?

Which stories are the *right* stories to tell?

How can I tell my stories better?

How can stories bring my people, my customers, and my other partners together?

How do stories connect to my most urgent initiatives, like *change management, knowledge management, culture and identity, engagement, branding, innovation, attracting talent, articulating vision and purpose, fund raising*, and more?

This is where *Circle of the 9 Muses: A Storytelling Field Guide for Innovators and Meaning Makers* comes in. This book is indeed a field guide, filled with ideas that are immediately actionable for bringing the wisdom of story into your most pressing work. It draws from my own experiments and experiences in helping leaders all around the world find, tell, and draw meaning from their stories. Importantly, it also draws from the best practices of some of the smartest thinkers, facilitators, and prophets in the global organizational story space. These are ideas that have been developed, tested, and refined in the practices of some of the most innovative business and social initiatives of our time.

Circle of the 9 Muses is about action. These pages are filled with ideas, processes, templates, activities, exercises, and more than a few flights of whimsy. To connect *Circle of the 9 Muses* to your work, you don't need to be a professional facilitator or an organizational learning consultant. Rather, this book is for anyone who leads other people . . . and who hopes to lead those people to a more human place where innovation thrives and opportunity abounds. As a leader who also happens to be a human being, you are already equipped with the basic capacities for bringing many of these ideas to your next team meeting, learning program, retreat . . . or any informal gathering in which you wish to unleash the collective genius of the team.

Ultimately, the intent of *Circle of the 9 Muses* is not to instruct you, but to remind you. Sure, you will discover lots and lots of new techniques for connecting story to your most urgent imperatives. But they are all based on the most innate human impulse for meaning making.

Behind all of the techniques and processes, *Circle of the 9 Muses* is really about permission: Permission to recapture your human voice. Permission to lead from your passion, emotion, and vulnerability. Permission to reveal your and your team's aspirations, beliefs, authentic selves, and the things you hold most dear by doing what every tribe, culture, and society has done since they began using language to create meaning around the camp fire: telling stories.

David Hutchens

March, 2015

Nashville, Tennessee

What's Inside

Circle of the 9 Muses contains dozens of tools and processes with nearly endless variations that can enable your work as a leader. As a field guide, *Circle of the 9 Muses* isn't meant to be read in order from front to back (although if that sounds like fun to you, then go for it). Instead, pick a tool or chapter or process that looks interesting to you. Each provides links to multiple other tools in the book, so you'll quickly forge your own unique path through these pages. Here's a peek at what you will find inside.

THE FUNDAMENTALS

You may wish to begin your explorations here. These are the processes and disciplines that are foundational to much of the material throughout this book.

A lot of leaders ask, "Which stories should I tell?" Tell these. This is a simple construct for helping leaders think about the kinds of stories they should be strategically finding and sharing in order to build their own leadership and develop the organization.

Page 31

When you place people in circles to tell stories to one another, it's like summoning the Greeks' nine muses who bring gifts of wisdom and knowledge. A story circle is a timeless construct of human interaction, but in organizational settings it requires some purposeful planning. Here's how to create a successful story circle for your next gathering.

Page 45

Stories are extremely sensitive to context and framing. How you ask for stories matters. Here you will explore the nuances of the framing question so that you can generate a rich story experience every time.

Page 59

A lot of leadership storytelling is spontaneous and rough around the edges; but there are times when you want to tell the most compelling story, in the most compelling way. Explore story theory from anthropologists, Hollywood script consultants, and folklorists. Then work through a step-by-step process that will imbue *your* stories with that *edge of your seat* quality.

Page 73

BRANCHING OUT

Ready to start connecting stories to the most urgent work of your team and organization? These innovative processes have been developed and tested in the most influential organizations in the world . . . and now we've made them actionable and accessible for leaders like you.

A natural extension of story circles, *twice-told stories* is a fun group process for helping the most compelling stories emerge. It provides a natural filtering mechanism and demonstrates the *viral* quality that stories can have. But there's much more to this exercise! It makes some dramatic statements about the bigger story that we are all living — and creating — together.

Page 103

Once the story has been told, the real work is just beginning. This exercise will help your team build its capacity for *meaning making* — having the important conversations about what they heard from the storyteller and her story. It will also help you to explore easy-to-implement ideas for responding to stories with conversations that matter.

Page 115

The story circle is at the heart of your work as a storytelling leader. The format is so basic and simple that it invites creative iterations and innovative approaches. Here are a few variations from the world's top story innovators that you can use to unleash your team's genius.

Page 131

Identify the voice of your brand, your offering, or even your own leadership by connecting it to *archetypes* — the deep story patterns that are encoded into our subconscious minds. The result of this exercise is a deep and shared awareness of who you are as the protagonist of your own story. The result? Stories that create indelible awareness among your many audiences.

Page 145

The ultimate destination of leadership is the future, and it's an urgent topic for your storytelling. In this fun and simple exercise from the discipline of scenario planning, members of your team or organization will identify possible scenarios for your work by crafting stories about the future.

Page 163

Encounter a remarkably simple, visually driven exercise for recreating the story of your (or your team's or your family's or your organization's) history. This is a fun activity that will give you a bird's-eye perspective of your experiences while also drawing fresh wisdom from them.

Page 171

Fractal Narratives

One of the roles of a leader is to define the bigger story that your team is living. When you define this broader *metanarrative*, you create an opportunity for team members to bring it to life with their individual stories. This practical exercise will provide you with some frameworks to define the larger story and invite others to be a part of it.

Page 181

Fractal Narratives & The Hero's Journey

Joseph Campbell's *Hero's Journey* is a massively influential story construct that is at the heart of the grand narratives told by ancient civilizations, world religions, novelists, and Hollywood hit makers. It can also be a powerful way to define the dramatic journey of your work so you can invite others to start telling their stories.

Page 189

Story Element Extraction

There's a lot of meaning in the stories that you and your colleagues have generated across the many exercises in *Circle of the 9 Muses*. This exercise provides team members with an active way to start discovering the buried themes, patterns and knowledge that lie hidden just beneath the surface.

Page 199

"We are *here*. We are going *there*." This *creative tension* construct is one of the fundamental cores of your leadership storytelling. This visually driven exercise is very easy to deliver, and yet it generates powerful insights into each team member's own capacity for leadership and change.

Page 207

It's a core task of leadership: identifying a course of action, and then influencing people to come along. So much strategy communication centers on goals, numbers, and metrics. By positioning the strategy as a narrative, you help connect it to the deepest aspirations of the people in the organization.

Page 215

This classic exercise uses storytelling and visual thinking to generate fresh innovation for your offerings. This simplified version of storyboarding is inspired by disciplined techniques employed by some of Silicon Valley's (and the world's) most influential innovation incubators.

Page 229

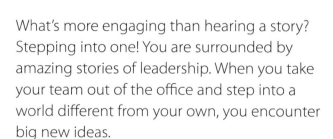

What's more engaging than hearing a story? Stepping into one! You are surrounded by amazing stories of leadership. When you take your team out of the office and step into a world different from your own, you encounter big new ideas.

Page 243

With digital tools (such as smartphones, tablet computers, and more) it has never been easier to craft and distribute your stories in fresh, compelling, and fun ways. The technology is changing fast, with new possibilities being generated all the time. This chapter will offer a peek at the possibilities and inspire your own exploration.

Page 255

Stepping into the Stream

I have a lot of people to thank. *Circle of the 9 Muses* is built on the practices and emerging thinking of the most innovative practitioners in organizational storytelling. In the earliest stages of brainstorming for this project, there were moments I was unsure of this approach. After all, I have a few ideas of my own and isn't that the whole reason one writes a book?

Those thoughts vanished the instant I stepped into the global community of story thought leaders.

To call this tribe *generous* may sound like empty praise. It isn't. It says everything about their orientation to their craft. When compiling this manuscript, I insisted that each collaborator should protect their own intellectual property and withhold their secret sauce if they felt even a hint of hesitation about sharing it with the world. It was a sensitivity they did not share. Several made the observation that story doesn't *belong* to anyone. Although many fields in management consulting have their own self-appointed gurus and geographic concentrations of ego, storytelling is timeless and boundaryless and its greatest practitioners see themselves as stewards who have simply waded out into a stream of ageless origin.

What a marvelous experience it is to collaborate in this community! Suddenly, Nashville, Tennessee felt like it was right next door to my friends in Israel, Denmark, New Zealand, London, Australia, South Africa, and many other far-flung places where brilliant people have dedicated their careers to experimenting with groundbreaking ideas.

And they have no hesitation in sharing those ideas with you.

Throughout *Circle of the 9 Muses*, I have taken great effort to attribute ideas to their sources. This was in some cases a maddening pursuit, with many practitioners offering iterations of iterations of something similar they heard someone else tried somewhere. How does one trace attribution to any given handful of water scooped from an ocean? If I have made errors in my efforts to acknowledge this community of collaborators, I ask for both your forgiveness and correction.

Detailed biographies of the many contributors appear in an Appendix of this book. Go take a look. You will want to work with them. Their deep wells of wisdom are just a click away. I urge you to step into their circles.

Briefly, here are those who have contributed their innovations to this work.

Here are the story practitioners who generously shared their time, their best ideas, their enthusiasm, and their friendship. You will find them referenced throughout many of the practices detailed in Circle of the 9 Muses:

- Mary Alice Arthur
- Madelyn Blair
- Bobette Buster
- Shawn Callahan
- Slash Coleman
- Paul Costello
- Karen Dietz
- Terrance Gargiulo
- Robbie Hutchens
- Michelle James
- Kat Koppett
- Per Kristiansen
- Cynthia Kurtz
- Jody Lentz
- Michael Margolis
- Christine Martell
- Thaler Pekar

- Barry Rellaford
- Limor Shiponi
- David Sibbet
- Lori Silverman
- Annette Simmons
- Paul Smith
- Graham Williams

Other friends and story practitioners whose great work has fueled my imagination:

- Bob Dickman
- Peter Durand
- Kendall Haven
- David Lee
- Raf Stevens

My Nashville musical storytellers:

- Marcus Hummon
- Billy Kirsch

Organizational storytelling does indeed have practitioners that I consider to be gurus. Above I listed those with whom I collaborated in the development of this book. Below are the thinkers who contributed only indirectly to this project. Some of them are no longer with us. But from afar, these have left their unmistakable fingerprints on the ideas you'll find herein. Most have books that you will find listed in the bibliography:

- Bruno Bettelheim

- David Boje

- Joseph Campbell

- Stephen Denning

- Robert McKee

- Gareth Morgan

- Carol Pearson

- Jim Signorelli

- Dave Snowden

- Christopher Vogler

My partners who have explored these ideas at some of the greatest learning organizations in the world, including:

The Conference Board, where we created the world's greatest "step into the story" learning experiences, with the Team USA Leadership Experience (at the U.S. Olympic Training Center), the Apollo Leadership Experience (at NASA's Johnson Space Center), and the Gettysburg Leadership Experience.

- Jeff Jackson

- Dick Richardson, my long-time friend and mentor in the learning space

- James Sayno, partner at the U.S. Olympic Committee, home of the storytelling program "Team USA Leadership Experience"

- Harv Hartman (retired) NASA historian for the Apollo Leadership Experience

INSEAD and CEDEP, who have provided a beautiful, globally inclusive learning playground in Fontainebleau, France. Here, learning leaders are experimenting with these ideas in an intoxicating environment of innovation. Merci beaucoup, mes amis:

- Jens Meyer

- Loic Sadoulet

- Frank Azimont

- Thomas Hinterseer

- Thierry Bonetto

- Sharon, Helen, and the rest of the terrific team that makes it happen

- Cam Danielson of Mesa Research Group

- Meryem Le Saget, who made a critical connection at precisely the right time.

FranklinCovey Speed of Trust Practice

- Stephen M. R. Covey, whose stories come from the heart.

The Tampa, Florida learning crowd:

- David Milliken and Robert Coates of Blueline Simulations

- Donna Burnette of Tango Learning, a longtime friend who is on the short list of "my tireless champions." *(Thank you.)*

- David Dauman of Solutions House

The Atlanta/Coca-Cola contingent:

- Teresa Hogan, who was there at the very beginning of all of this, and who pointed the way. Hugs and love to you, T; and all of my other Coke learning buddies (Dianne Culhane, Renee Moorefield; Joe Simonet; Amy White).

The Pegasus crowd: Man, those were the days, weren't they?

- Mark Alpert

- Ginny Wiley

- Janice Molloy

- Eric Kraus

And the rest of the tireless folks who made the Pegasus dream burn so brightly:

- Peter Senge, Daniel Kim, Robert Fritz

- Bobby Gombert who brought all those talking animals to life and charmed the world

- Otto, Boogie, and the other crazy protagonists from the *Learning Fables* who I consider to be friends. Those googly-eyed talking animals somehow persuaded the world's most effective leaders to put on puppet shows, dress up in weird costumes, make movies, mount stage productions, and otherwise abandon all normal sense of decorum in the pursuit of

organizational transformation through storytelling
and learning.

- All of those advertising agencies I worked at as a
young copywriter, where we agonized for hours and
over weekends over words, images, metaphors, and
stories for the purpose of leading people though the
stages of awareness, interest, desire, and action. It was
the best possible beginning to this journey.

Love to my family:

- Robbie, my coauthor of the glorious future story
which we are now stepping into.

- Emory and Ollie, who provide dramatic arcs, comic
relief, and subtext that is endlessly deep.

- Mom. Dad. *See? I told you this would work.*

9 Muse Story Recipes

Organizational story practitioners discover early in their work that there really aren't that many companies asking for help with storytelling. This is a painful realization, as it would be for anyone who discovers that the magic elixir they're selling isn't on the hearts and minds of everyone with a checkbook. But it's true. Many of the leaders I work with do not express a need for better stories, or more stories, or any stories at all. Some are even suspicious of story work.

What they ask for is something very different. They seek greater alignment. Deeper engagement (in the company and across their marketplace). Strategic alignment. Richer marketplace dialogue. The ability to manage change. The ability to archive the organization's deep wisdom. Influence. Relevance. Fire. *That's* what leaders are seeking.

Story is merely the way. It is the operating system that delivers an electric jolt of context and meaning that brings to life many of the most urgent imperatives of the organization.

What brings you to *Circle of the 9 Muses*? It may be that you are indeed looking for storytelling resources. (If so, welcome aboard, kindred spirit.) It is also likely that you have other outcomes in mind—with applications as diverse as branding, team development, change and strategy work, organizational development, and more. You're welcome here, too, as *Circle of the 9 Muses* is indeed a field guide, filled with ideas that can support you in your diverse leadership efforts.

In that spirit, the following *recipe cards* suggest opportunities for stringing together different *9 Muse* resources in different combinations to achieve your desired outcomes.

A word about the recipe metaphor, because it is the nature of metaphor to reveal our hidden assumptions about the world. In my bayou upbringing just outside of New Orleans, Louisiana, a recipe is merely a suggestion, and a jumping-off point for experimentation. This has been a point of difference between my literal, rule-following wife and me. Oh, it says to add a clove a garlic? Why don't we add six cloves of garlic and also a half-teaspoon of cayenne pepper? And let's throw in some brown sugar and see what happens. The resources in *Circle of the 9 Muses* are infinitely configurable, and invite your tinkering. In that spirit, then, these are basic recipes; suggestions. You're welcome to give it a try as written, but rewards await those who are willing to throw in a little okra, shrimp, Tabasco, or whatever you have on hand until the outcome is uniquely yours.

And as always, please share your ideas! Write to me at David@DavidHutchens.com

Branding Recipes

> **I want to identify the unique voice of my product, service, or offering.**

Use "Leadership Story Archetypes" to identify the unique "voice" of your offering and connect it to deeply felt human needs; host story circles around your values or use "Stories in Words" (from "Story Circle Variations") to refresh connection to your mission statement. Seek your customers' insights via "The Client Sets the Frame" (also in "Story Circle Variations.") Use "Story Element Extraction" to begin uncovering the deep meaning that is woven throughout your diverse stories.

> **I want to find stories that will engage my customers or marketplace.**

Create occasions for story circles, and begin collecting the "4 Core Stories" of your work, including stories of "identity" and "values in action." Use "Twice-Told Stories" so the group can begin to surface especially powerful stories together and also to begin creating a shared archive of stories. Explore "Digital Storytelling" for fresh ideas for bringing those stories to life.

> **I want to improve my "elevator pitch" or "About" page on my website**

Use "Leadership Story Archetypes" to identify the unique voice of your offering. Modify the pitch to different audiences using "Story Carousel," and use "Stories in Words" for new insights that come from the heart of your mission. (You will find both of those exercises in "Story Circle Variations"). Use the "Story Distilling" variation to start bringing the story down to its essence. Use "Capturing Fire" to begin improving the style, energy, and presentation dynamics of your story.

> **I want my constituents to be engaged and active in my offering.**

Host story circles in which you invite constituents to share their stories (NOT to tell them to embrace your story!) Use the story listening and meaning making methods in "Summoning the Muse" to create shared and deepened awareness around each others' stories. "Digital Storytelling" suggests lots of opportunities for easily and inexpensively capturing your customers' stories so that you can begin connecting them to your story. Then use "Story Element Extraction" to begin identifying the core truths that unite all stories. Explore "Strategy is a Story" and consider rendering your story visually using a story map.

Team Building/ Relationship Building Recipes

> ### We are a new team and need to get to know each other.

Consider creating a *third space* occasion (perhaps in a retreat setting) and use "Twice-Told Stories" to create affiliation with the broader team story. Get to know each other with "Visual Timelines." Use "Getting Personal" stories (from "Story Circle Variations") to bring your "whole person" to the team. Use the "Visual Timeline" to share the unique journeys that led each of you to this shared place. Talk about the future you will create together using "Creative Tension Pictures." Use "Leadership Story Archetypes" so each team member can explore his or her unique identity as the protagonist of their leadership story.

> ### We are stuck in conflict.

Be especially mindful how you frame the dialogue using "Story Prompts." Use "Creative Tension Pictures" for a powerful way to externalize the conflict with reduced defensiveness, and dialogue around the future you both desire. Host a story circle using a timeline (as described in "Fractal Narratives") as a mining structure; be vigilant about reinforcing the ground rules (no disagreement;

respond to a story with a story.) For deep conflicts, consider the intervention of an external facilitator.

> ### We are a strong team. Nothing is wrong. We just want to be even better.

Almost everything in *Circle of the 9 Muses* can help you! Be creative in establishing a *third space* or retreat for narrative work. Create multiple occasions for story circles; use "Fractal Narratives" to be more purposeful about creating the shared story and "Leadership Archetypes" for a penetrating conversation into the unique "voice" and strength of the team. Focus on future stories using "Creative Tension Pictures."

> ### I/my team needs inspiration, or to reconnect with my/our passion

Create a story circle and share your "Why I'm Here" stories. Tell "Stories in Words" to bring new energy to the mission. Tell "Twice-Told Stories" to connect individual stories to the bigger story you are living. Use the story listening and meaning making methods in "Summoning the Muse" to create shared and deepened awareness around each others' stories. Use "Creative Tension" pictures and make it a personal exercise: "Where I am today in my leadership" and "where I need to be."

Leadership, Strategy, and Change Management Recipes

> Things need to change around here. We need to create a shared understanding of where to go next.

Consider bringing a narrative flow to your strategy communications using "Strategy Is a Story," or invite teams to help define the strategy by creating storyboards as described in "Strategy Is a Story" storyboarding. Ask each member of the team to draw "Creative Tension Pictures" as it relates to the change. Have them take turns describing "Here's how I see our current reality . . . and also our desired future state." Use "Future Story Spine" to identify possible futures, and the paths that will take you there.

> I want people to lead with agility when the way forward isn't clear.

Be prepared for future possibilities by using the "Future Story Spine." Use the "Hero's Journey" (in "Fractal Stories") to put the current stories in the context of the *big picture* story. Use "Creative Tension Pictures" to enable people to define their own unique visions for moving forward.

> I have a big presentation coming up, and I want my audience to be blown away.

Consider your Four Core Stories for possible narratives that come from the heart of your leadership. Practice your stories with trusted colleagues using the harvester/witness construct in "Summoning the Muse." Then spend time thinking through the structure of your story in the chapter "Capturing Fire." (Hot tip: Look for opportunities to engage emotions as described in "The King and The Queen" section of "Capturing Fire.")

Organizational Development Recipes

> Actually, I'm one of those people who just wants more storytelling in my organization.

I like the way you think! Everything in *Circle of the 9 Muses* is game for your exploration, but you may want to begin with the basics: Host lots of Story Circles. Begin capturing the "Four Core Stories"; become skilled with "Story Prompts" and eliciting stories in effective ways; find multiple occasions for story circles, combined with larger metanarratives as laid out in the "Fractal Narratives." Those are the building blocks. Start there, and begin exploring and branching out!

We are trying to become more innovative.

Have team members "Create Your Own Creativity Model" (from "Innovation Storyboarding") for a deep discussion into the nature of creating in this team. Take a story field trip as described in "Step into a Story" for expansive thinking; then after you return to your organization use the "Innovation Storyboard," for defining new offerings or rethinking current offerings.

We need a more cohesion/a shared identity/awareness of one another's roles.

Have members create story boards around a topic like "A Day in our Life." (Ideas for designing this process can be found in "Storyboarding Frameworks.") Then present your storyboards to one another for deeper shared awareness of one another's roles. Host an "Organizational Movie Night" with employee-created videos, as described in "Digital Storytelling." Use Story Archetypes to identify the unique "voice" of your offering and connect it to deeply felt human needs. Host Story Circles around your values or using "Stories in Words" (from "Story Circle Variations") to refresh connection to your mission statement.

Part I

Fundamentals

Use the Four Core Stories when you want to think broadly about your role as a storytelling leader, to begin building the identity of your team and organization, and to create engagement around your most critical leadership tasks.

Chapter 1

THE 4 CORE STORIES

For this exercise, you will need:

- A quiet place and some time to reflect

- A method of capturing your stories, such as a word processor, a diary, or a note-taking application, such as Evernote

"Which stories should I tell?"

This was the question of a leader from a global luxury products organization based in Copenhagen.

Yes. That is the question.

He didn't ask, "How can I tell better stories?" or even "What dramatic details should I include in my stories?" His question was about selection rather than construction or content, and that's where we must begin.

A central conviction of *Circle of the 9 Muses* is that the storytelling leader is purposeful and strategic about selecting and sharing stories, even if he or she doesn't tell the story particularly well. Start with getting the right story at the right time for the right reason. Sure, your style of delivery has an impact, which I will talk about later, but for leaders I maintain that style is secondary. I always see people breathe a sigh of relief in my programs when I tell them, "This is not a lesson in presentation skills or becoming a better public speaker." You can stumble and stutter your way through an adequately delivered story, but if it is the right story, it can change your world.

A lot of storytelling is spontaneous. It happens in the hallways, over coffee, and at lunch. It is fluid and responsive to what is happening in the moment. But it becomes an act of influence when it is intentional, deliberate, and preconsidered. The strategic leader is always on the lookout for the narrative assets—the especially valuable stories—that are so important they need to be shared with constituents over and over. These are the core stories of your leadership.

Many frameworks suggest that there are certain categories of organizational stories. In her book *The Story Factor*, my friend Annette Simmons poses an influential framework that says leaders tell six primary kinds of stories in organizations.[1] Another colleague, Paul Smith, is a former Procter & Gamble researcher who wrote a book where he laid out 21 unique story types that leaders should be mindful of.[2]

So, which is right? Are there six kinds of stories? Are there 21?

There are probably a million types of stories that leaders in organizations can tell. But a review of story frameworks reveals common elements that are broadly comprehensive to the tasks of leadership—whether you are the chief executive officer (CEO) of a multinational organization, or you lead a team in a rural school district or small community organization.

These are the *Four Core Stories* of your work. And as a leader, you are the curator of your team's or organization's identity. Think about the curator of a museum. The

1. *The Story Factor: Inspiration, Influence, and Persuasion Through the Art of Storytelling*, 2nd ed., Basic Books, 2006
2. *Lead with a Story: A Guide to Crafting Business Narratives That Captivate, Convince, and Inspire*, AMACOM, 2012

curator's role is to make decisions about which images to hang on the wall and what stories to present to the public (e.g., Cubism in Italy). Likewise, as a leader your role is to constantly be on the lookout for these stories, collect new ones, and find opportunities to tell them over and over so that you can be purposeful about shaping your organizational system.

The Four Core Stories are:

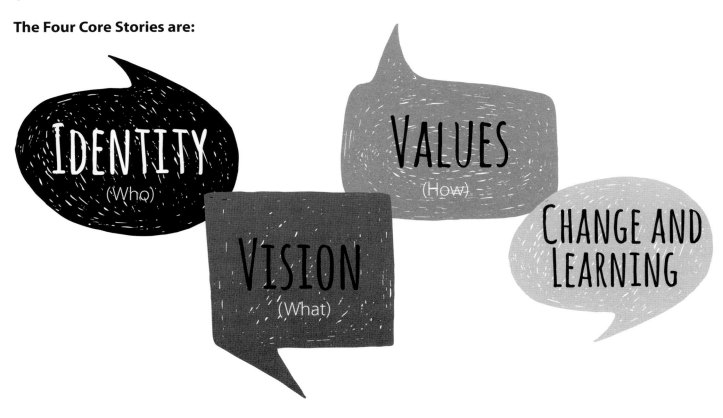

34

 Identity Stories

"What does it mean to be us?" This is the sacred center of storytelling. It's a question we answer in America every time we sing the story that is "The Star-Spangled Banner" or during a Passover Seder when the youngest child present invokes the *Haggadah*—the story of the exodus from Egypt—by saying, "Why is this night different from all other nights?"

One critical subset of the identity story is the *origin* story. When did your organization (or your team, your project, or your career) start? What was true at the beginning of the organization that is still true today? These stories hold unique power! The DNA of your identity is in there, and when you tell these stories, you refocus your colleagues on what's important in ways that are nearly impossible to argue with.

One of the great origin/identity stories comes from General Electric (GE). Here is how it articulates that story. (I know this because I was the copywriter for its website!)

> The year was 1876, America's centennial. It was also the year that Thomas Alva Edison opened a laboratory in Menlo Park, New Jersey. Out of that laboratory was to come perhaps the greatest invention of the age—a successful incandescent electric lamp. (A light bulb!) After a merger in 1892, he called his new organization General Electric. Today, that same spirit of innovation and discovery is still a part of everything we do.

Note the last sentence of the story. The teller of the story is being very explicit in saying, "This story says something that is still vital and true about us." Does this story get repeated within GE as a way of reinforcing its culture of innovation? You'd better believe it does.

Origin stories don't just happen at the beginning of the organization. Every time you start a new project or a new team, you have a new origin story. People have origin stories, too. Your parents probably told you their origin stories (although they probably didn't call them that), and if you have kids, you have probably passed on your sense of identity by telling your origin stories.

Of course, the identity is not only encoded in the origin. It also shows up in actions every day. Some of those actions are remarkable, and demonstrate *who we are when we are at our best.* Those, too, are important stories of identity.

Here's a wonderful story of identity that I heard just recently from a leader in a speech at a manufacturing organization I partnered with:

> The other day I was standing on the corner downtown waiting for the light to walk across the street, and I noticed that the guy standing next to me had one of his shoelaces untied. I said "Sir, your shoelace is untied. I don't want you to get hurt."
>
> The man thanked me, and then he said, "You must work for [the manufacturing company] here in town." And I said, "Yes, I do. How did you know that?" And the man said, "Everyone knows that your group talks about safety all the time." And that was a very proud moment for me as a leader. Throughout the streets of Copenhagen, we are known as people of safety.

The significant thing about this story is that it was a small moment—mundane, really—and yet this leader was mindful enough to recognize its importance. He thought to himself, *I should capture that story and I should share it with the organization. It makes an important statement about who we are.* Simply by telling the story, he creates the vision and boundaries of identity and establishes a vision for how the organization's values should spill out into public awareness. We create our reality through the words we speak. This is the heart of leadership storytelling.

In a few pages, you will find space to write down some of your identity and origin stories. You can start reflecting on them now. What stories reflect the identity of your organization? Your team or function? Your individual leadership? (And how about your family? Your childhood?) What are the origins of your organization, your team, and you? What was true at the beginning that is still true today? What are the events, conversations, and turning points— big or small—that say something about who you are?

Vision Stories

"Where are we going?" Your answer to that question is central to your leadership. Typically the answer comes in the form of a vision statement, which isn't so bad. But to truly invite people into your vision, do you know what would work even better? That's right. A story.

Stephen Denning was an executive at the World Bank in the early days of the knowledge management movement. As he shares in his classic management book *The Springboard*, he initially had a hard time gaining traction in this new idea of knowledge management within the World Bank, until one day when he changed his presentation and instead told a story. Here's how he presents that story in *The Springboard*:[3]

---

3. Stephen Denning, *The Springboard: How Storytelling Ignites Action in Knowledge-Era Organizations* (Routledge, 2000).

> In June 1995, a health worker in a tiny town in Zambia logged on to the website of the Centers for Disease Control in Atlanta, Georgia, and got an answer to a question on how to treat malaria. . . . This was in Zambia, one of the poorest countries in the world. But the most important part of this picture for us in the World Bank is this: the World Bank, isn't in the picture. The World Bank doesn't have its know-how accessible to all the millions of people who made decisions about poverty. But just imagine if it had. Think what an organization it could become.

Notice how Denning's vision for the World Bank is articulated in the form of a story about someone else! (Again, notice how the end of the story makes an explicit link to the listener and says, "Here's something I would like to draw out from the story.")

Sometimes to cast your vision for your desired future, you may need to reach to your past. Identify a time when you or your team were at your very best and exemplified the traits that need to be called forth again. I worked with one retailing organization where an executive told a story of how a few years earlier one of his teams responded to a community after a catastrophic flood. "That's who we are," he said at the conclusion of his story. "We are people of commitment and compassion. Those are the very same qualities we need to bring forth—again, here, today—to meet the challenges in front of us."

A *future* story is another type of vision story. In a future story, you simply articulate your desired future: What are customers doing? What innovations have you achieved? What rewards are you enjoying? How does it feel? A key aspect of the future story is to tell it in present-tense language—as if the desired future had already been achieved and is currently the reality. Check out the Future Story Spine (Chapter 9) or Creative Tension Pictures (Chapter 14) for two helpful processes for defining this future story.

 Values Stories

Almost every organization has a statement of values. And I've seen more than a few organizations where that values statement was a source of cynicism rather than vitality. That's the result when people perceive a disconnect between the espoused values and the actual values.

So your organization espouses a value for "quality"? For "excellence"? Are "people your greatest asset"? To keep the words from ringing hollow, bring them to life in a story. What does "quality" look like at *this* organization? What is unique about "customer service" at *this* organization? In what unique ways does "innovation" come to life at *this* organization?

These are the *how* stories of your work. When you tell these stories, you establish the behavioral boundaries for how people in the organization accomplish the mission. And at their best, the stories will have the effect of liberating behavior for innovation, rather than constraining behavior.

Zappos, the online shoe retailer, has quickly created legendary levels of customer passion by telling stories that go viral. (It captures these in its annual *Zappos Culture Book*, which customers may order for free from its website.) For example, if you do a Web search for "Zappos 10-hour customer service call," you'll encounter dozens of links, some relaying this now-famous viral story.

> On December 8, 2012, a customer service representative took a call that clocked in at a record-setting 10 hours and 29 minutes! The customer called to order a pair of Ugg boots, but in the conversation the service rep discovered that the customer was about to relocate to the Las Vegas area, where Zappos is located. They spent 10 hours exploring neighborhoods and other details of life in Vegas. At the end of the call, the customer purchased the pair of Ugg boots.
>
> "Sometimes people just need to call and talk," said a Zappos representative. "We don't judge. We just want to help." Zappos doesn't view the incident as bad news. It confirmed that the employee was following protocol, and that this was just another experience in being dedicated to customers.

Values stories are most fascinating when the corporate value is put to the test, when those ideals clash with the organization's need for expediency. You can sense that tension in the Zappos story, and it is inherently dramatic: How much did the organization invest in those 10 labor hours compared to the profit margin from a single pair of shoes? But the fact that the story pushes the value of *customer service* out into that gray area is what makes it so compelling. And you can be sure that the story's viral spread has ensured a return that is infinitely greater than the value of that single pair of shoes. (Indeed, this is intentional on the part of Zappos. It loves the press it gets from these "crazy" customer service stories. Wouldn't you?)

Here's another one that I heard from a story program participant at a food-manufacturing company in London:

> There was a report that one of our batches of product had been tampered with in a way that could make kids sick. I was shocked! I couldn't see how that was possible! And I was even more shocked when I got a call from Scotland Yard—and they told me they were treating this as an investigation into terrorism! So Scotland Yard came in and audited all of our processes, both for hiring and for manufacturing. They concluded there was no way a terrorist threat could have come from inside [the company].
>
> Later we discovered that there had been no tampering at all. But I will never forget what the detectives said. They said, "[The company's] processes are so sound, they cannot be compromised by a terrorist." Isn't that an amazing endorsement? One of our values here is quality. I've always known our quality standards were high. And now that has even been acknowledged by Scotland Yard.

One significant thing about the above story was that most of the other leaders in the large organization did not know about it. They were surprised that something so significant had taken place. One of the leaders reflected, "Why are we surprised? If we don't take opportunities to stop and share these stories with one another, there's all kinds of extraordinary events that we will never know about."

A big part of leadership is keeping an ear to the ground and listening for these stories of your values in action. Remember, you are the curator of identity. When you find these stories, share them! When you do, you create vivid but fluid boundaries for behavior all across the organization.

Stories of Change and Learning

I work with a lot of groups where I challenge them to identify stories of change and learning. It doesn't always go well. In some organizational cultures, it's a real risk to reveal something you did that failed. (Even if it is not a cultural risk, for some people who have carefully cultivated a specific image of themselves, it can be an unacceptable personal risk.) Sure, it's a risk to appear vulnerable. But if you wish to create a culture of learning and continual improvement, share these stories with a spirit of transparency, humility, and authenticity.

The Coca-Cola Company has a *brand archivist* (or *company storyteller*) who once told me this story of organizational learning:

> Back in the 1980s before we introduced New Coke [in an infamously failed product launch], we tested it endlessly with focus groups. Consumers were unanimous: New Coke tasted better. So why did it fail in the marketplace? Because we never asked the crucial question: *What if we got rid of Coca-Cola and replaced it with New Coke?* That would have revealed the deep, emotional connection people have about our brand. We thought they wanted better flavor. We discovered they want to maintain their emotional connection to our brand! It was a mistake that taught us not ignore the incredible brand loyalty we have cultivated for more than 100 years.

A key element of the change and learning story is the wisdom that is drawn out at the end. "I tried something. It didn't work. Now we have valuable knowledge that we didn't have before." The story is redemptive in that it turns the screwup into a source of valuable knowledge for other leaders.

Of course, you can always tell the story about someone else's failure! This is a story that my colleague Dick Richardson and I both tell as part of our work at the Apollo Leadership Development Experience—a program of The Conference Board that is hosted at Johnson Space Center in Houston and Kennedy Space Center in Cape Canaveral, Florida:

Wernher von Braun, the legendary leader of the rocket program at the National Aeronautics and Space Administration (NASA) during the 1950s and 1960s, was at a launch of a Mercury-Redstone rocket. He watched in horror as one test rocket (which did not contain a human pilot) lifted off, then veered off course and had to be detonated. Later as he was about to launch an investigation to find out what had gone wrong, a low-level maintenance guy came into von Braun's office and said "Sir, I think I may have had something to do with that." The maintenance guy explained that before the launch he went around the rocket with a wrench "just tightening things up." It turned out the guy tightened up the gimbals, which are the hinges that allow the rocket thrusters to shift ever so slightly side to side. It was a small action, but it was enough to alter the rocket's navigation. Von Braun said to the guy, "I'm calling a meeting of the entire team and I want you sitting in the front row." So you can imagine this guy was now thinking, *I'm going to my public execution*!

So the whole organization showed up, and von Braun called this poor guy up to the stage. He reached under the podium . . . and pulled out a bottle of champagne and handed it to the guy! He thanked the guy for bringing the problem forward, for not covering his butt, and von Braun said, "This is the only way we will be able to innovate." And that's true in our organizations, too. Without permission to fail, there will never be innovation.

What Are Your Core Stories?

Later in this book, you will have many opportunities to identify, craft, tell, and draw meaning from your Four Core Stories.

For now, just spend a few minutes warming up your storytelling engine by identifying some of your core stories. You don't need to construct formal stories out of them. Just write down some brief memories, giving each one a title. For example: "The time I challenged the client in Philly," "The day our team threw out the production guidelines and improvised," "Adopting our third child," and so on. See how many you can think of. Consider stories at the individual, team, and organizational levels. Go for quantity!

Identifying (or "mining") your stories requires purposeful thought.

On the next page, see how many examples of "core" stories you can think of.

Don't write the stories yet. Just capture titles for now.

Go for quantity.

Soon, this will feel natural to you . . . and you'll start recognizing leadership stories everywhere!

Think of Some Stories of *Identity*

- How did you or your team/project/organization begin? (Keep in mind that every new team or project is a new origin story.)

- What was true and valuable at the beginning that is still central to who you are today?

- Think of a time that you or your team/project/organization was operating at its best. What happened?

In my organization: ....

....

....

In my team:..

....

....

In my own life or personal leadership: ....

....

Now Think of Some Future *Vision* Stories

- What was a time when you saw the desired future action achieved in another organization? In another industry?

- When did someone display an action or characteristic that is now needed all across the organization?

- Tell a future story: Imagine that you have achieved your future. What are customers saying? How is your company different? What kind of innovation have you produced? What have you learned? How does the world look different? How does it feel?

In my organization: ....

....

....

In my team:..

....

....

In my own life or personal leadership: ....

....

Think of Some *Values* Stories

- What was a time when you (or someone else) lived or embodied what is most important to you?

- If you have a statement of values for your organization or team, take a fresh look at them. This is a high-leverage starting point for your storytelling. What are some times when you saw each of the values being lived in especially remarkable ways?

In my organization: ....
....
....

In my team:..
....
....

In my own life or personal leadership: ....
....
....

Ready to Tackle Some Stories of *Change and Learning*?

- When was a time that you or the team/organization blew it?

- When was a time that you changed thoughts, beliefs, and behaviors to accomplish something that was hard?

- When did you do something that didn't work . . . and now you are doing something differently and getting better results?

In my organization: ....
....
....

In my team:..
....
....

In my own life or personal leadership: ....
....
....

Three More Cores!

In an influential white paper, Annette Simmons proposed six stories that leaders should tell that, she says, "encompass the heart of all business communication." In different ways, the Four Cores in this chapter overlap with her framework. But she also advocates some others,[4] which I find myself turning to frequently in my own work. Here are three more cores, courtesy of Annette, to consider in your leadership.

Who I am.

Establish your personal character or competence by telling stories that illuminate who you are and why people should follow you. (You might have noticed I used the introduction of this book to do precisely that by telling just a few stories about my work and my experiences in the story realm.)

- Who are you? What makes you special? What qualities and experiences do you have that earn you the right to influence?

- What were the moments when you really exercised or tested your character or competence?

Why I'm here.

Michael Margolis, president of Story University, asks: "What are you most curious about? What riddle you are trying to solve? Why is that so personal for you? That's your core story."

Let people know why you are personally bought in to the work so that your passion can help awaken their passion.

- Was there a moment when you knew you wanted to be a part of this organization/project/team? When did you choose this job? What was going on when you chose it?

- What do you get out of this work besides money? Why do you go the extra mile? How was that conviction borne?

- Do you perhaps have some painful experience from your past that informs the work you do now? Are there personal reasons you feel urgency? What happened that brought you here?

I know what you are thinking.

Give voice to the secret suspicions or reluctance to change that your audience holds. Tell a story that frames their objection as completely rational and understandable—and then tell another story that establishes an alternative position. Once you earn trust by validating your audience, listeners are more likely to come along with you to explore the other side of the issue.

- What are the points of pain or resistance among your audience? (If you don't know, how can you find out?)

- When was a time you or someone else felt the same way? What happened to move you/them to a different position? How did you get from there to here?

4. Simmons, A. *Whoever Tells the Best Story Wins: How to Find, Develop, and Deliver Stories to Communicate with Power and Impact* (United States: AMACOM, 2007).

Where Do I Go Next?

The Four Core Stories is a simple construct that connects to the heart of your leadership. It will serve as a foundation for other activities and processes presented in this book.

So what's next?

- *Tell it!* Pick just one of the stories you identified, and find an occasion to share it. You could do this at the beginning of a team meeting, as part of your next presentation, or simply as an e-mail you send out to colleagues with the subject line "A story I wanted to share with you."

- *Find more!* The core stories are happening all around you. Stay alert! I was in a team meeting recently where I was moved by the ways we exposed our assumptions and mental models. I thought to myself, *This would be a good story to tell others*! I even said that out loud to the team, which had the effect of creating a nice moment of self-awareness and reflection. As you exercise this story awareness, it will quickly become a habit.

- *Capture it!* One might approach the search for these core stories in the same way that a miner might pan a stream with dreams of striking gold. You might carry

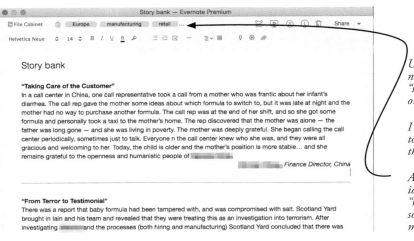

Using a tablet computer such as an iPad and note-taking software you can begin to build a "story bank" of the core narrative assets of your organization and leadership.

I use a note-taking app on the iPad called Evernote to quickly capture great stories when I come across them.

At the top, note how I "tagged" the stories with identifiers such as the industry ("retail" and "manufacturing") as well as location ("Europe") so that I can quickly search and find stories that match my context

44

a story journal around with you so that you are ready to capture stories when you discover them. My preference is to use my iPad and the app Evernote, which allows me to capture the story in any form (written or voice recorded) and then tag it for future search. (That is, based on my particular interests I might label it a "trust" story, "innovation," or "learning," along with the industry, such as "retail," "manufacturing," or "pharma." Thus, I can do a search for "innovation in retail" and retrieve several targeted stories.)

- *Improve it!* After you have identified a core story you would like to tell, head over to Chapter 4, "Capturing Fire," and begin applying some structural and stylistic elements to make it positively gripping.

- Use the Four Cores as a framework for *story mining*, that is, for digging up the great stories that your team members know. A great place to start is Chapter 11, "Fractal Narratives."

- This book offers several models for taking your *vision* stories to the next step. Look at the "Future Story Spine" (Chapter 9), "Creative Tension Pictures" (Chapter 14), or "Strategy Is a Story" (Chapter 15).

- If you wish to lead your team through an exercise on the Four Core Stories, you may download a four-page worksheet from www.DavidHutchens.com. It will help you present the Four Cores and then help your team members identify, craft, and tell their core stories.

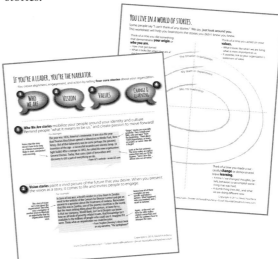

Use story circles as the core structure for all of your shared storytelling activities.

Story circles are the most fundamental structure for shared story sharing, sense making, community building—and even human survival and evolution.

Chapter 2

HOST A STORY CIRCLE

For this exercise, you will need:

- A comfortable space or third place (as described in "Find or Create a Third Place.")

- Chairs or cushions

- A reason to tell stories

Here's how to host a story circle:

Step 1: Sit in a circle, facing one another.

Step 2: Take turns telling stories.

That's all there is to it. Really. Class dismissed.

Recently I visited my teenage daughter, Emory's, high school on a pretty day, and I saw her and her friends sitting together on the grass just after lunch. They were in a circle facing one another and telling stories: stories about boys, about chemistry tests, about driving, and about

The story circle is the foundation of all of your narrative practices. It is an exceedingly simple structure that delivers incredibly robust data about the work, the organization, your shared leadership . . . and so much more.

music. No one instructed them to do this, and they didn't take any facilitator training on how to host a good story circle. But they looked deeply engaged to me. I suspect my daughter will never forget those conversations on the lawn.

A story circle is a universal organizational structure, one that is created spontaneously and naturally wherever Homo sapiens have gathered over the millennia. Since the beginning of humanity, every community that ever gathered around a fire naturally formed a circle—driven equally by a need to absorb the fire's warmth and to see one another's illuminated faces fully. King Arthur seated his knights at a round table where position was equalized and learning was a shared responsibility. And today, organizations all over the world are discovering the *group mind*, the emergent collective intelligence that is generated when its members purposefully engage themselves in the circle structure to tell stories.

In its purest form, a story circle operates a lot like my daughter's friends on the grass; there is no defined driver or outcome other than the human need to meet in a place of shared connection. But leaders are tasked with creating movement and alignment, so often some specific outcome is desired. Shawn Callahan, of the Australian firm Anecdote, brands his process as "anecdote circles,"[1] which are distinguished by a thematic framing, a strategic direction,

1. Anecdote provides an excellent, free guide available for download at http://www.wcasa.org/file_open.php?id=1097.

a targeted question, and a purposeful intent to draw usable meaning from the story.

Whether you call it a story circle, an anecdote circle, or something else, this chapter introduces you to one of the most fundamental building blocks of your story work. As you'll discover, story circles can be combined in endless configurations with other activities.

Here, we will stay focused on a single purpose: creating meaningful experiences where your team members can tell purposeful, value-creating stories toward some strategic end that you define.

Honestly, you could probably host a story circle right now without reading any further. After all, you do it all the time. Just set aside a little time, and follow the two-step process above.

Of course, a few nuances will make the experience even more valuable.

Decide How You Will Frame It

In an organizational context, a story is defined by purpose. Why are you bringing people together to tell stories? Here are some scenarios where I have applied story circles:

Innovation work

- A national association of librarians needed to uncover new, innovative ways of thinking about their changing roles and the value they offer in the instant-information age of the Google search bar.

Sales and marketing work

- A small nonprofit organization wanted to uncover emotional and inspiring stories of its impact in the community. (Its original intent was to use the stories for fund-raising and marketing, but it discovered the process to be equally productive for organizational development.)

- A bioscience sales organization known for its aggressive approach wanted to uncover new and fresh ways of thinking about how it engages with customers.

- A group of graduate students, facing a tough job market and their first experiences with interviewing for employment, wanted greater insight into their own stories of marketplace vocation. ("Who am I beyond my grade point average, and what is the change I wish to be in the world?")

Culture work

- A consumer products company had a new generation of young employees who did not know the company's history (recent or distant), and leaders wanted them to have an opportunity to connect their own stories to that history. (In the process, leadership was shocked to discover how many seasoned members of the organization were also unaware of the company's identity stories, and they expanded the scope of the offering.)

Strategy work

- A food products company was making difficult organizational changes and wanted to give all team members an opportunity to process their mixed feelings about the future while envisioning how their work might evolve.

- An engineering firm, facing declining market share, wanted project teams to envision new ways of thinking about their future and drive the conversation for defining the strategy.

Knowledge management and learning

- A multibillion-dollar energy firm in the Middle East wanted to capture the history, or institutional memory, of a complex project that it was still in the middle of, to identify key challenges and decisions that could be used in knowledge transfer for future employees.

- A medium-sized company wanted to do a better job at collaborating and learning from one another across functional lines.

- One of my colleagues uses story circles with small businesses in her community as an alternative to the traditional focus group for research purposes. That is, instead of bringing a group of (say) customers together and saying, "Do you like your spicy buffalo wings breaded or unbreaded?" she has them tell stories about their most special dining memories at sports bars. The data she gathers is so much more robust and enlightening than traditional customer surveys.

Team building

- A global retail organization wanted its technology leaders to develop stronger teams with members who were emotionally engaged and personally committed to the work.

- A small team in a small organization simply wanted to build their appreciation for one another during a retreat.

Organizational identity work and culture audits

- A global consulting firm wanted to help new employees in their onboarding process connect their dreams and aspirations to the mission and history of the firm.

That's just a sampling of the kinds of purposes where a story circle can generate a bottomless well of insight and learning. That said, if it is what your context requires there is nothing wrong with leaving the agenda as open as possible, with only the stated outcome of *increasing connection*.

You should expect story circles to serve as *divergent* structures that open up ideas and generate possibilities. It is a prime-the-pump experience, as opposed to putting the team in execution mode. The pure story circle experi-

ence should be framed in terms of creating possibilities, although it can certainly be connected with other exercises in this book for generating specific, actionable outcomes. (For some of those ideas, see the Story Recipes in the Introduction of this book.)

Articulate the frame—the big-picture *why*—of the session before you begin. Broad is good. When you invite participants, tell them the purpose: "We're going to set aside some time simply to *hear* one another, share our experi-

Come to the circle. This universal structure works in every culture and any context. Notice how much these storytellers and listeners are using their bodies and their hands. (Notice, too, the complete lack of smart phones, tablet computers, PowerPoint slide shows, or any other technology crutch.) This is the purest form of human connection and meaning making.

ences around the new product launch thus far, and begin imagining where we could all go together next."

A spirit of generosity should accompany this framing. Mary Alice Arthur is a leader (they call themselves *stewards*) in the global Art of Hosting[2] movement, and she says that the framing is really an *invitation*. "People *like* being invited," she says. "And people often don't have that feeling of invitation. Maybe that's why so many people are so forceful when they want to make a point—they don't feel listened to and they get that they are not really invited; therefore something in their psyche has to push their point into the conversation."

Find or Create a Third Space

Here's a sure way to kill your story circle. Have your participants come to the conference room, and say, "We are here to tell stories. But I know you're all busy, and another group needs us to clear the conference room by 3:45. So let's get to work. Ready? Start."

The more you structure the story circle like a meeting, the more you can expect to see meeting-like behaviors, such as participants self-editing, deferring to the senior people, *leaning back* disengagement, and conversation marked by short, imperative statements as people grit their teeth,

2. See http://www.artofhosting.org.

glance at the clock, and hope that their to-do lists aren't getting too much longer. An important first step in creating a story circle, then, is distancing the experience from people's expectations.

Starbucks says that its rapid growth can be attributed equally to its customers' insatiable thirst for coffee as well as their social hunger for a third space—an alternative location that is neither home nor work—where spontaneous encounters and social connections can emerge. The idea of the third space was popularized by sociologist Ray Oldenburg in his 1989 book, *The Great Good Place*. He says that the third space is defined not so much by its physical location but by its psychic location. A true third space is typically characterized by the presence of chance connections and unhindered dialogue, as in the famous French salons of the seventeenth century, which became hothouses of new ideas and social reform.

Storytelling needs space to breathe, and for that it needs a third space.

If we're going for the ideal scenario, we would find a third space that feels like a retreat, and is separated from our daily, distracting reality, that is relaxed, open, and flooded with natural light and surrounded by natural beauty or perhaps among inspiring architecture where the hum of exotic, urban energy draws out our best creative impulses.

Oh, but your only option is the old, windowless conference room in the basement? We can work with this. The third space can be symbolic. The idea is to do something that represents separation from the typical.

At the very least, I always have people push away from tables and desks and sit facing each other. I usually make a bit of a ceremony out of this: "No tables between us! We are going to be fully present and facing each other. Move your chairs into the empty spaces of this room. Move the furniture! Make a mess!" This has the effect of establishing a third space with an expectation for increased presence, even if you're not able to take more dramatic measures.

Even having a table of food and drinks can help create the sense that this is not a meeting, but something different, social, and open, where we can encounter one another in more human ways.

You can plug your laptop into the room's sound system and play some rock music as people walk in. (I like to play The Beatles. No one complains about The Beatles.) Music acts as a social lubricant. Social engagement increases in a room where music is playing.

If the weather is nice, and there is a nice grassy area outside, you should certainly seize that opportunity. It almost feels like playing hooky from work, which is a bit of a paradox because urgent work is taking place.

My colleague Barry Rellaford is a master facilitator for FranklinCovey, and I'll never forget his approach to creating a third space. He calls it "walking stories," and he

simply invites everyone to pair up and leave the room or the building and walk around the parking lot, around the hotel lobby, or down the street and back. This has several advantages. Because participants are side by side, it reduces eye contact, which may decrease vulnerability and increase a feeling of social ease and comfort,[3] and the walking increases heart rate and endorphins, which stimulate the brain to think more freely. It's a great way to create a third space, and because it is a dramatic pattern disrupter, the event tends to be extremely memorable. It also offers an elegant time management structure: "When you get to the corner of 18th Street, turn around and start heading back. That will be the second person's time to start their story." I can still recall vividly the first time I experienced walking stories when Barry sent us all out of the room on a sunny day in Salt Lake City. I was surprised how willing I was to share some personal things with my new friend walking next to me.

3. Mary Alice Arthur points out that this is a particularly good way for men to make contact. Social research shows that even from a young age boys prefer to engage with one other side by side with reduced eye contact whereas girls prefer to face one another. Mary Alice also mentioned that washing dishes after dinner is a great activity for couples for precisely this reason.

A "third space" for stories. At the European Center for Executive Development (CEDEP) in Fontainebleau, France, executives will take their story circles to the lovely wooded lawn when the weather is nice. It almost doesn't feel like work.

Decide Who Needs to Be There

This is up to you and depends greatly upon your objectives. But if you are in doubt, it is good to err on the side of diversity. Having participants from different functions, different regions, different levels, or different stakeholder groups can lead to enormous appreciation between groups that are normally separated by silos. My friends at Plexus Institute are creating exciting change in complex health-care environments by bringing surgeons, administrators, and even janitors and other environmental services staff into the same circle for shared learning. You'd be amazed by some of the surprising insights that surgeons can draw from the team that brings in the linens and wipes down the beds. And imagine the impact it has on the environmental services staff to feel truly heard by the leaders at the top of the organization.

Think outside the typical players! My colleague Christine Martell, creator of VisualsSpeak image prompts, says she is astounded by how often her clients have story sessions about the customer—but they fail to invite the customer to be a part of the event!

Sometimes when I work with groups, there is a good reason to keep members

These are examples of ground rules I use frequently, but your unique gathering may demand different rules. The principle is to keep them simple and minimal.

in their functional groups for the story circle. But when that's not a requirement, I always prefer randomizing the group so that people can hear stories from others in the organization whom they might otherwise never have the opportunity to talk to. These surprise connections tend to deliver the most impactful and transformational story experiences.

A story thrives in a diverse environment, and it can be a powerful way to knock down the walls between groups.

Set Ground Rules

When the session begins, frame the boundaries of conversation with some minimal ground rules. The rules should have the effect of liberating behavior—not limiting it.

Here are some examples of rules that I will often include on a flip chart.

- *Don't Disagree.* I always point out that stories are subjective, and that you may hear people tell stories with style or even content that you disagree with—or may not even like. As my dad always says when my mom starts correcting him, "Pat, this is my story!" (If you wish, this is a good place to talk about mental models and the fact that each of us views the world through a unique lens.)

- *Thank the Storyteller.* It may seem like a small thing, but it creates such a generous environment when every story you tell earns a response of "Thank you for sharing that with us." It can be a vulnerable feeling to share a story; affirmation is like sunlight to a spring garden. If participants forget to thank a storyteller, you can model the behavior. After you say "Thank you" to a story once or twice, the habit will quickly catch on.

- *Talk Like Yourself.* In most cases, I will emphasize that this story experience is not about performance. We aren't asking participants to become charismatic public speakers. "Just talk the way you always talk," I'll tell them, "even if you, stutter or say *um* and *ah* too much. I'd rather you tell the right story, a strategic story, than to tell the story well." I've discovered that people need this permission. It's amazing how I always feel the anxiety leave the room when people are released from story-crippling performance expectations.

The exception to this, of course, would be any scenario where you *are* focused on the quality of presenta-

tion and delivery—such as in a communications skills or media relations program.

- *The Rule of Two Feet.* My colleague Graham Williams uses this, and it is a recurring principle of Art of Hosting methodologies.[4] The rule of two feet is a dramatic statement that says, "You don't have to be here. Your presence is an act of free will, and we want this event to include people who want to be a part of it. At any point, if you feel like there is more value to be found elsewhere, you're welcome to leave." What a bold statement! And yet, it establishes an enormous amount of trust, neutralizes any feeling of coercion, and increases the commitment in the room: Simply by remaining present, the participants are testifying to the relevance of the event.

- *Respect Confidentiality.* If you anticipate that the story session may contain sensitive information, then make a statement about respecting confidentiality.

Communicate any other minimal ground rules that you think are important to the participants.

Also communicate any other expectations or unique procedural items. A story circle is the most basic structural

4. For some group methodologies, such as Open Space, the"Rule of Two Feet" is an important design principle for self-organizing meetings. In those cases, participants are *expected* to move about frequently in order to cross-pollinate ideas over multiple groups. For a traditional story circle as described here, that is not the intention.

54

Story circles are scalable. Whether I have just four people or a crowd of 1,000, the setup and facilitation is the same. The only adjustments are for space and number of chairs.

element in storytelling, and it can be combined in endless combinations with almost every other process in *Circle of the 9 Muses*. Do you intend to capture the stories on video or audio? Do participants need to capture story elements on flip charts? Are you going to ask them to write their stories down for input in a story bank or database? Will you include any feedback processes (such as those described in Chapter 6, "Summoning the Muse")? Are there other activities on the agenda? Make sure your participants know what is going to happen during the session and after their stories are told.

Put Participants in Groups

Smaller groups are better. Make it clear that everyone is expected to share. Most often, for a typical story circle I work with groups of four or five, rarely more than six. Three is a minimum. (Of course, one-on-one dialogues or interviews may leverage a story, but that is a different structure that we will explore elsewhere.)

If you have a large group with many participants, the smaller groups take on an added dynamic. Once the multiple groups start sharing stories at the same time, the room will fill with voices, laughter, and infectious energy.

Begin the Session and Manage the Time

What story do you want people to tell? Share a prompt or framing question. (You might wish to review Chapter 3, "Story Prompts" now.) Write it on a flip chart, or project it from your computer onto a large screen. I find that participants keep looking back to the framing question, examining each word as they begin searching their brains for the story they want to tell.

I ask whether there are any questions before getting started, and there usually aren't.

There will be an awkward moment at the beginning of the experience when people feel the pressure of starting the process with a story. I even tell my groups to expect that: "You will feel hesitancy at first. That's because we are putting a structure on something that you normally do naturally. But that awkwardness will pass quickly. So whoever has a story can go first. If you don't have a story yet, don't worry. It will come!"

Then just say, "Okay! Go!"

You will also manage the time for the session. I know many colleagues who impose no time structure for their story session, and they allow the day to unfold with its own self-organizing structure. However, I often find myself in workshop or meeting settings where it is important to manage time, so I'll tell members approximately how many minutes they have for their story. Three minutes is

a pretty fast story, but workable. Five minutes allows for a comfortable amount of detail. I find that 10 minutes is too generous for a single story and may result in a meandering or unfocused story. (Better to have two 5-minute stories than a single unfocused 10-minute story.)

You'll need to crunch the numbers based on how many participants you have and the time. At 5 minutes, a story circle of four people can share in a period of about half an hour. (Four people times 5 minutes is 20 minutes, plus extra padding for comments and conversation. Always pad with extra time!) If you are adding rounds of listener feedback or meaning harvest, as described in Chapter 6, "Summoning the Muse," you'll need to build in time for those conversations as well.

If you are not limited by time and you are creating a more open story session, it may still be advisable to run a single cycle at 30 minutes so that participants can practice telling their stories under constraints. Then you can run additional cycles of the story circle with those time limits loosened or removed.

So far I've taken quite a few pages to capture the nuances and details of the story circle, but in reality much of this will be invisible to participants. Story circles work best when they are brisk, loose, energetic, and not burdened by a lot of formality.

Your Role as Host

As host, your role includes some basic facilitation duties. These include answering any questions and monitoring the time and the progress of the story circles. If it looks like some teams are lagging, you can make announcements at the halfway and three-quarters points: "We are about halfway through our time now. Ten minutes left."

During the actual telling, I stand off to the side and become invisible. I don't want people telling stories *to me*. They are there to connect to one another.

Most important, your job is to believe sincerely in the wonder and value of every human being who is in the room with you. Believe it, and wonderful things will happen.

Ready to Get Started?

See? I told you this would be easy.

Building your skill in hosting a story circle is foundational. There's nothing more basic than bringing people together and asking them to tell stories.

It's basic, but it also takes a little bit of practice. You might want to try hosting a few story circles before you move on to the more advanced techniques (such as the fractal narratives or the archetype extraction). Make note of what works, and what doesn't. Graham Williams compares this work to fishing. Sometimes, you drop a line in the water and don't get any bites. When that happens, be still and remain present. The stories will come eventually.

And sometimes, there is a gift. Someone will bring something true, human, electrifying, and unforgettable. This doesn't always happen. I can't predict when it will or won't, and I can't predict who will bring it. But when it happens, you will cheer, you will cry, you will be shocked or astonished, and the experience will stay with you forever. When was the last time *that* happened to you in a business meeting?

In this chapter, I have dedicated many words to this process that, at the start, I claimed was very simple. Don't be intimidated. Yes, your story circle deserves all the disciplined planning and design you wish to bring to it. But you'll likely find your loose and spontaneous experiences just as rewarding and surprising.

In fact, if you haven't made any plans for lunch tomorrow, why not reach out to a few colleagues and friends right now and ask them whether they will meet with you to share some stories?

Where Do I Go from Here?

Story circles connect to everything in this book! This is the keystone—or, if you prefer your metaphors to be imbued with a living pulse, the heartbeat—of your leadership storytelling practice.

A natural next step is to simply turn the page and begin reading the next chapter, "Story Prompts," so that you can think more specifically about framing the story experience.

Use story prompts when you want to create an intentional experience that draws the *right* stories out of your team . . . and in a way that lets them share freely, naturally, and unselfconsciously.

Chapter 3

STORY PROMPTS

For this exercise, you will need:

- An upcoming event (either formal or spontaneous) where you are planning on asking for stories.

"If I were given three hours to tackle the world's most challenging problem, I would spend the first two and a half hours defining the questions."

Einstein is credited with saying that. I couldn't find any confirmation that he actually did, but quotes just take on an air of gravitas when attributed to Einstein. Regardless, it contains much wisdom about the sensitivity of questions in framing our understanding of the world.

Questions are especially sensitive in story work. A colleague of mine is a leader in a nonprofit organization here in Nashville. She recently told me that she tried to put some of these ideas to work by hosting a story session with her staff. "It didn't work," she said. "I asked for stories and everyone just sat there."

Stories happen naturally all the time, but eliciting them can be like calling a shy child who doesn't want to come out of her room. The paradox of this work is that story is a universal, ubiquitous, and ageless phenomenon—and yet it withers under the harsh glare of self-conscious awareness, demanding expectations, or organizational contexts that have pummeled us into speaking in bullet points as if our brains were structured like the PowerPoint decks we have become so addicted to.

It's easy to kill the story experience. Imagine we are at a cocktail party, standing around a high-top table with drinks and a group of friends. Imagine I point at you and say: "You know, a social engagement like this is a great opportunity to deepen our bonds through oral storytelling. I'd like for each of us to think of a 3-minute story that provides a humorous perspective on today's events at work. I'd like for you to go first, Paul. Ready? Begin."

How do you think that's going to work out? You probably *won't* tell a story. And you probably won't invite me to party with you again.

On the other hand, if I exercise just a little bit of emotional intelligence and allow the social dynamic to simply unfold, it is likely that everyone will do exactly what I described above. We will all naturally start telling stories with great energy, and those stories will tap the neural networks of our minds to deliver even more stories, until we are all bursting with things we want to contribute.

Framing is everything. Story work is incredibly sensitive to context, and how you position the story session will affect how—and whether—people will contribute. Here, then, are some best practices for setting a context or creating the container for narrative.

First, Some Don'ts

Let's say you've brought your team together, and you've decided that the topic of *trust* is one you'd like to explore through some stories.

Avoid saying things such as:

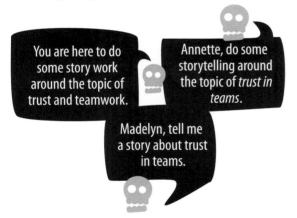

You can imagine how Annette and Madelyn might feel as I put them on the spot. *Story* and *storytelling* are loaded words for many people and immediately make them think of *performance*. "Oh, I'm a storyteller now? I guess I should be thinking of my characters, and the central conflict, and not rambling too much, making my voice sound less nasally, and making it compelling." See the problem here? There's a big difference between thinking about how to tell a story and simply telling a story. It's counterintuitive,

but asking for a story may not be the best way to produce a story.

Sometimes in this work I don't use the terms *story* or *storytelling* at all. Sometimes it is better just to start telling stories without calling attention to the fact that that's what we are doing. If I do use the term *storytelling*, I emphasize my preference for *purposeful* and spontaneous stories rather than *well-told* stories.

Here are two more prompts that are not likely to deliver stories:

The PowerPoint zombie disease has trained most of us to give correct answers. Yes, you can count on these prompts to put your team in the right conceptual space. But they won't elicit stories. Instead, people will say things like "To have trust in teams, you have to have clear accountabilities" and "It's hard to create trust in teams when people are being incentivized to different outcomes." Those are useful insights, sure, but they're not stories. If your intent is to generate stories, then you will need a different approach.

Dr. Karen Dietz describes another ineffective approach that may surprise you. Anyone who has ever studied journalism learned to interview people through the classic technique of asking questions that begin with these words:

Here are some other phrases that may deliver a perfectly lovely conversation but, for the reasons stated above, probably won't deliver a story:

If Lois Lane were interviewing witnesses to a robbery at the Bank of Metropolis, for example, those would indeed be great prompts. ("Who did you see?" "What did Lex Luthor use to blast open the safe?" "When did Superman arrive?") They would generate *descriptive statements* for her note taking so that she could go back to her desk at the *Daily Planet* and construct the story. ("Lex Luthor blasted the safe with Kryptonite." "Superman arrived after Luthor escaped out the back.")

If your intent is to reconstruct a story *later* from a series of descriptive statements, then these are great interviewing questions. But we are exploring ways of generating stories together in dialogue, and in that context these questions won't deliver what we seek.

Dr. Dietz sometimes has participants in her programs use these ineffective prompts to ask for stories and then make note of the responses they get. (They don't get stories!) Then she challenges them: "How would you modify those questions in a way that generates stories?"

Great question. How would *you* modify them?

Let's look at what works.

Paul Costello offers insight into story framing (and learning itself) when he says, "The best questions ask for an exploration rather than an explanation." Story work always opens up the space for dialogue. It is divergent. It does not provide immediate answers, but rather populates the conceptual space with a bottomless well of wisdom to be explored. Thus, your framing efforts should emerge from an orientation of exploration rather than finding the answer. (If quick answers are what you seek, you may not need stories at all. Just Google it.)

Here are some practices that will invite people into an exploratory story space.

Plant the Suggestion

Cynthia Kurtz, one of the pioneers in connecting storytelling to knowledge management efforts, says that she starts her story sessions by setting up a self-fulfilling prophecy. Imagine that we are still looking for stories on the subject of trust. Cynthia might say to a group, "I find that when you put people together in a circle, they naturally start telling stories. So tell me about a time you experienced a leader who extended trust to you."

See what she did with that first statement? She presented a statement of fact: "This is what people tend to do." Notice that she didn't instruct *this* group to tell stories. She sim-

ply describes an inclination that human beings have, and that's all. This plants a vision in the minds of participants and creates a self-fulfilling prophecy that influences the ensuing behaviors. I tried Cynthia's suggestion with one of my groups, and it worked just as she described.

"Tell Me about a Time . . ."

This is the classic story prompt. "*Tell me about a time* someone extended trust to you, and it made all the difference in your work."

When you say, "Tell me about a time," you move people's awareness to a linear, time-based continuum which is exactly where stories live. This prompt is historical and encourages people to scan over the timelines of their experiences for a specific event and the cascade of events that followed. Notice how the language in these examples reinforces that we are looking for a specific event:

Tell me about a time when a team failed because people couldn't let go of their old ways of thinking. What happened?

Tell me about a time you were proud that you made a difference for a customer.

Tell me about a time when you felt you were being truly vulnerable as a leader. What happened?

Notice that a couple of the examples above follow the *tell me about a time* prompt with the question "What happened?" This may seem redundant, but I think it serves a purpose in that it further orients people in story space. The question "What happened?" primes people to drop an anchor that is the catalyst event on their timeline and then begin noticing the ripple effect of events that followed.

Earlier we described that the journalistic "how" questions may not deliver stories. However, Thaler Pekar, an expert on story and persuasive communication, finds that "how" questions are a helpful assist for the reluctant story sharer. "If a teller is stuck," she explains, "follow up the *tell me about a time* prompt with *how did it happen?* This causes them to think of an unfolding of events, a pattern of causation—and stories!"

As we look at other ideas for prompting stories, notice how many of the examples that follow use some variation of *tell me about a time.*

Story Buckets

Annette Simmons says that in her experience, there are four prompts that are almost always effective at drawing out stories. "These four buckets aren't the only places to find stories," she says, "but they may be the easiest." Her four buckets are:

A time I shined | A time I blew it | A mentor | A book, movie, or current event

So, let's say you've brought a team together around the topic of "innovation." Having a menu of options can generate more productive brainstorming. You could place all four prompts up on a whiteboard and invite participants to pick one (whichever generates an idea for them first):

A time I shined: "We're talking about innovation today. Tell me about a time you were part of delivering something that was especially innovative. What did you do?"

A time I blew it: "Innovation is a fragile thing, and it is easy to compromise. Tell me about a time that you or your team failed to deliver the innovation you expected to deliver. What happened?"

A mentor: "Think of someone you respect most/the most innovative leader you ever knew, and tell me about a time that he or she produced something extraordinary. What did that leader do?"

Cynthia Kurtz phrases her mentor/leader question a little differently:

> Did you ever see somebody do something and think, "If *everybody* did that things would be a lot better around here?"
>
> Or did you ever think, "If everybody did that things would be a lot worse?" Tell me what happened.

She observes that this question roots the answer in *behavior* rather than the person's status.

A book, movie, or current event: "Think of a scene from a movie, a book, or the news that is a great example of people producing innovation. Tell me about the scene."

Extreme Prompts

Wherever there is a high point, low point, or turning point in your experience, you'll almost always find stories lurking there. As Paul Smith points out in his book *Lead with a Story*, this is why many of the most effective story prompts have *-est* adjectives in them:

> What is the craziest thing that has happened to you during a sales call? Tell me what happened.

> Share with me the toughest leadership challenge you have experienced in your career.

> Tell me about the scariest moment of your childhood.

> When did your team learn its hardest lesson while delivering Project Alpha? Tell us what happened.

> Tell me about the greatest team experience you've ever had.

> Share with me the time you produced the most creative thing you've done in your career. What happened?

It can be valuable to highlight contrast by invoking the opposite ends of a continuum at the same time: "Tell me about your worst team experience, and then tell me about the best. What happened in each?"

My wife and I sometimes do this as a quick check-in at the end of the day, especially if I'm out of town. Robbie will say, "What's high/low?" and I know that's shorthand for "Tell me the high point of your day today and the low point." It's a simple prompt that always brings us quickly into a conversation around the most important issues of the day. (I mentioned this technique at a story retreat in South Korea, and two executives laughed and said, "We do exactly the same thing at our house!" Storytelling and marriage are both universal.)

Emotional Prompts

One of the defining characteristics of a story is emotion, and in his Anecdote Circles e-book, Shawn Callahan points out that stories built around emotion are the ones we remember. Emotion belongs in our organizational communications as well, although we often don't find it there.

Slash Coleman says this is the very heart of organizational storytelling. Slash is an author and producer whose award-winning storytelling shows have been produced off Broadway and even been archived at the Smithsonian. For

Slash, whether he is stunning audiences in a theater or building story capability for business leaders, story work is always about emotion.

Slash's best-known production, *The Neon Man and Me*, found its way to television as a Public Broadcasting Service (PBS) Special. "I originally created the story to come to terms with my best friend's death," he says. "But, along the way it turned into an experiment of sorts." After retelling the story more than 1,400 times over seven years and documenting listener reactions, Slash became a student of the emotional content of stories.

Emotion is fertile ground for storytelling. Close your eyes and point to one of the "emotion" words below. What stories does the emotion word trigger?

Tell me about a time you felt . . .

inspired calm secure victimized melancholy gratified free embarrassed lonely energized smart provoked uncertain indecisive combative loved proud refreshed sexy liberated immortal astounded happy fascinated hesitant cruel determined wronged afraid dorky helpless strong amazed trapped restless grieved sad curious brave confident foolish uneasy surprised challenged alone attractive serene fortunate relieved jealous capable ambivalent abandoned satisfied defeated diminished angry rewarded alive vulnerable anxious scared untrusting

"If you ask about someone's best leader or best team experience," he says, "you're probably going to get one very specific story." He defines this type of story as an "identity story," where the person telling the story is grounded in a single narrative from the past. These stories typically come from our memory, tend to lack emotion, and have probably been repeated multiple times as the teller's way of shaping the identity of a person, thing, event, or even the self. As we've seen, such stories can indeed deliver great dividends of meaning. But Slash sees an opportunity.

"But let's say you ask a leader about a time they felt *dismissed* on a team," he says. "You'll probably get an emotional story, and much more. It produces a fluid stream of meaning: stories within stories." The teller experiences emotion through the telling; the listener (through the phenomenon of neural coupling) generates a parallel emotional state. Everyone shares the experience, and as Slash has discovered from his stance in the spotlight, it can be quite powerful. When you include emotion, Slash says, "even a story about walking to the curb to get the newspaper can become transcendent."

Notice how most of these prompts overtly use the word *feel* or *felt*:

> Tell me about a time you felt the power of the organization's value of *excellence* in a dramatic way. What happened?

> Tell me about a time when you realized you were cared about on this team.

> Tell me when you felt the proudest of your team/organization/marriage/family. What happened?

> Tell me about a time you felt diminished on a team. What happened?

Or, work other "feeling" words into your prompt. Slash often begins with the words on the previous page (drawn from the psychology of nonviolent communication) and you can too by simply closing your eyes and pointing to one at random.

Aspirational Prompts

In organizations, the most generative stories are the *aspirational* ones, the stories that capture us at our best. Rather than say, "Tell about a time you saw someone acting on our value of collaboration" (which may well deliver a mundane or even a negative story), an aspirational prompt would be, "Tell me about a time you saw someone acting on our value of collaboration *in a truly remarkable way.*" Do you want to find buried gold—the highest examples of daily leadership that you didn't even know were there in the organization? Aspirational prompts deliver the goods.

I always do this when telling stories about an organization's values. We don't want just any story about *quality*, for example. We want the dazzling stories of quality, for those are the ones that have something valuable to say about our identity.

I sometimes have groups resist this. "Yeah, but you don't know how screwed up things are around here," they say. "When we tell those happy-happy-joy-joy stories, we aren't being honest. No one is going to buy it." The fact is every organization has dysfunction, and there is always a group of employees perpetuating an antinarrative of the organization at its most toxic. The task of leadership is not to ignore the problems but to name them and deal with them. Those are very often current reality stories, whereas aspirational stories present the desired future state. (This is an idea called *creative tension*, and it is explored in Chapter 14, "Creative Tension Stories," later in this book.) In effect, by telling the aspirational story the leader says, "Yes, things are hard today. Now let's explore who we are when we are at our best." With these stories the leader establishes an attractor around which the organization can organize and grow. In this way, they become stories of vision. Speak your desired reality into existence.

Especially in culture building, branding, or engagement work, the extraordinary stories are the ones we want because they make the desired vision real and attainable. *Sure, we are not currently achieving the remarkable collaboration we need. But here's a story of a time we did, and it was a powerful thing to behold! Imagine if we could be that way all the time!*

Go Wide Open

Many of my story colleagues are perfectly comfortable going into story sessions without the safety net of a predefined topic. A wide-open narrative space allows the wisdom of the group to take the dialogue to wholly unexpected places. This is desirable when you want to foster emergence or a self-organizing group mind. (Make sure you tell the group that's what you are here to achieve.)

Kat Koppett is a master in the application of improvisational theatre techniques for management and the author of *Training to Imagine*. "You can trust the group to know what they care about, and what they want to talk about," she says, and offers a wonderful prompt for opening those possibilities. She begins with this question:

What are you curious about right now?

Invoking curiosity can be a powerful thing. Our curiosity hides in the corners of our minds, where we hold untested questions or little sparks of unexamined fascination. Curiosity is vulnerable and precious. We don't reveal our curiosity very often, and when we do, it can lead us off the main path of the typical, and down unexplored trails to places of unexpected surprise.

Kat will have each participant share his or her thoughts, and then she draws out any themes or patterns: "It sounds like we're wondering about how to support positive failure."

Then she makes the bridge to elicit stories:

Tell me about a time you saw someone wrestle with this. It can be a best-case example or a worst-case example.

Tell me about a time you saw a need in our organization that might have been transformed by that idea.

Have you ever seen a mentor or a leader do that well? What happened?

Go for the Heart

Most organizations have an *intimacy threshold*, a place where authentic engagement crosses over some invisible but collectively held boundary into a space of discomfort because it lands too close to the heart. For American businesspeople, that threshold tends to be higher than it is in European business cultures, where emotional vulnerability can more quickly undermine credibility. But this is just a matter of degree. Regardless of where your culture sets that dial, many leaders aren't used to revealing their hearts in the conference room.

I for one am a proponent of scooting right up to the edge of that threshold and then placing one toe over the other side (prompting some of my partners at INSEAD and CEDEP in Fontainebleau, France, to tease that I'm *so* American). I find that people usually squirm only for a moment, and then marvelous things begin to happen.

Bobette Buster is a world-renowned lecturer on stories, the language of cinema, and the economics of Hollywood. She is also a script consultant who has worked with Hollywood power houses, such as Pixar. My team invited her to share her perspectives with our group of storytellers, and she shared something that stuck with me. The most powerful stories—the transcendent ones—speak to the deepest human desires. "Cinema is the art form of transformation," Bobette says, and the stories that stay with us answer one of three questions that are at the heart of the human journey that we all share:

Will I find transformation?

These may be stories about reinvention, when I bravely chose to step into a new possibility; or redemption when my compromised or "sinful" identity was restored with new value.

How will I become fully alive?

These may be stories of finding liberation, transcendence, ecstasy, or meaning—or they may be cautionary tales, in which I became the living dead, so to speak, through wrong choices.

Where will I find hope?

Dare I entertain my deepest desires in the expectation they might be met? These are stories of times I lost hope, or found it, or both.

Here are some prompts that can invite people to share from the most precious areas of their lives. What stories do these trigger from your memory?

Share with me how you met your spouse, and how you knew you were falling in love.

What is the closest you have ever come to dying? Tell us what happened.

Tell me about a time someone believed in you.

Tell me about when you almost gave up—and how you found hope.

When did you encounter your greatest joy? I would love to hear about that time.

Was there a time you felt the most free? Tell me about what happened.

You can sense how these kinds of prompts would require you to share from the place of your deepest humanity. That may not be what you're seeking in the Monday morning staff meeting. I find that these conversations, if that is indeed what you seek, may benefit from some kind of separation from the demands of the normal work environment. (See the principles about the third space described in Chapter 2, "Story Circles.")

Stories Beget Stories

Author and consultant Terrence Gargiulo finds that the best way to create a context for sharing stories is, simply, to start with a story.

"The shortest distance between two people is a story," he says, "and so I begin my sessions by telling a story or a quick series of stories that are connected to our topic at hand. I have found that when people hear a collection of loosely interrelated stories that orbit the topic, they are quick to counter with stories of their own."

The prompts that we are exploring in this chapter are really focused on starting the story experience. Once the environment for story work has been correctly established, it takes on a life of its own.

"One story usually leads to another," Terrence explains. "This happens even if we are not thinking about it at a conscious level. Our minds replay our stories and treat them as precious jigsaw pieces of a never-ending puzzle. They become chains of cross-referenced experiences, opening a floodgate of meaning that can be explored in conversation with another person or in a reflective process with ourselves."

Where Do I Go from Here?

You can use these story prompts anywhere—at a meeting with one of your salespeople at a coffee shop, during an interview for a new team member, in a meeting with your staff in the conference room, or over dinner with your spouse and kids.

My mentor Dick Richardson used to do this when interviewing young managers at IBM. He would put down his pencil, look at the clock, and say, "Well, that's all of my interview questions but it will be a couple of minutes before it's time to leave. So, what are you planning on doing this weekend?" Of course, the interview wasn't really over, but the storytelling that followed produced the most important data of the event.

I do this in the car with my kids on the way home from the bus stop. "Tell me about a time that you laughed really hard today. What happened?" This gets much better results from a teenager than "How was your day?" (Although I've overused the prompt, and now my kids are on to me. *There goes Dad again trying to get us to tell stories . . .*)

Once you start defining the story prompt and imagining the conversation that will ensue, you will likely begin to think more broadly about what that shared experience should look like. If you are reading this book out of sequence and you have not yet reviewed the previous chapter, "Host a Story Circle," now is a good time to jump back there.

To dig deeper into the idea of framing stories for meaning, review the metanarrative structures in Chapters 11 and 12, "Fractal Narratives."

Use these ideas when you want to make your stories better! Improve your craft as a storyteller by drawing from the deep body of knowledge about what makes great stories. Pick a story that you want to make better, and connect it to timeless structures that are proven to connect.

For this exercise you will need:

- Awareness of a specific story that you would like to improve.

- Note that this exercise works even better if you share your progress with a trusted friend. Consider finding someone to share feedback as your story evolves through a series of incremental improvements.

Chapter 4

CAPTURING FIRE

BETTER STORIES! MORE IMPACT!

Elsewhere in Circle of the 9 Muses, *I have made the point that it is better to tell the right story, the strategically chosen story, than it is to tell the story well. That's true.*

But a killer, beautifully delivered story would be even better, right? This is especially true for leaders who communicate directly with the marketplace or the media. And if the CEO is going to be in the audience of your next presentation, it would be nice if you could knock it out of the park.

Fortunately, in our quest to develop knockout stories, there is no shortage of material to draw from. Professional story makers in Hollywood invest in a high-stakes pursuit of understanding which stories connect and why. (And it is a testament to the endless nuance of the craft that they still get it wrong so frequently.) Increasingly, organizational leaders are also tapping this deep body of knowledge as a path to influence, and screenwriting gurus, such as the legendary Robert McKee, are now presenting their insights to packed audiences of corporate executives.

For insight we can look back even further to the year 1863, when German playwright Gustav Freytag proposed a classic structure in his *Technik des Dramas.*

His definitive five-act structure for drama—which includes exposition (setup), rising action, climax, falling action, and denouement (wrap-up)—is so pervasive that it may strike modern story consumers as self-evident. And yet how often have you heard leaders fail to set up their story with audience-tailored exposition, articulate the most critical sequence of events in the rising action or climax, or bring the story to a satisfying close? Violations of this basic structure are epidemic. You will notice that Freytag's framework informs many of the techniques and templates provided in this chapter.

Throughout this chapter, we will travel across time and cultures to find wisdom that we can connect to your storytelling. And, of course, we will draw from my colleagues' and my own experiments in helping leaders all over the world tell better stories.

Although there are many, many paths into the world of stories, for the sake of simplicity we will explore it here in a step-by-step process in which you will consider one of your stories through a series of lenses.

Ready to get started?

Freytag's classic five-act story structure. It may be common sense . . . but in many organizations it is not common practice.

| Setup | Rising action | Climax | Falling action | Wrap up |

Your turn!

First, Pick a Story to Work On

Think of a story that you would like to improve. This could be a story you've told before or one that you have identified previously in a different exercise in this book. Perhaps you have an event coming up soon, and you'd like to grab your audience with a great story. (If you are stuck and can't think of one, you may wish to review Chapter 1, "The Four Core Stories.")

Have you thought of your story? Good. If you are working with a friend, take turns sharing your selections with one another—and then be ready to share your coaching and ideas as you work through the lenses that follow.

For the purpose of example, I'll use a story that a 25-year-old participant named Geoff shared in a session recently. Here's what Geoff originally said:

> There was one time when one of my coworkers—Marcela, who everyone here knows, because she manages the projects, and everyone loves her—when Marcela made a mistake on our project plan. She came up and told everyone about the mistake and she didn't try to hide it even though it was a big deal. I thought that was really awesome. I wish more people would do that.

Geoff's intuition was correct: This is a story that needs to be heard. It has something relevant to say about leadership and the culture of his organization. But Geoff also sensed that it could land with more purpose and impact, so we are going to run it through some different frameworks and techniques. We will come back to Geoff. And to your story.

Clarify Your Intent

Intent is the invisible driver behind everything you do. Your people may not see your intent, but they will always respond to it. Great leaders develop an ever-present self-awareness around their intent, and they habitually pause to clarify the authentic *why* behind every action they take.

To tell great stories, begin with intent. Why are you telling this story? What outcome do you expect? There are endless reasons to tell a story to your team or audience, but ultimately it is because you want them to *know* something, to *do* something, or to *feel* something. (Or some combination of the three.) More specifically, here are some of the most common outcomes that storytellers desire, with examples of the audience's possible responses:

Framing
"Okay, now I understand our theme or why we have been gathered here today." "I see the need or chain of events that have led to this moment."

Engagement
"I'm going to enjoy our time together in this event. This feels good. I am eager to see what will happen next."

Credibility
"This speaker knows what she is talking about. We should listen to her." "I trust the speaker's experience or character."

Empathy
"The speaker really gets me, and understands our world." "This speaker knows what we are up against."

Pain awareness
"Things are hard here. I would love to be delivered from the situation that the speaker just illustrated." "Is there a way to stop these bad feelings?"

Vision and aspiration
"I would love to be a part of the compelling future that the speaker just illustrated." "I want that to happen to me. This is something I'm willing to work for."

Disorientation and disruption
"Now I am second-guessing my ways of thinking or acting. I don't know what to do." "You mean there's a better way forward?"

Insight
"Aha!" "Now I see a way forward. You gave me some ideas of things I can do differently. This is something I can act on." "I see a useful behavior or idea that I didn't see before."

Fascination
"This is new." "This is a way of thinking I've never considered before. This is intriguing/exciting. I want to hear more about these new possibilities." "I am motivated to understand more."

Connection
"I'm proud to be a part of this team/organization. I feel good about what we have accomplished together. We are a part of something special." "What we are doing matters."

Your turn!

What Is Your Intent?

Think about the story you identified at the beginning of this chapter, and the context where you will share it. What is your intent in telling it? What kind of response do you want from your audience?

Choose one or more possible outcomes from the list. For now, you don't have to take action on the intent, or change your story. At least, not yet. Just hold this as an awareness. After we spend some time with your story, we will come back and double-check to see whether the results do indeed serve your intent.

At first, Geoff had a hard time identifying his intent for telling the story about Marcela admitting a mistake. He ultimately decided that in this event—an off-site, two-day learning retreat with his colleagues—he wanted to drive *insight*: "If everyone would just admit their mistakes," he said, "it would make our work go so much smoother. It would save money too." Great choice. His story has the benefit of featuring a single easy-to-replicate behavior, which is always helpful when we are in the realm of insight.

After additional reflection, Geoff also decided that he also wanted people to feel *connection*: "This is a special place where people can feel safe admitting mistakes. It wasn't like that at my other job. My team here deserves to feel good about that." Armed with this awareness around his intent, Geoff said he immediately felt a rush

of excitement and urgency—which is a familiar state for people who are fueled by purpose.

Now select one or more outcomes that you desire for your story from this list:

I want my story to produce:

Framing	Disorientation and disruption
Engagement	
	Insight
Credibility	
	Fascination
Empathy	
	Connection
Pain awareness	
	Something else:
Vision and aspiration	

Again, hold this awareness. We will double-check your intent at the end of our process.

Connect Your Story to Universal Plots

There are no new stories. Human beings keep telling and living the same stories over and over. This may sound limiting, but the opposite is true. Once you begin to recognize the universal stories that surround us, it is tremendously liberating as a storyteller. For example, you may recognize that your last sales call was actually a reenactment of the classic David and Goliath theme. Or perhaps your failed project was the story of a winged Icarus flying too close to the sun (with only the names and a few other details switched out). When you tell your stories with that kind of archetypal awareness, you elevate even the most modest stories and connect to your audience's primal need states. Story theorist Robert McKee says, "Stereotyped stories stay home. Archetypal stories travel."[1]

Many story theorists have proposed frameworks that suggest that a fixed number of dramatic plots keep re-occurring in stories. For example, in his book *The Seven Basic Plots: Why We Tell Stories*, author Christopher Booker makes a persuasive case that every story falls into one of seven plots. In the influential *Save the Cat! The Last Book on Screenwriting You'll Ever Need*, Blake Snyder says that movies all fall into one of 10 basic frameworks.

These attempts to create a story taxonomy aren't limited to modern-day Hollywood. In 1895, the French dramatist Georges Polti presented a more nuanced framework with *les trente-six situations dramatiques*—the 36 dramatic situations.[2]

If this were a class in screenwriting or novel writing, all of Booker's, Snyder's, Polti's, and others' material would be fair game. However, my experience in leadership storytelling suggests that most of the time we will draw from a more limited palette. That's because leadership stories tend to be aspirational. They don't typically deal with, oh, adultery, the accidental murder of your brother, or finding out that your mortal enemy is actually your father in disguise. In our efforts to create organizational alignment, there is far more power in the stories of virtue rewarded than there are in the shadowy tales of the salacious, the unseemly, or the macabre.[3]

---

1. *Story: Substance, Structure, Style and the Principles of Screenwriting*, ReganBooks, 1997

2. Polti based his work on the writing of the great German writer Johann Goethe, who in turn says he based his thinking on the work of an Italian dramatist of the 1700s named Carlo Gozzi. Interestingly, all three writers ended up with a list of exactly 36 dramatic scenarios, and claimed they were unable to think of a 37th. In the appendix, you'll find descriptions of Booker's seven plots, Snyder's 10 frameworks, and Polti's 36 dramatic situations.

3. That's not to say there is never a place for leaders to tell stories of betrayal and revenge, for example. There are certainly opportunities to explore the darker parts of human nature in the business world to great effect—especially when doing some truth telling about a past or current reality. (Nonetheless I would caution against telling stories of eroticism and adultery on your next earnings call!) But for the purposes of this chapter, we will remain focused on the virtuous future stories.

On the following pages you will find my library of leadership story frameworks, informed by the great thinking of those I've already mentioned, and cultivated through my experiences applying the frameworks to leaders. This list is certainly not comprehensive, but I find that it covers most of the leadership bases.

It begins with the granddaddy of leadership storytelling, which drives all the examples that will follow. This master template, called *The Quest,* flows like this:

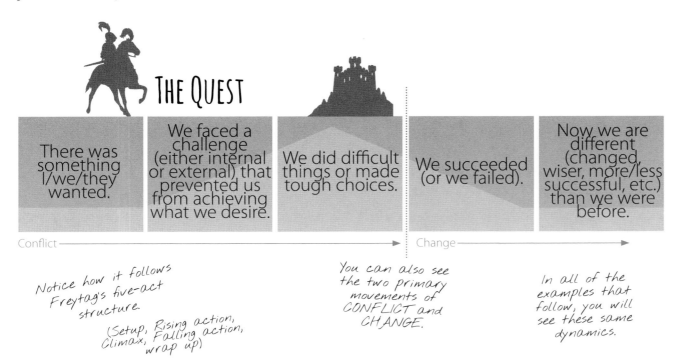

THE QUEST

There was something I/we/they wanted.

We faced a challenge (either internal or external) that prevented us from achieving what we desire.

We did difficult things or made tough choices.

We succeeded (or we failed).

Now we are different (changed, wiser, more/less successful, etc.) than we were before.

Conflict —————————————————————→ Change —————————————→

Notice how it follows Freytag's five-act structure.

(Setup, Rising action, Climax, Falling action, wrap up)

You can also see the two primary movements of CONFLICT and CHANGE.

In all of the examples that follow, you will see these same dynamics.

80

Note how the *The Quest* is built on two movements of conflict and change. In fact, these are the core building blocks of all storytelling.[4]

Michael Margolis, chief executive officer (CEO) of Get Storied, says that if you can find the conflict in your narrative, you find the hook to grab your audience. "Your greatest source of untapped power," he says, "is the place in your story that needs to be reconciled."

Every living creature with a limbic system and an instinct for self-preservation experiences its world through the lenses of conflict and change. Influential Hollywood story guru Bobette Buster says that our insatiable appetite for transformation is what draws us perpetually to the movies. Simply pausing to consider your story through these primal lenses will elevate its urgency. In my story, where is the conflict? What are the forces that are working against me/us? What are the stakes? What is changing (or how are you being changed)? What will be different when we win (or lose?)

In business stories, the conflict may come in the form of a competitor, a tough customer, or a difficult boss. But dig deeper and you'll find that the real source of conflict is probably *us*: our beliefs, mental models, and behaviors, which got us into this mess and which must now change.

What was the conflict? What changed? If your intent is to tell better stories, answering those questions is your first point of leverage.

Again, the simple Quest template as laid out on the previous page never seems to become tiresome. You have seen it, heard it, and read it countless times and it is endlessly evergreen. It is also open to tremendous variation. Let's expand our palette of choices with the following archetypes, and see if you can think of examples from your own experiences.

Note that the following examples are all positioned in the collective first person: *we*. This is for the sake of illustration. Let your story dictate whether the protagonist is *them*, *you*, *me*, *her*, and so on.

Key:

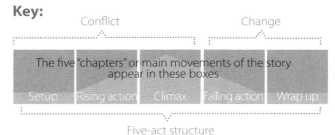

Five-act structure

---

4. Or to be more specific, conflict and change are the building blocks of Western storytelling. The idea that transformation is a result of conflict is embedded deeply into not only how we consume stories but also our very philosophy of life. But some Eastern traditions, such as the Japanese narrative tradition of Kishōtenketsu, offer a tantalizing alternative: a plot that has no conflict. It's an idea that is almost inconceivable to most Western thinkers. Given that the readers of this book are most likely products of Western cultural influences, I won't attempt to wade into those waters. At least, not here and not today. Buy me a beer and let's talk.

THE HEROIC ACT

| We came up against a formidable threat. | There were moments we were not confident of the outcome. | We demonstrated amazing virtues (such as passion, dedication, courage, ingenuity, etc.) | We triumphed, and now our world is better. | We have new awareness of who we are and what we can do. |

Example: *The Hobbit*
Business example: "How our underdog firm landed the big account."

THE THREAT AMONG US
("MONSTER IN THE HOUSE")

| An unanticipated threat entered our business. | It caused disruption / destruction. | We had to gather our wits and resources quickly. We suffered loss. | We demonstrated resilience. It took effort, but we ejected the threat. | Today we are stronger and more secure against such threats. |

Examples: *Alien, Jaws*
Business example: "The week that a software bug crashed our servers and brought our sales to a halt."

THE EXTRAORDINARY WORLD
("FISH OUT OF WATER")

| We found ourselves in a fascinating place where the rules were different (such as in a different culture, in the presence of powerful groups, in the media, in a very different industry, etc.) | What usually worked in our "normal" world, didn't work here. | We had to learn new skills and behaviors, improvise, and respond in the moment. | We navigated through the situation. | Today we are changed; more capable, more aware, and more resilient. |

Movie example: Harry Potter arrives at Hogwarts for the first time
Business examples: "The time we were called in to testify before Congress." "Launching our new stores in Asia."

82

Impossible Odds

| We encountered an adversary with significantly more strength, resources, or power. | The odds were against us, and the stakes were high. | We operated from a place of truth and integrity. | We were victorious over the established power. | Today we have the confidence of knowing our convictions / capabilities have been tested. |

Examples: David and Goliath; Harry Potter battles Voldemort
Business example: "Our small firm's new product went up against the industry leader and won."

Speaking Truth to Power (The Standoff)

| We found ourselves at odds with someone influential, powerful, or intimidating. | We were confident in our truth, and knew it would be a source of conflict. | We spoke up/stood by our principles or our truth without fear (or in spite of fear). | We may have won, or we may have lost. | We kept our integrity, and demonstrated that we are people of values and conviction. |

Examples: Dorothy stands up to the great and powerful Oz; the anonymous Tiananmen Square protester (who stood before the line of tanks)
Business example: "Everyone gasped the day I challenged the CEO . . . but he listened!"

The Noble Stand

| We faced a challenge that put our values to the test. | It would have been more practical, less expensive, or less disruptive if we had compromised. | There was a moment of confrontation that required our commitment, courage. | We stood by our values. We did not compromise, despite the cost. | Now we are seeing even greater rewards. |

Example: "I am Spartacus!"; Atticus Finch in *To Kill a Mockingbird*
Business example: "The time we voluntarily recalled our product even though customers were pleased with the quality."

Virtue Rewarded at Last

We encountered tribulation—possibly for a very long time.	We battled hard times and wanted to give up.	We refused to abandon our ideals, hope, faith, or integrity.	Finally we achieved liberation.	Now our virtue is recognized and rewarded.

Examples: Nelson Mandela; *The Shawshank Redemption*; George Bailey (played by Jimmy Stewart) in *It's a Wonderful Life*; Prince Charming takes Cinderella away from the evil stepmother

Business example: "The time our customer left us for a low-cost provider . . . and later came back to us and said they were wrong."

The Rite of Passage

We set out to accomplish something; our eyes were fixed on a goal.	We encountered a series of challenges that tested our capabilities and endurance.	We responded to each surprising development by summoning different capabilities.	We had some victories, and we also suffered loss.	We achieved (or missed) the goal, but found that the true value came from the journey.

Examples: An athlete training for the Olympics; *Rocky*; *Stand By Me*

Business example: "How I survived my first two years on Wall Street."

The Fatal Flaw

We were confident. We expected to succeed.	We entered a situation that we were unprepared for.	Our hidden vulnerability was our undoing.	We fell.	Today we have deeper self-awareness or a plan for going forward. We are ready to try again and win.

Example: Achilles' heel

Business examples: "I thought the company-wide software implementation would go fine. Here's why I was wrong."
"How I lost my first job at the ad agency."

Journey to the Heart

Our business as usual was disrupted by a situation demanding a more human response.	We demonstrated "softer" capabilities (such as vulnerability, love, compassion, or kindness).	Someone's life was changed.	Everyone was touched or moved.	Today we see ourselves differently, or are inviting those same human characteristics into other parts of our work.

Example: *How the Grinch Stole Christmas*

Business examples: "Our response to the family when one of our team members died." "The time our team rallied around one of our struggling customers." "After the local flood/earthquake/tornado, our people responded with amazing dedication and resilience."

Resurrection or Redemption
(Internal Setback)

We experienced failure, loss, disappointment, or embarrassment.	We were down but not out.	We took action, or changed the meaning of the bad event.	The event became a source of value, learning, and change.	Today, the loss makes us better. We are thankful for the challenge we experienced.

Example: Luke Skywalker must soldier on after the death of Obi-Wan Kenobi

Business example: "The day our biggest account fired us and went with our competitor, but we didn't quit."

The Point of No Return
(External Setback)

There was a cataclysmic action, decision, or event.	The world was fundamentally changed and we can never go back.	We were forced to learn new ways of acting and thinking.	Now we are adjusting to (or thriving in) the new normal.	We are ready for what is next.

Examples: *War of the Worlds* or any zombie virus apocalypse story; Bluto's (John Belushi's) famous speech in *Animal House*: "Did you say 'over'? Nothing is over until we decide it is!"

Business example: "Rebuilding our team after the layoffs."

Wish Fulfillment, or The Dream Comes True

We received the thing we always dreamed of.	There was a cost or surprise repercussions.	We struggled.	We experienced some wins and also some losses.	We are wiser today, and that wisdom was hard-earned.

Examples: Aladdin negotiating with the genie, Faust's deal with the devil
Business example: "After we went public and were flush with cash, that's when things became difficult . . ."

The Lonely Path of the Visionary

We were driven by our own vision to do something new.	We encountered critics, people who couldn't see what we saw, and other barriers.	We made sacrifices alone for the thing we believed in.	We unveiled our brilliant creation (to acclaim or to derision).	Today, our world is improved because of our vision, and we are recognized, fulfilled, or rewarded for our vision and belief.

Examples: Thomas Edison invents the light bulb in his Menlo Park laboratory.
Business example: "Everyone thought we were crazy for rebuilding our core offering from scratch . . . but then the market changed and we were hailed as heroes for being ahead of the curve."

The Enigma

A series of events started interrupting our world. We could not explain the events.	We took a series of actions to identify the cause of the events.	With ingenuity and persistence, we figured out what it was.	We took action and restored order.	Now we understand our world better, and are stronger as we face the future.

Examples: Most detective mysteries or police procedurals such as television's *Law & Order*
Business example: "Last year, our new accounts mysteriously dropped 50 percent, and here's how we figured out the cause."

Choose a Plot Archetype

Earlier you identified a story that you want to tell. Now it's time to elevate that story by connecting it to one of the plots presented in this chapter. Which of these best matches the story that you identified? (Note that *The Quest* is the broadest plot. Use it if the others don't quite match.)

☐ The Quest
☐ Extra-ordinary world
☐ Noble Stand
☐ Fatal Flaw
☐ Point of No Return
☐ The Enigma

☐ Heroic Act
☐ Impossible Odds
☐ Virtue Rewarded at Last
☐ Journey to the Heart
☐ Wish Fulfillment

☐ Threat Among Us
☐ Speaking Truth to Power
☐ Rite of Passage
☐ Resurrection/Redemption
☐ Lonely Path of the Visionary

Additional Plots

Want more? This chapter presents only a handful of the most inclusive story archetypes. You may draw from many others, including:

The Trials of Job. "Just when we thought it couldn't get any worse, it did. This has taught us a lot."

The Big Misunderstanding. "We took action based on poor communication or assumptions, and it caused a mess we had to clean up."

The Dodged Bullet. "If we had made a different decision, things would be much worse now."

The Big Screwup. "We made a mistake through sheer human error. We got bad results. We changed our system, thinking, or behavior, and now we are getting good results."

The Tragedy. "How we lost it all, and began to recover and find a new way forward in the face of loss."

Rags to Riches. "How we went from nothing to our current success." (Many gangster movies, such as *Scarface*, are rags-to-riches tales using antiheroes.)

Deliverance. "Someone asked us for help and we took him or her out of a bad situation." Or, "Someone rescued us."

The Deal with the Devil. "We made a commitment, and it demanded much more of us than we anticipated."

The Innocent Accused. "Someone accused us of wrongdoing and we paid a price, even though we were innocent."

Revolt. "We were mad as hell at the system or the prevailing powers, and we chose not to take it anymore!"

Remember Geoff's story about Marcela admitting a mistake? He decided that was a story of *The Noble Stand*, although he couldn't initially see how it aligned perfectly. (The Noble Stand includes a "confrontation." He said, "What was the confrontation? Marcela just came up and admitted her mistake. There wasn't really a conflict." I pushed back: "Are you sure about that?" I reminded him that very often, the conflict is internal and invisible.)

After you've selected a framework, go back and look at the stages. Now write your story so that it follows the stages.

Geoff looked at the template for The Noble Stand and reworked his story:

The Noble Stand

We faced a challenge that put our values to the test.	It would have been more practical/less expensive/less disruptive if we had done nothing.	There was a moment of confrontation that required our commitment, courage.	We stood by our values. We did not compromise, despite the cost.	Now we are seeing even greater rewards.
Well, Marcela manages some of the biggest and most significant projects in our company. That means she is in charge of assigning timelines, money, and resources to the most important work we are doing. One day she discovered that she made a critical error. It would have meant my team would need to throw away a *lot* of work.	There were probably ways she could have covered her butt on this. She could have asked the client to change their timeline. Or she could have taken some resources from a different team. Or maybe she could have just put the blame on Production or somebody. Because this was an expensive mistake!	I can only image that bad moment when Marcela realized what had happened. What would *you* have done? Well, I know what Marcela did.	She came to us right away, and she told everyone what she did. She completely owned it. She doesn't hide from the truth, even when she is the one in the hot seat.	We did have to change our work and we lost a lot of hours. But no one got mad at Marcela. Everyone was impressed by how she handled it. If she had waited, it would have been much worse. She saved us money by coming forward like she did.

Now it's your turn! Write out your story like Geoff did above so that it aligns to the framework you identified.

Other Story Structures: FWA*

Story theory is deep. There is no shortage of plots, frameworks, and structures to think about. If you wish to step away from the plot archetypes described in this chapter, there are other ways to go. Here are some acronym-driven approaches that are simple, memorable, and easy to act upon.

In *Lead with a Story*, Paul Smith makes a good case that the easiest way to shape your story is with the acronym CAR. It stands for:

Context:

So, there we were, sitting in the conference room on the eighth floor, when the door burst open . . .

Action:

Amy shouted, "We won the Epic account!" And then . . .

Result:

. . . In the end, all of our hard work paid off, and here is the new innovation we produced . . .

Does your memory have room for another letter? Dr. Karen Dietz offers another acronym called STAR, which reminds you to bring conflict (Trouble) into the story:

Situation:

So, there we were, sitting in the conference room on the eighth floor, when the door burst open . . .

Trouble:

Amy shouted, "We won the Epic account!" But then she said, "There's just one problem . . ."

Action:

So we spent all night reviewing the code, the project plans, and the budget . . .

Result:

. . . In the end, all of our hard work paid off, and here is the new innovation we produced . . .

Dr. Dietz also suggests adding two more elements to turn STAR into STARQE (pronounced "stark" as in "the stark data and truth"). The Q and E stand for *Quantification* and *Evaluation,* and they bring data-driven discipline and learning to your story.

Quantification:

In total, that was more than 100 labor hours of troubleshooting that resulted in more than $3 million in added revenue . . .

Evaluation:

So I learned from all of this that even the most established processes are vulnerable, and we must never be overconfident . . .

So next time you need to construct a story quickly, just remember:

CAR
- Context
- Action
- Result

STAR
- Situation
- Trouble
- Action
- Result

STARQE
- Situation
- Trouble
- Action
- Result
- Quantification
- Evaluation

*Fun With Acronyms

Declare Your Intent

Earlier you identified your intent for telling your story. Geoff had identified *insight* and *connection* as his dual reasons for telling the story.

Do you think his story accomplishes this?

I think it is on the right track. But intent is most powerful when it is declared. As my colleague Barry Rellaford described once, intent is like the turn signal on your car. The reason you turn on the blinker when you are about to take a right turn is to declare your intent to the people behind you: "When I get to the next intersection, I intend to turn right, which means I am about to apply my brakes and slow down." Now that other drivers know your intent, they can modify their behaviors and put on their brakes without plowing into your rear. (Have you ever gotten mad when someone didn't signal? "Use your blinker, jerk!" We don't like to be surprised by undeclared intent.)

Don't assume that everyone in the audience will automatically intuit your intent. Your story is more powerful if you put on your blinker and declare it. This can be a simple statement that you add to the end of the story.

Here are two statements that Geoff added to the end of his story to declare his intent to produce *insight* and *connection*:

> We did have to change our work, and we lost a lot of hours. But no one got mad at Marcela. Everyone was impressed by how she handled it. If she had waited, it would have been much worse. She saved us money by coming forward like she did.
>
> *Original version . . .*

> So, there's a reason I told you this story. It's a story about owning our mistakes. It's such a simple thing to step up and say, "I own this." No matter what the cost is. And look what a big difference it makes. This is what allows our team to be as agile and innovative as we are.
>
> *. . . plus Insight . . .*

> And the other thing is, this is a great place to work. At my last job, everyone covered their butts. But the thing Marcela proves is that this is a place where you can admit mistakes and no one will dogpile you. Everyone will support you! That is pretty awesome, and rare.
>
> *. . . and Connection*

This kind of overt connection is unwelcome in most entertainment storytelling, where it may be seen as moralizing. But in leadership storytelling, our mandate is not to entertain but to align. And you cannot assume that the audience will draw the connections you intended. You have to turn on your blinker and say the words. In doing so, you draw a container around the meaning and define the space for further exploration.[5]

Take a few minutes now and add the statement of intent at the end of your story.

....
5. Of course, stories can go to work on your audience when you declare no intent or make no overt connections. Sometimes it is equally powerful simply to tell the story and allow each audience member to be affected by it in his or her own way. But too many leaders miss the opportunity to make these connections . . . or to invite their team into the dialogue (which you will explore in the next chapter).

Other Tips and Techniques for Better Stories

You just took a rather broad approach to thinking about the form of your story. Of course, you can take many other steps to make your story truly unforgettable. Here are a few tips that are low-hanging fruit: easy to implement, while delivering big a impact.

As you consider these techniques, determine which ones might bring even more punch to your story.

Technique 1: Throw 'Em Right into the Action

I hear a lot of new storytellers begin their stories with long, agonizing preambles in which they tell their audience *about* the story. "Well, my boss asked me to tell a story, so I'm going to tell you about something that happened at our last regional meeting in Atlanta. Everyone here has been to those meetings, right? So you will know what I'm talking about. And you'll appreciate how unexpected this was. I know I didn't expect it. So, okay. Here's what happened . . ."

Agonizing, right? Nothing loses an audience faster than telling *about* a story without actually telling it.

Instead, invite your audience into the story immediately. Just put them right into the action! This is easy to do. Think of the beginning of your story. Close your eyes and

imagine the scene. And then just start describing it. To orient your thoughts in a specific sense of place, you may find it helpful to use the phrase (or some variation) "So, there I was . . ."

So there we were, still finding our seats at the regional meeting in Atlanta. The lights haven't even gone down yet, and suddenly someone starts yelling something from the back of the auditorium . . .

I was dead asleep in my bed, 4:00 in the morning, and my phone rings . . .

It was just after breakfast and the temperature was already 103 degrees Fahrenheit in Saudi Arabia, and there I was sweating on the street corner in a full business suit . . .

Notice how each of those draws the audience into the narrative immediately. No preamble. No explanations or clues of what you're about to hear. Place them in the story and trust the audience's imaginations to engage.

♚ ♛ Technique 2:
Add Emotion ("The King
and the Queen")

Stories are containers for emotion. There is an important opportunity here that many leaders miss.

I've seen many leaders go to great lengths to strip out any emotion from their stories. They fear that emotion is too unprofessional, too self-revealing, too soft, or too vulnerable. My European colleagues fear that using emotion is too American.

And yet, more than any other detail in your story, emotion is what engages your audience. If you strip out the emotion, you remove engagement. It's that simple.

E. M. Forster, the great English novelist and essayist who gave us *A Passage to India, A Room with a View*, and more, famously said, "A story is nothing more than a fact plus an emotion."[6]

Forster illustrates this memorably. If I were to say to you, "The queen died and the king died," that is a fact.

But if I said, "The queen died and the king died *of grief*," that is a story.

See how the simple addition of an emotion transformed the data into an experience? Perhaps it triggered your own experiences with grief. "Yes. I remember. I know how that feels." A flood of emotional information arrives in an instant.

Your mind experiences emotion in the amygdala, which is the brain's fight-or-flight center; the amygdala then signals the hippocampus—the seat of executive functioning—with the message, "This is important. You'd better save it so that we can retrieve it later." This is why your dog won't tangle with a skunk a second time.

This emotional experience also has the effect of lifting the audience out of the present and putting them in a different shared experience that Graham Williams describes as "narrative transport." This is a powerful effect, and at its best it bears similarity to a trance or hypnotic state. Graham says he recalls watching the movie *The Elephant Man* in a theater and being unexpectedly seized with sobs that he could not control. "At some level I had entered the story," he says. "Perhaps I identified with Joseph Merrick's ugly duckling situation. I certainly experienced overwhelming empathy with him, and anger at what society can do to individuals."

Granted, your goal may not be for your audience of leaders to become overcome by an uncontrollable fit of crying. (Although think for a moment about what a powerful

6. Quoted in *Lead with a Story: A Guide to Crafting Business Narratives That Captivate, Convince, and Inspire*, Paul Smith, AMACOM, 2012

92

event that would be and the opportunity it would offer to disrupt mental models and redirect action.)

Many leaders avoid enhancing their stories with emotional declarations—especially with the vulnerable emotions, such as uncertainty, anxiety, or fear—because of the unpredictability of emotion. But rather than compromise your strength, it becomes its own unique source of strength and credibility.

In terms of your storytelling, this can be very easy to do. Simply include short, declarative statements of emotion:

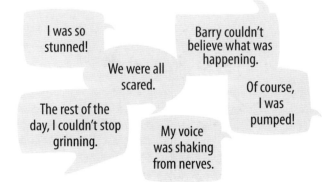

See how simple that is? Notice how each of those short statements provides powerful triggers that indicate how your audience should process your story emotionally. Emotion brings the audience along with you.

Earlier in *Circle of the 9 Muses*, we shared the Zappos 10-hour customer service call story. That story did not include any emotional statements. Here it is again with some emotional statements (with new content highlighted in bold text):

On December 8, 2012, a customer service representative took a call that clocked in at a record-setting 10 hours and 29 minutes! The customer called to order a pair of Ugg boots, but in the conversation the service rep discovered that the customer was about to relocate to the Las Vegas area, where Zappos is located. They spent 10 hours exploring neighborhoods and other details of life in Vegas. **The whole time, the customer service guy is just relaxed, and smiling.** At the end of the call, the customer purchased the pair of Ugg boots. **Think about that. Ten hours! When I first heard this story, I couldn't believe it. I was incredulous. I thought, "That guy wasted company resources." But the response from the company stunned me even more. Here's what they said . . .**

In the example above, note that the emotional statements are applied to the customer service protagonist ("the customer service guy is just relaxed, and smiling"). They also connect to the storyteller ("I couldn't believe it," etc.). Thus, the audience is allowed to empathize with the values-driven customer service agent, as well as the story-teller who is calling out his or her own reaction to the tension in the story. In the process, the storyteller gives voice and validation to the invisible reactions of the audience.

You can imagine how an effective delivery of the above story might also include facial expressions, body posture, and verbal inflections to help bring the emotion to life even more!

Technique 3: Add Sensory and Motion Information

Similar to the use of emotional statements, when you add sensory or motor information to your story, it activates the parts of the brain called, respectively, the sensory cortex and motor cortex.

I already suggested this in my example about Saudi Arabia a few pages back, which is a story from my own experience that I told to a group. In fact, let's add a little more sensory information:

> It was just after breakfast and the temperature was already 103 degrees Fahrenheit in Saudi Arabia, and I was standing on the street corner wearing a full business suit. The downtown buildings, with their black marble facades, had absorbed the heat and were now radiating it like ovens. I could *see* the heat coming off the streets in waves . . .

Similarly, notice how these quick statements of smell, sight, touch, taste, and sound activate the corresponding regions of your sensory cortex. Pay attention to how you experience these statements:

> For our meeting they led us to the basement of this old building, where it smelled like mildew and cigarette smoke . . .

> Every time the elevator outside my office went *ping!* I just knew the doors were about to open and unleash another angry customer on us.

> When the auditor shook my hand, his grip was like iron and his skin was tough like a farmer's.

> Her office smelled like that fancy lavender soap from bathrooms.

This also works with action statements, which create a little adrenaline release by triggering the motor cortex of the brain:

> I handed the engagement survey results to Denise, but instead of looking at it, she just threw it toward the trash can like *this* . . .

> So there we were, this team of sales reps, huffing and puffing and running down the concourse at LaGuardia at top speed in our heels . . .

> I asked Gerald if he remembered to get the blueprints, and he *slammed* on the brakes, and I hear the car tires squeal, and my heart stops because I'm thinking, *I'm gonna die.*

Notice how that last statement is a triple hit of motor, sensory, *and* emotional information!

Story thought leader Annette Simmons advocates mixing sensory information. These sensory mash-ups create a moment of surprise that prompts your mind to take an extra step to reconcile the metaphors:

> My mentor reassured me, with his velvet voice . . .

> When she told her story, the room was electric!

> She kept tossing out recommendations, and each had the substance of cotton candy . . .

Technique 4: The "MacGuffin," or Gleaming Detail

The great film director Alfred Hitchcock ("the Master of Suspense") often constructed his films' most dramatic moments around some visual object that became the physical embodiment of the film's action and themes. He called this item the "MacGuffin," and he said that it didn't even matter what it was. In *North by Northwest*, that film's most suspenseful moments hinge on a metal cigarette lighter; and once you've seen *Notorious* you never forget that key

to the wine cellar, and its dangerous journey as it is passed from Ingrid Bergman to Cary Grant.

A few months ago in Paris, an executive in one of my story programs held up a pair of socks and said, "I want to tell you about a leader who changed my entire perspective of leadership with this pair of socks." (Aren't you intrigued? Our audience certainly was.)

Another leader told a story he called "the white box," which was a box in the break room of a manufacturing facility in which employees could make anonymous donations that would later be distributed to other employees in times of great need. His telling of the story was powerful, as he allowed the audience to follow the white box from the break room to a hospital where an employee was in intensive care. Today, thanks to that memorable telling of the story, one can simply say "white box" anywhere in the manufacturing division, and it is a universally recognized metaphor for the company's culture of caring for its employees. (And likewise, for my group in Paris, one can now simply say "gym socks," and everyone will smile in instant recognition.)

Is there a MacGuffin (or "gleaming detail" as Bobette Buster calls it) that can become the embodiment of your story? Perhaps it is a crystal paperweight from your desk; a label that says, "Hello My Name Is . . ."; an old floppy disk with faded writing on the label; or a handwritten thank-you note from a customer. If so, describe it, use it, show it, and build your story on it. The image of the object will become an easy-to-recall metaphor that cements the story indelibly in your audience's minds.

Technique 5: Play with the Timeline

Christopher Nolan's movie *Memento* is famous for starting at the end of its story and working backward in time as an amnesiac seeks to discover the cause of his wife's murder. And Quentin Tarantino's influential *Pulp Fiction* thrillingly leapfrogs back and forth across its timeline in a way that disorients but somehow feels just right emotionally.

I'm not suggesting that your business story attempt the same dazzling acrobatics as those innovative movies. But I have certainly heard storytellers make some simple leaps across the timeline to great effect.

For example, you might start with the end and then go back and tell the story sequentially:

> We watched the FedEx cargo flight take off and disappear into the sky. Somewhere on that plane was a special order of $1 million of valve fittings that had just come off our line in Nashville. John and I looked at each other, kind of dazed, sweat still running down our backs, because we knew we had come within 10 minutes of blowing the whole deal.
>
> How did we get that close to screwing up the biggest deal in our company's history? It all began a week earlier, the previous Monday, and we were at our facility in Portland . . .

The above story, by telegraphing the ending first, creates a tension that the remainder of the story will resolve.

Another approach: Tell the beginning. Tell the end. Then fill in the middle.

> We started at our kitchen table with two computers and a phone line. Now here we are with a $6 million buyout offer from our competitor. The ride in between was a wild one!

Set up parallel timelines:

> At 3:00 in New York, my team sat staring at the phone waiting for it to ring. At the exact same time, two time zones away, our production manager was waiting for the word to fire up the assembly line.
>
> And meanwhile, our competitor was sitting in the customer's office in Palo Alto making a counteroffer.

Make dramatic leaps across time and settings. Stanley Kubrick's 1968 movie, *2001: A Space Odyssey*, contains the most famous jump cut in the history of cinema, from a bone flung violently into the air by a prehistoric ape to a similarly shaped space station floating in the heavens in some unimaginable future. The jarring shifts in time and setting prompt the audience to search for the theme or connecting idea. You may recall that I did something similar in the introduction of this book, which begins with me on a date with my wife before catapulting back 30,000 years in time.

I heard one leader begin a story about his team by saying, "The story of our new safety initiative actually begins 150 years ago at Fort Sumter, South Carolina, with the first shot fired in the American Civil War." The entire room leaned forward in anticipation, hungry to hear how their story connected to that historical event.

Technique 6: Make It Shorter!

This is an easy one. Are you sure you need all of those words? You probably don't.

Remember that although there are notable exceptions, leadership storytelling is often rather brief. (Note that many of the examples scattered across the chapters of this book are no more than a paragraph in length.)

In his memoir, *On Writing*, horror novelist Stephen King exhorts aspiring storytellers to edit their own beautiful words mercilessly. "Kill your darlings, kill your darlings, even when it breaks your egocentric little scribbler's heart, kill your darlings," he says.

Capture your story in a word processor. Make note of the word count.

Can you remove 25 percent of the words?

What would happen if you cut it by 50 percent?

Give it a try. Or even better, let your spouse or partner do it for you. Weep for your brilliant words that have been forever lost; then marvel at the improved product that results.

Your turn!

Provide Some Final Polish to Your Story

As you review the six previous techniques, which ones do you think might offer additional improvement to your story? Here is how Geoff's story might have connected to each.

Throw 'Em Right into the Action.

> So there we were in the executive conference room, with empty sushi trays scattered around the big mahogany table. It was quiet, and everyone had their head down into their spreadsheets, when Marcela comes in . . .

Add Emotion (The King and the Queen).

> Before she even opened her mouth to speak, there was something about her. I just had this strong feeling of, *Oh, no, something's about to blow up.*

> I looked over at Amir, and his face was frozen and his eyes were wide. My stomach sank.

Add Sensory and Motion Information.

> The room was filled with the click-click-click of everyone typing away on their laptops, but when Marcela walked in with that look on her face it became instantly silent.

The "MacGuffin," or Gleaming Detail

> See this? It's a printout of a typical production schedule. But you may notice there's something different about this one. It is covered with frantic red editing marks. This is the document that Marcela brought to us when we were in the middle of planning for our product launch.

Play with the Timeline.

> It was 7:30 on a Wednesday evening, and the cleaning crew was vacuuming the office and turning out lights, but we were still in the conference room, and you could just smell anxiety in hanging in the air. How did we get here? It all began four hours earlier, when . . .

Make It Shorter.

You can see how, if we were to apply all of the techniques presented here, Geoff's simple story could quickly become bloated. And especially because Geoff's story is making a relatively straightforward point without dire stakes, this one doesn't need a lot of fanfare. A final pass over the story will allow an opportunity to bring it down to its essence.

Let's take a look at Geoff's final story on the next page.

Bringing It All Together: Geoff's Story

Let's take one last look at where Geoff's story landed. I like how it takes an easy-to-overlook moment in the life of a team and transforms it into a nice moment of learning and shared identity for the organization.

Follows "The Noble Stand" archetype

Throw 'em right into the action

More emotional data

Connection to teller's intent: Insight and Connection

Emotional and sensory information

The MacGuffin

I was sitting in the conference room with Amir and the others on the project team, and we were working on the final phase of the Alpha implementation, when Marcela—our project manager—came into the room. Even before she said anything, I saw the look on her face and my stomach sank and I thought, *Something is wrong*. And she held up *this* project plan, and you can see her edits all over it, and said, "Guys, I've made a critical error." It was a planning mistake that meant we would have to scrap more than 100 labor hours of work.

You could feel the team's panic rising, like a fever. But Marcela stood there, like a rock, making direct eye contact, and owning it. Think about that. She could have covered her butt, or changed the timeline of the client, or shifted around some resources to hide it. But instead she had the conviction to come face us within minutes of discovering her mistake. And just as amazing, the team immediately supported her. No blame, no finger-pointing.

The reason I'm telling you this story is, I've worked at places where everyone covers their butts and people who make mistakes get dogpiled. What we have here is rare. And as long as we can be that up-front with each other, and that supportive, I think we will keep delivering the innovation that our clients expect from us. Guys, we've got something special here. I'm proud to be part of this team with Marcela, and with you.

Story climax, conflict resolved

Great job, Geoff!

Where Do I Go from Here?

I think you're ready to tell your knockout story!

Go find an audience or occasion to tell your story. Test it out, make note of the response you get . . . and, if necessary, adjust it again to make it even stronger!

If you would like additional tools that can enrich your storytelling, check out leadership story archetypes (Chapter 8). This will offer richer insight into the identity and role of the protagonist of your story, or provide insight into your role or the unique voice of the teller.

PART II

BRANCHING OUT

Use this when you would like to enrich your story circle with a little more structure, to demonstrate the importance of each individual's voice in an organization, and to create a simple way for rich stories to begin bubbling up into the full group's awareness.

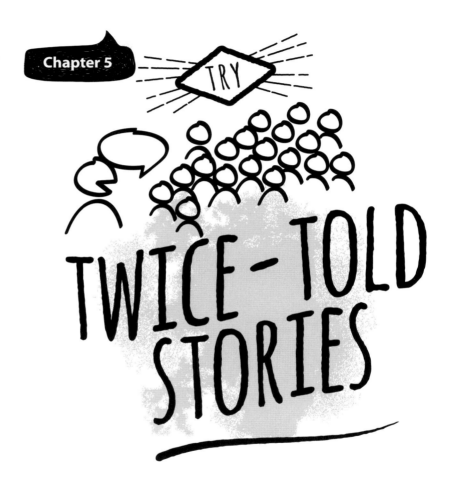

Chapter 5

TRY

TWICE-TOLD STORIES

For this exercise you will need:

- A story circle experience as described in Chapter 2

- At least two story groups with a total of at least seven or eight people (with no limit on the maximum)

- One flip chart for each story circle (If you have 16 people, they will be divided into four story circles, so you will need four flip charts, each preferably with its own stand.)

- Markers and tape

Twice-told stories is another classic story-sharing construct, and it has become a centerpiece of many of the story experiences that I host. The idea behind twice-told stories is very simple. If you have at least two story circles sharing their experiences at the same time, the room will be full of energy and sound as those concurrent story conversations fill the space. Members of one story circle may well think to themselves, *I wonder what kinds of stories my colleagues are telling over in the other group.* With twice-told stories, they will find out! Each group will have an opportunity to hear selected stories from the other groups—and a simple filtering process will ensure that especially rich, impactful, or urgent stories will be selected to share again with the entire room.

In fact, in its purest form that's really all there is to twice-told stories. Simply ask each story group to select its best story, and then have each of those tellers come to the front of the room to tell his or her story a second time—only this time to the full group.

But there are some exciting ways to facilitate this, and this chapter follows an elegant format that finds its genesis in the work of Paul Costello, with contributions from Dr. Madelyn Blair and Dr. Karen Dietz. Costello calls his process "Living Stories," which he has been practicing for more than 20 years at New Story Leadership. He works with young leaders all over the world to build future stories in war-torn societies marred by old, toxic stories. Costello and Blair have taught this process as part of The Center for Narrative Studies,[1] and they have agreed to share it here with you.

As described in this chapter, Twice-Told Stories makes several impactful statements:

- It illustrates the viral dynamic of story dissemination, in which some stories prove stickier, so to speak, and are selected by the social system as being somehow vital to the organization.

- It creates a powerful awareness that all the individual stories within the organization are all elements of the larger story that the members of the organization are living together. This is a great "from me to we" exercise.

- It creates an awareness of inclusion. No matter who I am in the organization, I see how my voice exists within a rich spectrum of other voices that are creating our organizational identity.

- It can serve as a simple way to begin capturing and archiving stories.

There are a few steps to this exercise, but it is really quite simple. Here's how it works.

....

1. Learn more at www.StoryWise.com.

Explain the Process to Your Story Circles

After you have organized your Story Circles (as described in Chapter 2), but before they begin sharing their stories, explain the steps. Here's how I explain the steps:

The First Teller Tells a Story.

The story circles will begin as they traditionally do. Explain this first step: "John, let's say you agree to go first. You'll begin by telling your story."

Group Members Suggest Titles (Teller's Choice).

"Group members, after John tells his story, don't forget to thank him! Then take turns suggesting a title for his story. The title can be funny, or exaggerated, or straightforward. A compelling title is good, because it will increase the interest from members of the other groups. But ultimately, this is John's story, so John gets to choose his title. John, you can us one of the titles generated by your teammates, or you can come up with a completely different one on your own."[2]

Capture the Title on the Flip Chart.

"Write the title of John's story on your flip chart."

Repeat until Everyone's Story Is on the Flip Chart.

"Now it is the next person's turn to tell their story. You will go around the circle and repeat the process. When you are done with the story circle, you will have four fascinating story titles on your flip chart." (Or three, five, or six, depending on how many people are in the story circle.)

Ask whether there are any questions. If not, begin the story circles.

The process begins with a story circle, only this time participants will assign a title to each story and then capture the titles on a flip chart.

----

2. Note that this process can include listening and meaning making processes, such as the Harvester/Witness construct described in Chapter 6, "Summoning the Muse." The group would simply harvest and witness before suggesting titles.

Begin the Story Circles

Allow enough time for the groups to complete multiple rounds of the process described above. Remain mindful of the progress that the story circles are making. If necessary, help them manage time. ("We are at the halfway mark. Fifteen minutes left.") Because you will be able to see each group post their story titles to flip charts, you will have a clear visual cue to each group's progress. For example, you can see that the group in the picture below is now exactly halfway through their process.

Giving a title to a story has a subtly powerful effect. It gives the story an identity so that it becomes its own distinct thing, like a suitcase loaded with valuable artifacts of knowledge, ready to travel.

Close the Story Circle Experience and Select One Story to Retell

After the story circles have ended, explain to the story groups what will happen next. "Look around the room. There are a lot of stories that were told today! I bet you're wondering what some of your colleagues said. Let's find out."

Have each team select one story that will be shared with the larger group. I think the phrasing of this instruction is important. I do *not* ask the team to select the best story or their favorite story. This implies a judgment about the *quality* of the stories, and we're not interested in judging quality.

Instead, say, "Of these stories, which one do you think the rest of the room *needs to hear the most*?" Yes, this criterion is ambiguous and that is by design. If the team asks for clarity, instruct them to interpret the instruction however they wish. But I almost never encounter resistance. The group always knows intuitively which story needs to be heard! The story that the larger group needs to hear the most may be defined by urgency or by some special connection to the organization's most challenging problem—or it may be a story that greatly moved the team emotionally. Trust the team's collective intelligence. They will choose correctly.

Paul Costello says he has heard some team members complain that choosing a single story isn't "fair."

Costello explains that whether it is fair or not, story is *always* subject to a selection process. Communities always decide which stories have power. This, too, can be a rich topic of exploration: What criteria are the community using? Whose stories are being heard? Whose stories are being suppressed? What does this say about the power dynamics of the community? Are there steps that must be taken to restore justice?

Recently I had a team tell me that they truly had a four-way tie and that they couldn't choose one story over the others. They asked whether they could read their four titles out loud and have the larger group vote on the one that sounded the most intriguing. It was a fun solution that produced a lot of laughter and energy. It also reinforced the idea that creative, skillful use of language can add to the value and intrinsic interest of a story.

Now each story group has selected one of its stories to present to the larger group, which means that teller gets to tell his or her story a second time. I always point this out to people. "If you wish, you can tell your story exactly the way you told it to your group. Or, you may be thinking there are things you'd like to change or present differently. It is up to you." This gives participants an opportunity to begin thinking about presentation, style, and crafting. But improvement is not the driving focus.

Create the Story Theater and Begin!

This is another small gesture that should not be skipped because it makes a significant statement. Until this point, your story circles have probably been scattered about the meeting space, along with their flip charts. Instruct all the teams to take their flip chart stand (or flip chart page) and put them all together in a common area, such as against a wall. The idea is to see all the flip chart pages side by side. This invites participants to scan all the pages and see all the story titles—their own and those of the other groups, including several stories that they won't get to hear.

Next, invite all participants to either move their seats or stand in front of the wall with the flip charts in a theater crescent configuration. Thus, as each teller shares his or

Bring all of the flip charts to the front of the room and arrange them where the group can see all of the titles. Have the first storyteller step up. Show time!

The listeners in this photo fascinate me. Even though we can see only their backs, their postures communicate a lot. How do you think they are experiencing this event?

her story, all participants will be able to see him or her easily, as well as the full panorama of story titles.

Invite the first teller to step forward. Ask him or her to read *all* the story titles that his or her group generated. (This will create intrigue and interest.) Then invite the teller to tell *his or her* story.

After the teller is done, be sure to applaud and thank the teller. If you are comfortable doing so, you may make some appreciative observations about the teller's personal presence as well as content.

Repeat the process for all the groups until each group has shared its chosen story.

The Critical Epilogue: Name the Bigger Story

This is yet another symbolic gesture that has big implications.

Let's pause and reflect on what the participants have experienced at this point. They have had a chance to share a story with a small group, heard one of their colleagues repeat a story to the full group, heard a series of stories from other groups, and, importantly, seen the titles of many other stories that they haven't heard yet.

Something significant is happening here that you should not overlook.

At the beginning of the exercise, participants were naturally self-focused on the challenge of telling a story to their colleagues. For some this may have been a source of performance anxiety or social pressure. But at this point in the exercise, participants now see the title of *their* individual stories alongside the titles of many others' stories. This makes a big impact, and participants will palpably feel a shift from individual self-awareness to collective self-awareness. *My story is not isolated. It exists alongside all of these other stories . . . and together they all come together to create a bigger story. It's the story of us. Our work, our identity, and what we are creating together.*

I make it a point to draw that out explicitly.

To drive this point home, Paul Costello does something with groups that I now do as well. Take a marker, open a new flip chart page, and say to the team, "We need to come up with one final title. Imagine each of your stories is a chapter in a book. *What is the title of the book?*"

I find that the titles people generate tend to be somewhat predictable: "The Story of Our Values in Action," "Leading with Quality and Excellence at Company X," and so on. And that's fine.

Individual stories all come together to create a bigger story. To define and name that shared story is an act of leadership.

The point here is not to generate something brilliantly creative but to create the awareness of a larger story and to validate that larger story by giving it a name. (In that way, this exercise connects to Chapter 11, "Fractal Narratives.") You may only need to capture three or four ideas, because participants will sense the significance of this gesture almost immediately.

If you do wish to capture richer titles, and bring your team into a deeper discussion about the bigger story of us, Dr. Madelyn Blair recommends breaking the team into pairs and having them discuss title ideas. Their ideas will be much richer, and the process allows them to reflect more deeply on the idea of our shared story.

This is a celebratory moment. Congratulate all the participants, and encourage them to give themselves a round of applause. Sometimes, participants get excited and say, "Hey, we really *should* turn this into a book!" Whether these stories would make a compelling book (and whether you wish to get involved) is for you to decide. I just point out to people how this is a sign that they are energized and invested in their collective story. They are justified in wanting their stories to live and be heard.

In my work this activity always seems to end right before lunch. I encourage participants to continue to share their stories with one another over lunch, and to ask questions about some of those other intriguing titles!

Modifying the Exercise
for Different-Sized Groups

This exercise is sensitive to numbers. It doesn't automatically scale upward or downward based on how many people participate. You'll need to make some adjustments.

Twice-told stories works ideally with a group of nine to 30 participants, with at least three story circles, and ideally no more than 10.

If you have a small group of three to five participants, the exercise will need to be modified. Keep everyone together in a single story circle. Have participants share their stories and generate titles on a single flip chart page. Because there are no other groups and therefore no other stories to hear, you will skip the story theater experience. Instead, go straight to the conversation about each story title being a chapter, and have the small group of participants generate ideas for the title of the book. Draw out the same points about individual contributions to the collective story, as described.

If you have six to eight participants, create two small groups. Run the exercise as described. However, when you get to the story theater, it may be a little anticlimactic to hear only two stories. Have the two selected storytellers take their turns, and then ask whether anyone else would like to volunteer—or whether anyone would like to volunteer a teammate. This may have the effect of bringing in a couple of more stories, or it may even result in everyone sharing. It's all good.

If you have a very large group, you'll need to do some pruning. Let's say you have 60 participants. If you place participants into groups of five, that gives you 12 story circles. Each story circle will need around 30 to 40 minutes to share their stories; then once everyone comes together, it would take well over an hour (12 stories at 5 minutes each) to hear each group's story in the story theater. If you have created a story retreat, in which participants expect to spend an entire day telling and sharing stories, then this may be acceptable. In a workshop setting with an active agenda, that feels a little long.

There are several options. Let's say you have 12 groups. If you have both the space and the time, you can create two separate story theaters in different rooms of 6 groups each. At the end, each can select a single story, so that when you bring the 12 groups back together each will hear the single story from the other. (This further illustrates the "emergent" selection process that is constantly happening with stories in social groups.)

Alternatively, you may simply wish to break up the 12 or more stories across the event. ("Let's hear eight stories now. We'll hear two more over dinner tonight, and the rest tomorrow morning.")

Capture It Visually!

Twice-told stories deliver value. You will start to hear the valuable, surprising, important stories of the organization. Some of these may even become the precious *narrative assets* that are told over and over, shaping how people view and experience the organization. Maybe you should capture some of those stories!

But how? Dr. Karen Dietz and I agreed that we are not fans of filming stories. In many contexts video cameras can be intrusive, and may cause a performance anxiety that compromises the story experience.

However, we have both had tremendous success with *graphic facilitation*. A graphic facilitator is a trained professional who is present in the room and captures the content of the stories in visual format. These images are powerful for aiding recall of the event after the fact. At the end of the story experience, expect to see participants pull out their smartphones to take photos of these images, which they will cherish as valuable knowledge artifacts that testify to the stories they told and meaning they created.

Graphic facilitation is a fast-growing discipline, and there are probably some experienced practitioners in your city. Do a Google search for graphic facilitators in your area.

It's fascinating work. If you're ready to take an even deeper dive into the application of visual-thinking techniques in your story work, look no further than the brilliant and pioneering work of David Sibbet, author of *Visual Meetings* (John Wiley & Sons, 2010), *Visual Teams* (John Wiley & Sons, 2011), and *Visual Leaders* (John Wiley & Sons, 2012).

Working quietly on the margins of the room, a graphic facilitator can capture the stories being told in a dramatic, visual, metaphorical presentation. When participants review these images later, it is amazing how much these images aid in recall. Participants will remember not only the story details but also the emotions they experienced when they told or heard the stories. (This image is a capture of ideas that I shared with the group. You might recognize some of the messages!)

Or limit the number of stories by asking for volunteers: "We don't have to hear from everybody today. Which teams feel especially motivated to have one of their members share their story with the larger group?" This serves as another level of filtering that will help the most urgent stories rise to the top.

Another Delivery Option

In the process described above, the facilitator introduces the idea that these stories might be imagined as chapters in a book. This is done as a creative exercise to make a point.

Paul Costello says his aim is to lead the listeners to become an "interpretive community," and he, Blair, and Dietz have several creative ways to keep listeners immersed in the content. They will break the large group of participants back into groups. (They can remain with their original story circles, or you may wish to mix them up to bring some fresh energy into the exercise.)

There are several questions that Paul asks to engage the interpretive imagination, including:

> If Hollywood made a movie out of this larger story, what kind of movie would it be? Tell me about the movie. Would it be a comedy? A tragedy? A drama? Why?

> What actors would be best in the key roles? (Who here would be played by Brad Pitt or Meryl Streep?)

> Would the movie have a sequel or a prequel? What would those movies be about?

Sometimes, Costello, Blair and Dietz will have the teams pursue the idea of imagining their collective stories as books by working on different assignments:

One team will create a cover for the book. Using a flip chart and markers, they will imagine what the front of the book looks like—including the image, any creative thinking they wish to do about authorship, best seller status, and other elements one typically finds on the cover of a book.

Another team will write a review of the book. Imagine someone—perhaps a literary critic, a famous business consultant, or someone completely unexpected—read this book about your organization. What did the reader say? How did the book make him or her feel? What made it strong?

Another team will create testimonials. This will be a series of short quotes from famous people, all saying positive things about the book. Why did they love it? Why do they recommend it to others?

As you might imagine, this exercise is a lot of fun and generates laughter and energy. But there's more going on here than just whimsical brainstorming. Costello says this is a process of *defamiliarization*. By running the story through these many filters, participants find themselves standing outside of the story where they can examine it with objective curiosity. "It's like finding the Dead Sea Scrolls," Costello says, "and reading about a lost community where all we have is this limited evidence to piece together a missing narrative." More important, it keeps participants immersed in the idea that they are living a broader story while exercising their critical role as an interpretive community.

Where Do I Go from Here?

Because you are in the mind-set of enriching your story circle experience, you can add another level of engagement through the meaning-making exercises described in the next chapter, "Summoning the Muse."

Use these ideas when you want to build your team's capacity for directed listening and drawing meaning out of stories, while giving your storytellers an opportunity to think about their own stories in fresh ways through the perceptions of their peers.

For this exercise you will need:

- A context where your team can hear and talk about stories (I suggest integrating these activities whenever you host story circles, as described in Chapter 2, "Host a Story Circle.")

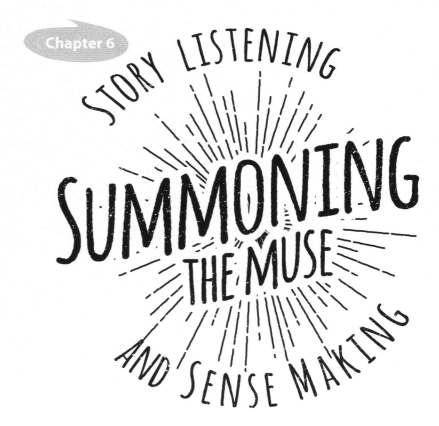

STORY LISTENING

SUMMONING THE MUSE AND SENSE MAKING

I remember when my kids were young, and we saw the Pixar animated movie *The Incredibles* in a movie theater. We talked about the movie in the car on the way home.

"I like how all of the people in the family had different powers," my son, Ollie, said. "I liked how Dash was super fast."

I asked, "Why do you think the little boy's power was speed?"

Without missing a beat, Ollie said, "Because little kids are hyper!"

I sensed that we had stumbled on something good here. I pressed: "What about the daddy?"

"He was strong, because all daddies are strong and protect their family!"

"What about Violet, the teenage sister?"

He had to think about that one for a second. "She could turn invisible. Girls don't want anyone to look at them and they get embarrassed. That's why she turned invisible."

"And the mom?"

"She could stretch! That's because moms have to do a lot. They have to do everything at the same time."

Pretty impressive. At a very young age, Ollie was already demonstrating an ability to look beneath the surface of a story to draw out its buried meaning. This is called *subtext*, and in good writing it is entirely intentional.

Some people think they aren't insightful or artsy enough to draw out subtext or interpret stories. "I barely passed my English Literature course in college. This isn't my thing."

I beg to differ. I often introduce exercises with the teams I work with to prove how easily they can shift from being passive story receivers to active makers of meaning.

The truth is we are all experts at meaning making. You do it all the time—even when you are unaware you are doing it.

Our minds are relentless at taking unconnected facts and filling in the spaces between them with patterns and meaning. If anything, we are *too* good at this. In his book *Thinking, Fast and Slow*, Nobel Prize–winning economist and behaviorist Daniel Kahneman shows that the brain's insistence on generating stories from random data can lead us astray. It is responsible for some of our more troubling impulses, from generating conspiracy theories to stereotyping of social or ethnic groups. This tendency,

Kahneman says, is also the source of irrational and unpredictable events that drive financial markets.

The phenomenon of *pareidolia* is one example of this. It is the reason you tend to see human faces in random visual data, whether it is a surprised face in an American power outlet or the face of a religious figure in the specks of a baked flour tortilla.

Sometimes when I work with groups that seem uncertain in their ability for meaning making, I'll start with an exercise. I tell or read a story from an organization or brand that they know well, such as Nike or Walmart.

For example, here's a great one from my friends at The Coca-Cola Company which will serve our purpose well:

I bet your eyes went right to it! The famous image of the Cydonia region of Mars was captured by the Viking I orbiter and released by the National Aeronautics and Space Administration (NASA) in 1976. People instantly saw and were captivated by "the face on Mars." Many were convinced it was evidence of extraterrestrial intelligence, but it's really evidence of your mind's brilliant capacity for assigning meaning to data.

118

> Coca-Cola was born in Atlanta, Georgia, on May 8, 1886. Dr. John Stith Pemberton, a local pharmacist, produced the syrup for Coca-Cola in a three-legged kettle in his backyard. He carried a jug of the new product down the street to Jacobs' Pharmacy, where it was sampled, pronounced "excellent," and placed on sale for five cents a glass as a soda fountain drink.
>
> Carbonated water was teamed with the new syrup to produce a tonic that was at once "Delicious and Refreshing," a theme that continues to echo today wherever Coca-Cola is enjoyed.[1]

I will read the story out loud to my group and then say, "The Coca-Cola Company must think this story is important for people to hear, because a statue of Doc Pemberton greets millions of visitors to the Coca-Cola museum in Atlanta. *So what does this story tell you about Coca-Cola? What do you know is true about Coca-Cola because of this?*"

People will be quiet for a moment, but it never takes long for them to start making connections. For the Doc Pemberton story, people will typically say things like this:

Well, it started in a soda fountain. There's a social aspect to Coke.

It was mixed up in a backyard. It has never been a snooty drink. It's for everyone.

He said it was refreshing. Coke always talks about the feeling.

It was called "excellent" at the very first taste. They make a big deal out of excellence, and their secret formula.

Yeah, it makes me think of the old Mean Joe Greene commercial. Mean Joe drinks the Coke and it makes him feel good and he gives his football jersey to the little kid.

It's kind of ironic that Doc Pemberton was a pharmacist, which implies that Coke "the tonic" makes you healthier but it has high fructose corn syrup and that's bad for kids!

Regarding that last statement above: I find that the audience almost always "goes negative" in this exercise, and starts testing for the shadow side of the story. This is an important part of the process, and there's no reason to be defensive. Wherever stories are being told, you should

1. You may recognize this as an origin story, which is one of the "Four Core Stories" we explored in the Chapter 1.

expect that audiences are evaluating: "Which part of this story can I trust? Where are the dark corners? Am I being manipulated?"

The fascinating thing about this exercise is just how long you could keep going with it. Even after people come up with four or five things, I say, "What else?" and then someone draws out some other fascinating connection that has never occurred to me. The point is they could keep unpacking the meaning and it would be relatively effortless.

After, when I ask the audience, "Was that a difficult exercise, or an easy one?" they will unanimously say "Easy!" It is a wondrous moment to realize how effortlessly the mind speaks the language of story. You almost don't even have to try.

Something important is happening in this simple exercise. The act of having this collective conversation—and of making meaning together—is a significant event. This conversation brings people together. Story practitioner Mary Alice Arthur says, "When we share a story and then explore that story together, we are creating shared wisdom and that acts as a collective root system between us. And people who are a part of that have more commitment to you, to us, and to the work we are doing together. When I experience that, you have more than my mind. You might have my heart, my strength, and my purpose too."

Now It's Your Turn

To warm up your team's meaning-making muscle, tell a story connected to a famous brand. Again, origin stories work especially well. If you like, you're welcome to use the Doc Pemberton story exactly as presented above.

Then ask the same question that I asked:

What does this story tell you about this brand? What do you know is true about the brand because of this story?

Then simply host the conversation for a few minutes as participants take turns making connections to the story. At the conclusion, call attention to the phenomenon of meaning making, and how easy it was for the audience to exercise. "See? That wasn't hard at all. You are experts at meaning making. In a little while, when we hear stories from one another, I'm going to ask you to continue making connections like that!"

In the lobby at the World of Coca-Cola museum in Atlanta, Georgia, visitors can see a sculpture of pharmacist John "Doc" Pemberton mixing up the very first batch of Coca-Cola syrup. The Coca-Cola Company is particularly skilled at leveraging its narrative assets for the purpose of brand building.

Meaninglistening and *Storymaking* with Your Team's Stories

I don't much care for the word *storytelling*. To make this confession now that we are this deep into the book feels a bit awkward, but there it is. The word is loaded with problems.

The trouble begins with the first part of the word: *story*. American businesspeople associate *story* with the fairy tales they read to their children at bedtime. The associations aren't any better for my European friends, for whom *story* might be a synonym for a lie, particularly when told with a certain swagger over a pint of Guinness. No wonder there is suspicion toward storytelling in organizations.

But my bigger hesitation is with that second part of the word. *Telling* always makes me cringe just a little bit, and part of that may be my background in organizational learning, where transformation is never the product of a one-way transaction. Telling is something you *do to* other people, and it disregards at least half of the complex social transaction that takes place whenever stories are being shared.

I'm a fan of new words (*neologisms*) that illuminate new possibilities that were right there in front of us all along, and it would be a lovely thing indeed if every member of the team embraced his or her role in shaping the team's reality. How about if we call it *meaninglistening*? Or, even better would be a word that suggests the active participation of all sides, such as *storymaking*. Maybe then we might recognize that once a story has been told, that is not the end of the conversation. Michael Margolis, chief executive officer (CEO) of Get Storied, says, "Transformation requires a witness. That's why we have to tell our story." And that means we have to have a witness. After the telling, we're just getting started. The really good stuff comes next.

Mary Alice Arthur is one of the stewards of the Art of Hosting movement around the world, which is focused on helping people host and take part in participatory leadership that leads to wiser action. Participatory leadership depends on active engagement from everyone, and as with storytelling, conversations that really matter depend on the twin skills of communicating and listening.

"People don't take the role of listening very seriously," she says. "But it's the most important part of the experience. I love the Chinese character for *listen* because it has the elements of *heart, one, ear, king,* and *a thousand* in it. What if we listened to each person as if they were a king and as if we had a heart of a thousand ears and with one pointed focus?"

"Ting"—the Chinese character meaning "to listen"

"Everyone thinks the teller leads the listeners," she says. "But it is the listeners who lead the teller. It becomes a self-fulfilling prophecy. When the listeners expect the best intentions, wisdom, humanity, and beauty of the storyteller, they will receive it. They can help to create a better story. The audience holds the power."

I especially like how Dr. Karen Dietz boils it down to an unforgettable axiom: *Listen the best possible story out of someone.*

Today, some of the wisest and most innovative story practitioners around the world are experimenting with social constructs for listening and meaning making. Some of them, such as Mary Alice Arthur and Paul Costello, have been perfecting their crafts over many years of disciplined experimentation and practice.

But you can begin to exercise this capability with your team in a simplified form.

Most often, when I host story circles I use a simple method modified from Mary Alice's Art of Hosting principles. It's called the harvester/witness construct. The advantages of this modified approach are that it is fast (just a few minutes of dialogue for each team member), it is simple (team members can easily embrace the roles and get to work), and it is *appreciative* (it focuses on what is true and good). As a leader, you don't need to be a therapist or a facilitator to host these conversations.

Roll the Dice!

I sometimes make a similar point about the ease of creating a story using the wonderful toy Rory's Story Cubes, which is widely available in many toy stores and bookstores. Simply roll the story dice, and then challenge one another to tell a story using the randomly generated icons on the dice. It's a fun way to marvel at your own mind's capacity for quickly generating narratives from random data.

Another fun exercise is to give each team member one die, begin with the phrase "Once upon a time . . ." and have the first member pick up the story based on the image on his or her die. Then, going around the circle, all other team members use their dice to build on the story. This can be a fun warm-up exercise before launching into a story circle. It also works as a pointed illustration of *social constructivism*—our human capacity for co-creating a shared reality through language.

You can try it now: What story would you create using the four dice images at the bottom of the photo?

At its heart, the harvester/witness model is based on a simple principle that drives shared listening and meaning making: *Every time you host a storyteller, give your listeners a job.* When listeners have a job, they have more focus.

Here's How It Works

Let's say you have a story circle of four participants. If one participant is the storyteller, everyone else is a listener, right?

Thus, in our group of three, we have a teller, a harvester, a witness, and an observer.

Teller

"Let me tell you a story . . ."

Harvester

"I heard something in your story . . ."

"I noticed some themes in what you said . . ."

Witness

"I noticed something about you . . ."

"I noticed something about my (or our) reactions . . ."

"I noticed something about the overall experience . . ."

Observer

For this round, just take it all in and enjoy.

The role of the *harvester* is to draw (or harvest) meaning from the content of the story. Participants are always intimidated by this role at first, but it is actually quite simple to do. This is where the listener says things such as "I heard something in what you just said," "That story made me think of something," "I think that was really a story about trust," "In your story, I think you revealed the key to why our teams are underperforming," and so on. (In Aristotle's art of rhetoric, these insights would point to *pathos*.)

The role of the *witness* is to comment on the person of the storyteller. The witness says, "I noticed something about *you* when you told the story." This is appreciative feedback, not critical. It may be, "I notice you become more passionate when you talk about your team. I can tell you believe in them," "You have a quiet way of establishing authority," or "I notice how you are equally attentive to both the people and the numbers in your story." This has the effect of fostering the teller's self-awareness of his or her own presence and voice. (Aristotle calls this *ethos*.)

The role of the *observer* is to remain actively engaged and practice listening deeply to the story while noticing any other dynamics that stand out in this story circle. (I often assign this role to manage time. If you have time for

Listen Better

Listening certainly begins with *presence* and the audience's decision to fully receive the gift the storyteller is giving. This receptivity for quiet, internal transformation (*meaning-listening*) becomes the bridge to collective listening and dialogue that follows (*story-making*).

Robbie Hutchens is a family therapist[2] who says that people jump to meaning making much too quickly. "The goal of listening," she says, "is to become an expert in the other person's story."

In fact, Robbie says meaning making is impossible if you have not first encountered the other person without bias. "When listening there's a temptation to start thinking of how you are going to respond, but that's not listening. If you have listened with presence and openness, you don't have to plan a response. Response will be automatic, and come from a place of deep empathy."

Deep practitioners of dialogue enter into the experience with an orientation that dialogue practitioners call "reflective openness."[3]

To practice reflective openness, adopt these awarenesses:

- My conclusions are my current best thinking. There are possibilities I don't see.

- My rank or position does not matter in this conversation. We are all the same.

- I will silence my judgments while others tell their stories.

- I can learn a lot from another's story.

- I expect this conversation to change me.

- I do not expect to "win."

....
2. Yep. I married her. Free therapy!

....
3. This is an idea I explore in my Learning Fable *Listening to the Volcano*. It also draws from the work of mental models as explored in the Learning Fable *Shadows of the Neanderthal*.

additional rounds of feedback, you can have multiple harvesters and witnesses in place of observers.)

I will project a slide on the wall or create a flip chart to summarize the three roles, because participants tend to feel uncertain about this at first. ("So, remind me what my role as *harvester* is again . . . ?")

If you have done an exercise using the Coke Doc Pemberton story (or other story) as described previously, you can use that experience to reassure participants: "You have already demonstrated your natural ability for this! Your responses to the Coke story are the kinds of responses we are looking for again."

In a story circle setting, each member of the circle will have an opportunity to serve in each role. For round 1, you will be a teller and then receive feedback from a harvester and from a witness. In round 2, everyone will shift, and you will be a harvester for a story that you hear. In round 3, you'll shift again. And so on. Each round tends to last approximately 10 minutes, so a group of four will need 40 minutes for a story circle with harvester/witness feedback.

Here's how I quickly introduce the roles on a flip chart. Because story is a timeless approach to connection and change, it pairs well with "old school" technology. With a few flip charts and markers, you can host an entire session with no projectors, slides, or other digital technology.

Taking It Deeper: A Geography of Meaning

If you are willing to dedicate some more time and exercise some more facilitation, you and your team can dig even deeper into their stories.

Paul Costello is a Washington, DC–based story expert who has been recognized by the U.S. Congress for his peacemaking efforts with young leaders from conflict-torn regions in Ireland, South Africa, and the Middle East. He does this through a hosted story-listening process that he calls *narrative room*. "People leap to meaning too quickly," he says, and his methodology seeks to identify *where* meaning is made. "Not *how*, but *where*," he clarifies, "and yes, meaning has its own geography." Costello's spatial terminology is informed by theological training and the interpretive process of hermeneutics which says that listening happens in three dimensions:[4] from behind the story text (which corresponds to our witness role), from within the story text (which is the harvester role), and in front of the text (which introduces a new role, connector).

In this listening construct, after the teller tells his or her story, the listeners will spend much more time in analysis. Working as a team, they will work through these three sets of questions (which you are free to use as shown here or modify to suit your needs).

....

4. Cynthia Kurtz has a very similar construct, which she labels as *story function, form,* and *phenomenon,* which correspond to Paul's *behind, within,* and *in front* construct.

This analysis—a *witness* perspective—plays out in the body of the listener, and it focuses on story as a felt experience before it is a rational, meaning-making experience.

- Who is the teller?

- What does the teller bring with him or her to this moment?

- What is his or her intent? Why did the teller tell this story?

- What did you appreciate about the teller as he or she told this story?

- Were there some parts of this story that you already knew? Were there parts that don't match or that add new information to what you already knew?

- What feelings did you experience during the story? What surprised you?

- Where did you feel the story in your body?

- What metaphors would you use to describe the story? If the story were a musical style, what style would it be (jazz, rock, etc.)?

This is a *harvester* perspective and is similar to a literary critical analysis of character, plot, and structure. It's a level of analysis that one might normally reserve for a great short story in a college literature class. ("This stuns the teller," Costello says, "who is thinking *all I did was tell a simple story*.")

- What happened in the story?

- What was the conflict or tension in the story?

- (Think about the feelings the listener articulated in the previous stage.) Where in the story did that feeling come from?

- What changed? Who changed? (And how?)

- What were the risks you heard in the story?

- What were the strengths you heard in the story?

- What values did you hear in the story?

- What leadership behaviors did you hear?

- What discoveries happened? Where were the breakthroughs? What made the breakthroughs possible?

This introduces a new listening role that we have not explored yet: *connector.* Here the audience is transparent about their own reading of the story, and the teller gets to observe them truly playing with the story. (Costello says, "I know it is working if there is laughter, which is a sign of release.")

- What does the story connect to? What does it make you think of?

- What are the themes of this story (e.g., "The power of collaboration," "The risk of vulnerability," etc.)?

- What does it tell you about our team/organization? (To what extent were the events of the story typical or atypical of our world?)

- What does this reveal about us that is unique to us?

- What assumptions, beliefs, or mental models does this story reveal? To what extent are these also present in our team or organizational system?

- What new possibilities does this story have to offer our team? What would happen if some of the key behaviors or mental models in the story were brought to life elsewhere in our team/organization?

- What do we want others to hear from this story?

- If the team is gathered to discuss a specific theme (such as innovation, trust, operational excellence, etc.), where did you hear that theme in the story? What did the story illuminate about our theme?

How deep you are willing to go into this dialogue depends on your time limitations! If you are skilled in facilitating, you could spend a few hours digging deep into a single story, or you could impose time constraints of 30 minutes for each story. Thus, after hearing a single story, the members of the story circle will spend 10 minutes examining the questions from behind, 10 minutes within, and 10 minutes in front for a total of 30 minutes.

Paul Costello says the effect of this experience on the teller of the story can be quite profound. She will experience a phenomenon that Paul calls "story ejection." That is, she will begin to feel as if she is standing outside her own story, observing herself and the other story characters through a startlingly objective lens, and considering nearly endless new meanings to the story. He even recommends having the teller physically move his or her chair outside of the circle after the telling and not make eye contact with any of the listeners. This gives listeners full freedom to play and interpret, while the teller "eavesdrops" on the response. This is part of the power of his narrative room experience, as young leaders from war-torn regions begin to view one another with a hard-earned empathy, while releasing the fiercely guarded meanings they have always assigned to their stories. "What I have found is that people wake up to the treasures they have in their own stories," he says. "It gives participants a new space for entering their own story where they can discover the nearly endless fluidity of meaning," he says.

For Thaler Pekar, an expert in the use of story for identity and persuasion, that link to the listener's story is exactly the point. Thaler bridges this conversation by asking listeners, "What story from your own life were you reminded of?" Thaler told me she shares my distaste for the word "storytelling," and says she prefers "storysharing." She explains, "Sharing a story usually prompts your audience to recall similar memories or aspirations. When you hear someone else's story, you are neurologically triggered to search your own memories for resonant connections."

Option: Use the Archetype Cards

Use the archetypes presented in this book as another easy entry into story listening. After the teller has finished the story, others in the story circle will take turns laying down three archetype cards that call out the voice of the story. "That story you just told, Barry, felt to me like a *creator/prophet* story and here is why . . ." See "Using Archetypes as a Directed Listening Framework" as described in Chapter 8.

See Chapter 8 to explore using 9 Muse Archetypes in meaning-making conversations.

The Power of the Spontaneous Invitation

Earlier we looked at the simple principle of giving listeners a role. This idea can be exercised spontaneously to make your stories much more engaging. Anytime you are speaking to a group, before you tell a story give listeners a role: "I want to tell you about something that happened in the leadership team last week. As you listen, see if you can identify why I might have been surprised."

Did you catch that? It was a subtle invitation, but the speaker gave everyone in the audience a job—and in the process created anticipation and engagement. It's a small thing and only takes a little bit of forethought. But the impact on the story experience (and the dialogue that follows) is significant.

The formula is "I'm about to tell you about X. See if you can connect to meaning Y."

Here's another one. "I want to tell you about something remarkable Kristina did at the feedback session yesterday. After I do, I want you to tell me what impact this should have on how we think about our feedback process."

I've done this with my kids, Emory and Ollie, at the dinner table. "I'm going to tell you about a phone call I had today. See if you can figure out the part where Daddy felt really embarrassed!" When I do that, Emory and Ollie lean forward in their seats, eyes glued to me, like I'm the greatest storyteller in the world. But really, all the energy is coming from their active engagement as makers of meaning.

Meaning Making and Individual Conversations

In this chapter, we are focusing on group conversations generated in story circles. However, these conversations can happen between you and colleagues or direct reports. Dr. Dietz demonstrates how these one-to-one story-listening conversations can be powerful paths to developing people. Here's how Karen describes it:

1. Decide on the story you want to hear (see Chapter 3, "Story Prompts"). For example, "Tell me about the project you are most proud of. What happened?"

2. Listen to the story delightedly. Don't get caught up in what you are going to say next, the piece of advice you can give, or the story you want to share in return. Suspend all agendas and simply listen to the story for the joy of listening.

3. When the teller is finished with his or her story, acknowledge him or her and ask a few reflective questions that deepen understanding. Avoid *information* questions (who, what, when, where, why, and how) until later. Instead, pick one or two of these to ask: *What do you like most about this story? What do you think this story really means to you? What do you think you learned from this experience? What kinds of decisions have you made based on this experience? Is there anything else you want me to know about this story?*

4. Thank the teller for his or her input. Acknowledge all the things you appreciate about the story, the way the story was told, the teller, what you learned, and what it means to you. Do not skip this step—ever.

5. Sometimes the conversation sparks a story that *you* will want to share in return. Don't hesitate to share it if it adds to the relationship and feels right.

6. If you feel so moved and you feel it is appropriate, you can offer an action step you will take. Thank the person again and conclude the conversation.

Dr. Dietz says, "Try this out and experience a qualitative difference in your conversations. What do leaders gain when using this process? Deeper relationships, trust, empathy, respect, authenticity, and a richer understanding of the organization. What's not to love about that?"

"For Lack of a System": A Story from Lori Silverman

How can we help people realize that they create meaning from each and every story that they hear? Lori Silverman is a story practitioner who has written extensively on the subject. To help people identify the elements of a compelling story, she uses this story which she captured from a colleague. The following is Lori's story, told in her words (as adapted from original version published in Stories Trainers Tell: 55 Ready to Use Stories to Make Training Stick, *Jossey-Bass/Pfeiffer, p. 288).*

My friend, Larry English, is a thought leader in the information quality industry. He received a request from an insurance company that needed to understand its risks—exactly what it was paying for through its claims.

The first thing Larry did was to put together a team. They decided to collect medical diagnosis codes from all the claims that had been filed for the last five years. In each region of the company, they collected and analyzed this data. Then it was put together into a report for review at a meeting.

"Oh boy. This oughta be interesting," Larry muttered to himself under his breath before turning to the team and said, "Hey everyone, before we dive into it, does anyone have any overall observations?"

"Larry, something seems not quite right."

"I agree. The data from one of the regions looks really suspect."

"Larry, you need to talk to our sponsor about this."

After a long silence, a small voice in the back of the room said, "Maybe we did something wrong. Maybe we didn't collect this data correctly or analyze it properly. Before we take any action, maybe we should recollect and reanalyze the information.

"Yes, you're right!" everyone chimed in.

So they went back to this one region of the company and recollected and reanalyzed the data. But after doing so, the analysis looked exactly the same as the first round.

What the team had noticed is that one region of the company appeared to have a high incidence of hemorrhoid codes—so high that it was way outside the normal distribution. There appeared to be some sort of an epidemic the company didn't know about. Once again the small voice in the room chirped up. "Maybe we should go talk to the claims supervisor who's responsible for this region."

"Great idea," everyone said.

They got in touch with the regional claims supervisor and explained what they'd found. Larry asked her what she knew about the situation. She growled, "That's our data. What are you doing looking at our data? No one else should be looking at it."

Larry replied, "You do realize that the actuarial staff uses that data."

She sighed deeply. "That's the data that we use to pay claims. I didn't know anybody else saw it. We use that particular code to identify claimants who are *PITAs* — you know — a 'pain in the ass.' How else are we to identify problem customers who we need to approach with special caution? If we have to get back in touch with them, this code helps us recognize that there was some sort of problem. This way we're better prepared to deal with the situation."

I asked Larry what he did when he heard her say this. He said, "I wondered if I'd been labeled a PITA by her staff when I'd called in to complain about a problem with one of my claims." I then asked, "What did you learn from this situation?" He replied, " Every time you think you have the perfect solution to a problem, you need to realize there are often unintended negative consequences that go along with it. As a result, you need to 'consider the consequences' of all solutions before you implement them."

What about you? How many problems are you trying to solve right now? When you come up with possible solutions, you, too need to "consider the consequences" of each and every one of them before you go to implement an answer.

Now that you've explored some meaning making ideas, give it a try! Lori's story on the previous page is rich with meaning ready to be explored. What are some themes that you hear *inside* the text? What connections to you make *in front of* the text?

Here are some of the layers of that Lori says her groups will typically share. What else did you hear?

Go to the source of the problem.

Get information before taking action.

Figure out what's causing outliers.

Listen to the small voice in the back of the room.

Don't be afraid to speak up.

Don't overreact!

Listen closely to the supervisor who created the workaround to solve her problem.

Where Do I Go from Here?

If you have a lot of stories, what is the meaning that is common across them? Story Element Extraction offers a structured process for drawing out and then capturing the deep and surprising metathemes shared by the many stories your people tell.

Review the Leadership Storytelling Archetypes as an additional construct for identifying the identity of stories (or reflecting on the teller).

Other activities in *Circle of the 9 Muses* will exercise the capability for meaning making, including the Visual Timeline and Creative Tension Pictures.

Use these ideas when you want other ways of bringing energy, engagement, and awareness to the basic story circle. These ideas might also inspire you to create your own unique story processes!

Chapter 7

STORY CIRCLE

VARIATIONS

Riffs, Jams, Jazz Licks, and Sitar Solos

For this exercise, you will need:

- An upcoming event (either formal or spontaneous) where you are planning on asking for stories.

Story work is like jazz, with endless riffs, variations, improvisations, and enough fresh ideas to fill 10 more volumes of books like this one. Some of the most innovative work in organizational learning is happening today in the field of organizational narrative. The spirit of experimentation in the story community (and certainly among the collaborators to this book) is intoxicating. I can imagine the rush of The Beatles in the studio assembling *Sgt. Pepper's Lonely Hearts Club Band*, and the *try anything* spirit that created a new set of rules and led an entire culture on a journey of discovery. (Yes, I am Paul McCartney in this fantasy. You can be George.)

Here are some ideas to spur your thinking.

Visual Story Mining

With this exercise, I am honored to introduce one of my favorite story practitioners to you. Limor Shiponi is among the wisest and most challenging thinkers in the global business storytelling scene, and her approach to story is deeply informed by her Israeli culture. "Everything meets here in Israel," she says of her culture, "and so there is impossible complexity coming into the stories. It is so dense it spits out diamonds."

Earlier in *Circle of the 9 Muses,* we explored the difficulty that some groups have in warming up to a story session. Limor has experienced that, too, and she suggests this exercise as a way of priming the pump for a group of storytellers. "People don't always respond to 'tell me a story'" she says, "for the reason they can't imagine themselves speaking in front of others in the form of story. This exercise is great for "clearing the story throat"—and for any time that you wish to find stories."

Here's how it works.

Place your team members in pairs at tables.

Give each couple a group of 10 visual prompts. For example, you could use "Rory's Story Cubes" (as featured in Chapter 6), or a set of metaphorical images such as those provided by VisualsSpeak (as featured in Chapter 14.) You could also use a group of random objects, or a stack of images cut from magazines. Limor says that simple images are best.

ROUND 1:
FREE ASSOCIATION

Pick up an image, look at it, and tell the other person what it makes you think of. It can be anything at all. Take turns going back and forth until you've gone through all 10 images.

ROUND 2:
THINK OF ORGANIZATIONS

Now shuffle the images and distribute them again. Once again, take turns sharing what each image makes you think of . . . only this time generate the associations *from your organizational experience*. Think broadly over your entire career, and answer quickly without overthinking it.

This looks dreary, like our time billing process!

Okay, I'll write that down.

ROUND 3:
THINK OF THIS ORGANIZATION

By now, both team members should be "warmed up" and generating ideas freely. Do a third round . . . only this time think about associations to *your current organization*.

Another difference this time is that your partner will write down what you say.

At the end of this round, you will have a page with the 10 things your partner said about this job; and he or she will have the 10 things *you* said.

Trade papers and review what you said.

Now it's time to tell a story! Pick one item from your page, and simply tell a story about it.

Limor says this exercise does a couple of things. First, the three rounds progresses from complete associative freedom to a sharpening of focus. It warms up the "filtering" muscle. In addition, they become comfortable "scanning" their experiences, and by the time they have the page with their ten thoughts about this job, they are already in a metaphorical/narrative mindset and can begin generating surprising connections about their current work.

"It is now easy for them to tell stories," Limor says, "because they've already heard their own voice speaking in the story domain."

Stories in Words

Terrence Gargiulo has written prolifically on how to use stories in organizational contexts. He says that individual words are containers of stories. "Words are how we index and retrieve our experiences," he says. "A word can encapsulate a whole universe of stories. Words open the door to our memories and recollections. Words are the links to stimulating these associations."

Let's test it now. Think about this word:

Success.

Pause for a moment and reflect on it. The relay boards in your brain are going crazy right now, retrieving associations, feelings, memories, experiences, and stories.

Dr. Madelyn Blair has developed a process based on this idea. There's a body of thought known as *social constructivism*, which says that we create our reality through our language and that this comes about through a complex, collaborative process. We assign meaning to our words, we come to shared agreement on the meaning, and then we bring them to life in community.

This leads to a curious phenomenon in which some words, used over and over, actually lose their meaning and their power—much like the old rechargeable battery in your cell phone that has lost its ability to hold a charge.

Dr. Blair offers a provocative example: "I daresay that in America, the word *freedom* has just about lost its mean-

ing," she says. That is, it has been used, manipulated, and loaded so much that it has become difficult to use it in dialogue because there is little shared agreement on what it means.

In this exercise, you'll use your company's mission statement (or vision statement or team goal) to infuse your most important work with new meaning and new urgency. Even if your organization has a mission statement that is a legitimate source of vitality and life, there are likely some dead battery words in there. ("What do we mean by *excellence,* anyway?")

To prepare for the exercise, distribute copies of your company's mission statement or project it on a screen. Read it aloud, and then explain that over time words tend to lose their ability to hold a charge.

Then give these instructions to your team members:

Pick a single word from the mission statement. It can be any word at all. (Some participants may make unconventional choices. I was with a group that chose the word *the* from their mission statement, which may sound like a trivial choice. But their mission statement

Your company mission statement is likely to have a few "dead battery" words. Charge them with new meaning!

included the phrase "we will be *the* provider of healthcare in our community," and they wondered whether the word *the* was loaded with outdated assumptions of singularity and preeminence that were sending a confusing message in their new age of collaborative partnerships.)

Option: For the above step, Dr. Blair says that sometimes she allows participants to regroup based on the word they chose. "The group that chose the word *service* is meeting in the back; likewise, if you chose the word *excellence*, then bring your chair over to the *excellence* group in the front left corner." This takes an extra minute or two, but it brings team members into a deeper dialogue with others around a single shared word.

Now think of a personal story related to that word. This is a story from your world or your life. Don't try to connect it to the organization. "I chose the word *service* and it reminded me of a story about my grandfather being drafted into the army . . ."

Get in groups of four (or three, or two, depending on what works best for the size of your group). Your story should take 2 or 3 minutes to tell.

Monitor the time and room dynamics to make sure all participants have time to tell their stories in their groups.

If you have several groups, ask them each to select one member to repeat his or her story to the larger group.

Afterward, debrief by making these points and asking these questions:

When words lose their meaning, our role as leaders is to enliven those words—to *recharge* them—by telling stories that infuse them with new meaning.

The stories you just heard might, on the surface, have little to do with our mission statement. (Some of you might not have actually even *said* the word you chose, but your story was *inspired* by the word.) The stories brought new depth to how you think about some of the key words in our statement, didn't they?

Give me some examples of ways that you are thinking differently about some of the words in our mission statement. "What does the story about Granddad being drafted reveal to you about the meaning of the word *service*?"

How can these ideas change how we think about our mission? What new meaning do they bring to our mission?

Thaler Pekar, an expert on story and organizational identity, suggests asking for stories about the *absence* of the word, as well. For example, "When have you experienced a lack of service?"

Note that this exercise could be combined with Story Element Extraction (Chapter 13) to help participants identify the themes that span across their many stories.

The Client Sets the Frame

Here's another one from Limor Shiponi. Limor says she is constantly amazed by the exclusionary nature of story circles in almost every culture. Wherever there are story circles, it is notable who is *not* present!

Why don't you ask your customer or client which stories matter? Here's how Limor manages this process.

Have at least 10 participants individually call their customers or clients in advance of the session, and ask them a single question:

> How would you describe what is best about working with my team (or my function or organization)?

Based on the customer or client response, each person should capture key *characteristics and phrases* on sticky notes. One idea per note.

For example, let's say Limor called her customer, asked him or her to describe working with her, and as a result captured these ideas on sticky notes:

When Limor and her colleagues come together for the story circle, each will put his or her sticky notes up on the wall. Each will take turns presenting what he or she heard from customers, as well as the key phrases.

Next, participants will regroup all the sticky notes according to similarity. (Thus, Limor's notes will become mixed in with everyone else's.) You will now have several affinity groups of notes with similar themes. Identify the big theme for each of these groups.

Pause for a moment and consider these themes. This exercise may yield some surprises! After all, what *you* assume is valuable about your offerings may or may not match what your customers actually find valuable.

Now take turns telling your own stories about the themes. So in the example here, participants will take turns answering the prompt: "Tell me about a time that you acted as a truth teller for our client." The participant should tell a unique story, and not simply rehash the scenarios or points that the customer referred to in the original call.

Thus, in this process each member of the team will now have a new mental model about his or her own value offering because it was illuminated by customers and then brought to vivid life in the stories of the team.

Invite the Witness

Don't stop with customers. Who else should be present? Consider bringing in your stakeholders and retired leaders. It's surprising how often people will explore stories without inviting the perspectives of the people whom the story is about. So bring them in.

What if the witnesses have died or are simply unavailable? Bring in the witness to the witness. I recently helped a six-decade-old health-care firm capture its origin stories. The founder had died several years ago, but his 90-year-old widow was alive. We invited her to the office and captured video of her telling stories about her late husband's values and his intent in establishing the organization. The exercise was as much a gift to the widow as it was to the entire organization, which might otherwise have lost those memories forever.

Leaders have asked me specifically whether it is appropriate to tell someone else's story. The answer is absolutely. However, it is not appropriate to tell the story from *the other person's point of view*. Instead, tell the story from your perspective as a witness. "I heard a leader tell this amazing story the other day. He said. . . . And here is how it affected me to hear him tell that story . . ."

Story Distilling

This is a great exercise in pruning a story down to its essence. The purpose is not so much to make a story better by editing it (although it may certainly have that effect) but to prompt a teller to unearth the core meaning of a story.

Let's say you and a colleague have each told the other a 5-minute story. Say to the other person, "Let's tell those same stories again . . . but this time we have to do it in *2* minutes." Take turns telling your 2-minute story. Use a timer!

Then do it again. "This time, we have to tell our same stories in 30 seconds!"

Then do it again in two sentences, then a single sentence.

Finally, it is always fun (and surprisingly meaningful) to conclude by *telling the story in a single word.*

Dr. Blair details a wonderful process for advancing this conversation over a series of e-mails with a friend in her e-book *Essays in Two Voices*. It is a rich exercise not just in editing but also in packing a growing awareness into a dramatically decreasing linguistic container. Her book *Essays in Two Voices* is in the bibliography and is available for purchase on Amazon.com.

Audience Carousel

After you have hosted a story event in which participants have told stories, issue them this challenge: "You just told a great story to your colleagues in this room. Without even thinking about it, you tailored your communication to your audience. You made split decisions about what details to include and which to leave out, based on who is sitting in front of you. What would have been different about your story if you had told it to different audiences? Let's find out!"

Invite each participant to tell his or her story again, but this time imagine someone different is in the group:

A customer	*A competitor*	*A 13-year-old boy*
Legal counsel	*A potential investor or donor*	*(Or others relevant to your context)*

Depending on the time and number of participants, you may have each participant tell his or her story multiple times for each fictional audience member—or you may draw names from a hat and have each participant tell his or her story only once to the selected fictional member.

One outcome of this exercise is that it demonstrates how fluid stories can be. It can be tempting to fall back on our favorite stories and tell them the same way, every time. But our role is to engage people, and that means bringing fresh perspective to the story every time we tell it, based on the audience.

Getting Personal: Stories and Significant Experiences

Annette Simmons, surely one of the most influential thinkers in organizational storytelling, says that this unexpected approach to story circles is her favorite. In this story experience, she asks questions to solicit stories that *have nothing to do with business or the organization*.

"We've assumed for so long that business isn't personal," she says. "But it is. How can it not be? Doing a great job demands personal commitment. We *want* people to take it personally."

The twist to Annette's process is that she demonstrates that these personal stories do indeed have links to the work and the organization that are urgent and vital.

This process works best when there's a gathering of around 15 to 20 people but can succeed with groups of 300 or more.

Number the four corners of the room that you are in. Place a piece of paper labeled *1, 2, 3,* and *4* in each corner.

Tell participants that you are going to ask a yes/no question, and if their answer is yes, they will go stand in corner number 1.

The question is: "Who here has met a big celebrity?" Those who say they have will go stand in corner number 1.

Go over to the group (with a microphone if the room is large) and quickly poll the group: "Whom did you meet?" Follow your intuition and pick someone who seems especially engaged (or who has met a *really cool* celebrity.) Invite that person to tell the story. "Wow, you actually met Bruce Springsteen? Tell us about that! What happened?"

After that person has told his or her story, *you as facilitator will connect that story to an organizational meaning*. This requires some skill, although it is much easier if you think in terms of the Four Core Stories presented in the first chapter of this book. "Jane, that was an amazing story about meeting Bruce Springsteen and how you connected personally to his vision in 'Born in the USA.' Can you see how that is really a story about *values*?" (Or change, vision, or identity.)

Now tell the group you are about to ask another question, and those who raise their hand must go to corner 2. (This will include some people currently in corner 1, as well as some people who are still seated. Shuffling people about like this brings a lot of energy into the room.)

The new question is: "Who here has ever buried a pet?"

Repeat the process above: Poll group 2, pick one person to tell his or her story, and then connect the story to one of the Four Cores (or make some other organizational connection.) Note that the buried pet stories are unique for their ability to generate both laughter and tears—sometimes simultaneously.

"At every step of the way," Annette says of her process, "I'm helping the audience see that *these are brilliant stories*. Even the simplest ones are loaded with meaning."

Repeat the process as many times as you wish. (After the fourth story, reassign corner 1 so that the people who are still sitting there can sit down and new storytellers can move into the space.)

Here are some personal prompts that Annette and I have used with success:

- Who has met a big celebrity?

- Who has buried a pet?

- Who has been to a concert in the past year?

- Who started working in a paying job before they were 14 years old?

- Has anyone ever won first place in an athletic event?

- Who here has gotten scared in the middle of the night at summer camp?

You can debrief the activity by calling out these points:

- You have millions of stories!

- People say that we should leave our personal stories off the job. Why are these stories relevant to us at work? (Let the participants tell you why these stories are important.)

- Why is it important to bring our whole selves to work?

- Is it appropriate to bring emotion into our jobs? Why or why not?

Show and Tell ("Relics")

Terrence Gargiulo has written extensively about storytelling as a leadership skill, and has worked with leaders all around the world. He describes a process he calls "Relics" as a fun and simple way to elicit stories.

Simply ask participants to show a personal object to the others in the story circle, and then tell a story about it. This can be an object from their purse or wallet, such as a driver's license, a frequent flyer membership card, or a photo. Or, you can ask participants in advance to bring an object with them from home or from their desk at work. Because these objects are personal, members of the story circle will have instant recall of the stories associated with them.

"The objects by themselves have no power," Terrence explains. "They are triggers for our memories and experiences. They are gatekeepers to layers of subjective meaning."

This simple exercise has a surprising ability to connect people to one another. I remember a time I shared a story about a gift card that was in my wallet, and the story I told resulted in smiles, nods, and immediate connection in a circle of people I had just met. Terrence says, "Sharing a personal object and the stories associated with it opens us up to each other. The boundaries we are accustomed to maintaining between ourselves and others come down. We become more real and accessible to each other, and it satisfies one of our greatest needs—to feel accepted by others and connected to them."

Capture Family Legacies

My wife, Robbie, spontaneously did this at dinner one night, and I was caught off guard by the unexpected power of the event—and how easy it is to replicate.

Next time your relatives are over for a meal (especially if it is a festive occasion, such as Thanksgiving in America), ask them whether you can capture a story. Prop your video phone up against a glass, press record, and *use a very specific story prompt* to elicit a specific story:

"Mom and Dad, tell us about that time you got lost while driving to your honeymoon."

"I know when I was born there were some real scares for our family. Tell me about that. What happened?"

"Grandma, you made a brave journey to start a new life in a new country where you didn't know anybody. Tell me what happened during that first year."

"Aunt Marcy, tell us again how you met Uncle Harry at the state fair."

"Dad, tell us about the famous *salmon incident* at that fancy hotel in Boston."

Even stories about seemingly trivial events will be loaded with treasure. The storytellers will quickly forget they are being recorded, and as they tell their stories their individual personalities—in all of their beautiful, maddening, human glory—will emerge. One day your relatives may be gone, and it is very possible these recordings will stand among your family's most cherished possessions.

Those are just a few ideas. (And, of course, there are many more to follow.) What other ideas do you have? Let me know what you have tried, and what you have learned. Write to me at David@DavidHutchens.com.

Use this exercise to clarify the voice of your brand or offering; when you wish to uncover deep, timeless, and universal patterns that lie buried in your own personal leadership story; or you wish to link your offering to your audience's most deeply held archetypal needs.

For this exercise you will need:

- A document that describes the 16 archetypes as they are described in this chapter

- A set of blank index cards (or large sticky notes that are approximately the size of an index card). Alternatively, you may purchase a set of archetype cards from www.DavidHutchens.com.

LEADERSHIP
STORY
ARCHETYPES

Why are people universally fascinated by personalities, such as Princess Diana, Steve Jobs, or Nelson Mandela? And why do we feel such deep connections to brands, such as Coca-Cola or Nike?

The theory of *archetypes* suggests that there are deep, timeless patterns of identity that all human beings respond to. This is why stories such as the Greek myths or Grimm's fairy tales have been preserved over the centuries. According to Carl Jung, the Swiss psychiatrist who founded the field of analytical psychology, these patterns are subconscious and universal. Jung even proposed that these patterns are biological and inherited. Think about that for a second. Your baby was born, Jung might suggest, with a predisposition to love Bilbo Baggins.

Stories that trigger these buried, archetypal patterns are incredibly engaging. Imagine if *your* stories could engage people at the same level as *Star Wars* or *Harry Potter*!

This exercise touches upon the deep body of knowledge that is Jungian theory. Together, you and your team will identify the archetypes that lie buried in your stories, in your team, in your offerings—or perhaps even in your personal identities as leaders. This knowledge will give you a powerful platform for communicating the essence of your identity and your value proposition to your many audiences.

Best of all, you'll find that this exercise is fun, inherently compelling to your participants, and able to deliver big ideas in a short time.

Our Cast of Characters

Archetypes can hold deep meaning, whether they are individual symbols (such as images of fire, earth, and water) or linear narratives (such as the narrative archetypes we explored in Chapter 3, "Capturing Fire," or Joseph Campbell's monomyth in Chapter 12).

In this exercise we will explore archetypes as a cast of characters. Jung proposed that these universal characters live inside each of us, occupying the ground floor of our constructed identities and defining who we are. Somewhere deep in your subconscious you are a little bit of King Arthur (the hero archetype). You also have a little bit of the Big Bad Wolf (the shapeshifter/predator archetype). Although there are nearly limitless archetypal symbols to draw from, branding experts such as Margaret Mark, Carol S. Pearson, and Jim Signorelli have proposed a more limited and manageable lineup of the most common archetypes for leadership and branding purposes.[1]

....

1. Mark, Margaret, and Carol S. Pearson, *The Hero and the Outlaw: Building Extraordinary Brands Through the Power of Archetypes.* New York: McGraw-Hill, 2001.

Signorelli, J. (2014). *StoryBranding 2.0: Creating Standout Brands Through the Purpose of Story.* United States: Greenleaf Book Group LLC.

For our exercise, I propose a lineup of 16 archetypes that I find most helpful for identifying leadership and brand voice. They are:

Let's take a closer look at these characters and get to know them a little better before we start inviting them to draw meaning from our stories.

You'll see that each of the archetypes on the following pages includes these details:

- *Examples.* Personalities (both real and fictitious) and organizations or brands that are representative of the archetype. Note that these are my own interpretations, and they are informed by my American experience. I expect and hope my examples would lead to disagreement and discussion.

- *The Quest.* Every archetype is on a journey to accomplish something. This is the goal that the archetype (and you, your team, and your brand) seeks.

- *Response to the Dragon.* Every archetype encounters trials and setbacks on its journey. And every archetype has its own way of dealing with the dragon. This suggests your team's or your brand's unique source of strength and growth.

- *The Gift (or Elixir).* At the end of his or her journey, the character has a hard-won gift to bring back to the ordinary world. In Joseph Campbell's construct, this would be called "the elixir," the potion or truth that holds powerful properties. In terms of your story or brand, this is at the heart of the value you offer to your stakeholders and marketplace.

- *The Shadow Side.* Every strength is also a liability, and your archetype has an Achilles' heel that may be the source of its downfall. These vulnerabilities in your team or brand strategy are a potent topic for self-analysis.

Soon we will explore the process for bringing this exercise to life in your team. But first, spend a few minutes getting to know the 16 archetypes. As you review these, notice how quickly you are able to connect with them and think of examples! You'll find it easy to start putting them to work immediately:

See whether you can think of additional examples from the archetype-rich stories *Star Wars*, *Harry Potter*, or *The Lord of the Rings*. (I've provided a few to get you started.)

As you review these the first time, which archetypes does your intuition gravitate toward? Which ones do you think are most descriptive of you? (For example, in much of my own career journey, I might describe myself as a creator/rebel.)

The 16 Archetypes of the *9 Muses*

	THE CAREGIVER	THE COMPANION
Examples	Mother Teresa; Goodwill Industries International; Johnson & Johnson; State Farm insurance	R2-D2 and C-3PO (or Ron Weasley); FranklinCovey DayPlanner; Apple's Siri virtual voice assistant
The Quest	Seeks to heal the wounds of others or self	To provide ready companionship and support to those tasked with urgent things
The Gift	Alleviates suffering and leads others to greater wholeness	Enables heroes to perform at their peak, provides care, support, loyalty, and life at the hero's most challenging moments
Response to the Dragon	Finds its source of pain and attends to it, brings health to the surrounding system so that the dragon is no longer enabled	Stands beside the hero without fleeing and endures whatever the hero must endure
The Shadow Side	Martyrdom, need for a dysfunction to attend to, resentment toward those complicit in perpetuating dysfunction	Offering "blind support", failing to set or challenge the vision, offering reliable resources for an ill-advised mission

Examples Martha Stewart; The Home Depot; LEGO

The Quest To create things that are new; To live a life of vision and new possibility

The Gift Brings things of value and beauty into existence; Equips others to exercise their own creative voices

Response to the Dragon Creates ingenious snares, and unexpected solutions

The Shadow Side Perfectionism; Chronic discontent with current reality; Fixing things that weren't broken

THE EVERY MAN

Examples George Bailey (from *It's a Wonderful Life*); Ford pickup trucks; John Deere tractors; Walmart

The Quest To bring value and honor to the masses using humble tools

The Gift Assigns nobility to common virtues, "earthy" values, and humility; Creates belonging and solidarity

Response to the Dragon Rolls up sleeves and goes to battle with expectation of self sacrifice; Gives to the greater good at the expense of self

The Shadow Side Feeling of being marginalized; Identity sublimated in service of the whole; Resentment toward the "haves"

Examples Make-a-Wish Foundation (and many other nonprofits); MacArthur "Genius" Grant; The Powerball lottery

The Quest To watch over those who are vulnerable; To save the day by providing good things, just in time

The Gift Provides resources and opportunities to those who might otherwise not have them

Response to the Dragon Bestows resources upon the afflicted so that they may be armed against the dragon

The Shadow Side Gives and then leaves; Providing token gifts without true sustainable support; Creating dependence without teaching self reliance

	the HERO	the Innocent	the Jester
Examples	Luke Skywalker; US Marine Corps or Navy SEALs; Nike or Adidas	Forrest Gump, Pee-wee Herman, Mr. Rogers, Jello brand pudding, Disneyland	Jon Stewart (of *The Daily Show*); Mark Twain; *Saturday Night Live*
The Quest	To accomplish the most difficult goals that are beyond the reach of "ordinary" people through strengths and competence	To move through life with a sense of uncomplicated wonder	To create laughter— often in the pursuit of illuminating deeper truths
The Gift	Through extraordinary acts of courage, creates a better world for other to enjoy; Enables others to discover their own inner strength	A path to deep wisdom by connecting with purity; attainment of transcendence through the simplest of virtues; Connects others to these simple virtues	Provides laughter and enjoyment; Holds up a mirror to society; Enables people to see the truth of their own lives without defensiveness
Response to the Dragon	Draw their swords and lead the way into battle without fear	Outwit the dragon, perhaps inadvertently, by maintaining an almost childlike faith in deeply held principles; Expose the compromised/dark side of the dragon	Expose and neutralize it through satire
The Shadow Side	Arrogance; lack of empathy for the weak or the wounded; "Needs" a battle to fight	Naiveté; Difficulty in embracing ambiguity, complexity, and gray areas of life	Frivolity of the time-wasting sort; Revealing others but absolving self

Examples — Don Juan; Hallmark Cards; Chanel No. 5; L'Oréal

The Quest — Transcendence through beauty, relationship, or sensual experience

The Gift — Strong loyalty and sense of union; Intimacy with others; Invite others to escape from the mundane through heightened feeling

Response to the Dragon — "Seduce" it, or convert the challenge into a lovely experience

The Shadow Side — Hedonism; Enmeshment with the other at the risk of losing the self (codependency)

Examples — Yoda; Oprah Winfrey; Oxford University; *Harvard Business Review*

The Quest — To pass wisdom along to others

The Gift — Leads other to truth; Enables other to build capabilities or find their true potential

Response to the Dragon — Encourages others to face the trial as a path to enlightenment

The Shadow Side — Focus on abstract truth without appreciation for pragmatic truth; A "teacher" who can't "do."

Examples — Al Gore (*An Inconvenient Truth*), Billy Graham, Centers for Disease Control and Prevention, any number of futurist think tanks

The Quest — To discern the forces that shape our current or our future reality, to speak their truth whether it is welcome or not

The Gift — Gives the people an opportunity to capitalize on their changing world (or to turn from their wicked ways)

Response to the Dragon — Predicts the dragon's arrival and puts contingency plans in place

The Shadow Side — Wallowing in "I told you so"s, pious arrogance, leaves those struggling to fend for themselves, may be rejected by those unwilling to receive truth

	the Rebel		**THE RULER**		**the SEEKER**
Examples	Hunter S. Thompson; Harley-Davidson; Las Vegas Convention and Visitors Authority ("What happens in Vegas stays in Vegas")	**Examples**	Warren Buffett; Bill Gates; Richard Branson; Microsoft	**Example**	Capt. James T. Kirk (*Star Trek*); Condé Nast; Patagonia; Royal Caribbean Cruise Lines; NASA; Jeep
The Quest	To experience freedom by throwing off the chains of convention	**The Quest**	To master the system, and accrue wealth, power, and resources	**The Quest**	To explore new worlds, uncharted paths, and fresh experiences
The Gift	Lead others to find their buried, authentic voices	**The Gift**	An equitable and benevolent kingdom where others can access resources and opportunity	**The Gift**	Lead others to encounter a larger world; Maintain faith in the mission when the journey become perilous
Response to the Dragon	Seek revenge and hurt the dragon back; or propose contrarian strategies to slay the dragon	**Response to the Dragon**	Marshall power and forces to overcome it	**Response to the Dragon**	Anticipate the dragon as a necessary part of the journey; Seek growth from encounter with the dragon
The Shadow Side	Taking pleasure in creating disruption, chaos, or shock to others; Alienates others	**The Shadow Side**	Using power in service of the self; Being driven to acquire more without concern for consequences to others	**The Shadow Side**	Rejection of society/ separation from the tribe; Life as a hermit; Allergic to boredom or status quo

154

Examples	Ken Burns; The Smithsonian Institute; *The New York Times*; TEDx talks
The Quest	To inform, captivate, and move others by weaving compelling narratives
The Gift	Holds up a mirror that allows the audience to see itself more fully; Tells stories that foster sense of community and shared self awareness; Gives community a richer sense of who we are by reminding us who we used to be; Carries the memory of who we are to the future
Response to the Dragon	Casts it as a character in the larger narrative so that future generations might understand what we experienced
The Shadow Side	Withdrawal; Narrating events without participating in them; "Revising" history to validate own truth

Examples	Gandalf (or Dumbledore); Steve Jobs; Deepak Chopra; Apple Computer
The Quest	To master the laws of the hidden universe in order to conjure miraculous things
The Gift	Interrupts our mundane reality with amazing tools that enable us to do more, be more
Response to the Dragon	Outwit it with amazing spells
The Shadow Side	May unleash a Pandora's Box of unintended consequences

Putting the Archetypes to Work

In this exercise, you and your team will find fresh ways of thinking about your brand, story, or offering by looking to the 16 archetypes for inspiration.

Identify the Frame for Conversation

As is usually the case with story work, you need to define the frame first. When you and your team get together, what exactly is the subject for your analysis? Options can be:

Our brand. Invite team members to think broadly about the brand—recognizing that the brand is much more than just the logo and tagline of your product or organization, but rather it is the full range of stories and experiences that your customer associates with your brand. (It is sobering to remember that the brand is not what we say it is in our communications; it is what our customer perceives it to be!)

Our story (or stories). It may be that you have a story or a group of stories that you have generated using other processes in *Circle of the 9 Muses*. Select a small handful of those stories to analyze for deeper understanding using the archetypes.

Our offering. Whatever you are responsible for delivering in your work (either to internal customers or to external customers) is, in effect, its own brand. For example, I was on a project team to create a training program, and we used this exercise to better articulate the identity and personality of the learning experience we were developing.

Me. (Or us.) The archetypes are a great way to think about yourself or your team! If you choose to go this way, you'll want to define this specifically. "We are talking about our identity as a team since we formed eight months ago." "We are talking about our lives together since we were married in 1996." "Think of your identity as a leader in your current role." I even did this exercise in the kitchen with my 12-year-old son, Ollie, and instructed him to think about his experience as a middle schooler. (And we had an unexpectedly powerful conversation!)

Present the Archetypes

Verbally spend a few minutes explaining what an archetype is. This can be a very basic explanation, much like the one that I provide at the beginning of this tool. You are welcome to borrow my words if you wish.

Next, share the 16 archetypes. You are welcome to copy the text from this book for use within your meeting. If you do, please include a statement that says "Copyright 2015, David Hutchens."

I have also developed a deck of 9 Muse Archetype Cards, which are available for purchase on my website. (Note that the cards are my preferred way to go! They make the exercise kinesthetic and introduce an element of fun, which makes it easier for people to think creatively.)

The deck of "9 Muse Archetype Cards" makes this exercise fun and tactile. Learn more at www.DavidHutchens.com

Place Participants in Groups

The exact number of participants isn't very sensitive for this exercise. You can group people in pairs (like my son and I did at the kitchen table) or in teams of five or six. Note that everyone will take turns sharing his or her perspective, so to keep the conversation manageable you might wish to keep the groups to six members or fewer.

Have Participants Each Identify Three Archetypes and Write Them on Sticky Notes or Index Cards

Each member should spend a few minutes individually reviewing the archetypes on the handouts (or on the 9 Muse Archetype Cards). Tell each person to identify three archetypes that best represent the brand, story, or offering. Lay them on the table in order of importance. That is, which archetype is the *primary* character of the brand? Which one is *secondary*? Which is the *tertiary* archetype?

The primary and secondary types are the most informative, especially when combined. For example, many health-care professionals may predictably identify themselves as the caregiver. The nuance comes with the addition of secondary archetypes: Are they caregiver/prophets, or perhaps caregiver/rebels? This becomes quite a rich conversation—especially when identifying possible marketplace positioning for brands. (See Mark and Pearson's *The Hero and the Outlaw*.)

People often use the third type for reoccurring characteristics. The third card allows you to say things like "But there have been a couple of special times when we operated as the innocent . . ."

Write your three archetypes on sticky notes or index cards. If you are using the 9 Muse Archetype Cards deck, simply take those three cards from your deck.

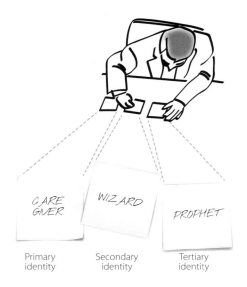

Primary identity   Secondary identity   Tertiary identity

Each team member will identify three archetypes. The sequence is important!

Present Your Cards

Take turns. Have the first participant visually lay the sticky notes or cards on the table, in sequence. Participants should explain why they chose the primary archetype and then the secondary and tertiary types. They are free to expound on this a bit and provide their reasons, examples, and stories.

Repeat until all members have presented their archetypes.

Analyze and Discuss What Just Happened

You may wish to use these questions or come up with some of your own:

• Which archetype(s) came up most consistently?

• What did you hear that you expected to hear?

• What did you hear that surprised you?

• Look at the "Gift" or need state that your primary archetypes offer to your customers. Does this give you any new ways of thinking about the value that you deliver?

- Look at the "Responses to the Dragon" and at "The Shadow Side." How well do these match your experiences? What stories do you have that support this?

- Look at your communications that describe your offering. (Perhaps these are marketing materials or the "About Us" page of your website.) Is the current language consistent with the archetypal identity you identified? How might you update the way you describe your offering so that it better connects to archetypal images?

Taking It into the Future: The Transformational Question

Remember that the theory of archetypes says that our subconscious selves are a home to all of these identities. Some just show up more often in our daily world while others are buried a little more deeply. I grew up in New Orleans, Louisiana, where the celebration of Mardi Gras provides an annual opportunity for revelers to put on masks and become someone else during the season of carnival. This has become widely misunderstood as an act of debauchery, but its roots are sacred. It's a way of acknowledging that we contain multitudes. I'm a business person and a leader, but I'm also a spoiled child, a laughing fool, a free-spirited artist, and a lusty drunkard. I contain all of these identities, both light and dark, and rather than attempt to banish them—a fool's mission that is a path to dysfunction—I will reveal them and embrace them. (And in the process, I rob the shadow archetypes of much of their power over me.)[2]

In your organization and in your leadership, it is the beginning of transformation and liberation to say, "We are not bound to our current identities. Who shall we become?"

So, as you and your teammates face one another, draw cards (or post sticky notes) in answer to these questions:

- What does our context demand of us? Which identity is missing? Which part of myself (or ourselves) do we need to summon and exercise? Who do I (we) need to become?

- *How?* What will it look like behaviorally when I begin exercising those different identities? What actions must we take to call forth and embody this identity?

- What resources, opportunities, and accountabilities do I need to bring that identity to life?

2. By design, the 9 Muse archetypes don't include any lusty drunkards. That would be a relevant conversation, but we will save it for another time. Instead we are focusing on an intentionally selected cast of characters that can drive value-creating leadership conversations.

Using Archetypes as a Directed Listening Framework

This is something I've been experimenting with and the results are intriguing. Archetypes have a unique ability to lead people deep into their stories. Here's a process that, when I tried it, caught me off guard with its power:

1. Identify your three personal archetypes as described above.

2. Place people in groups of three or four members.

3. Have all participants lay their three archetype cards in front of them facing the others (so that the cards are probably upside-down to the teller.)

4. Now invite them to mentally set aside the archetypes. Ask them a framing question for a story. (I often use a "Tell me about a time you were at your best in your work" kind of question. See the Story Prompts in Chapter 3 for additional ideas.) Specifically say to participants, "I know you just spent a lot of time thinking about your three archetypes. But set those ideas aside in your mind for now. You do not need to try to weave archetype language into your story. Just tell your story the way you normally would."

5. Prepare the audience to listen to the story. The listeners' job is to give the storyteller feedback based on the teller's archetypes. So for example, if the teller has ear-lier identified herself as a creator/caregiver/jester, the audience should listen for any elements in the story consistent with that. Tell them that the content may be in the actual words that the storyteller uses—but it may also be in the style, presence, or nonverbals of the storyteller. It may even be revealed in the negative space of the things the teller didn't say.

6. Thus, everyone will take turns. One will tell a story and then receive surprising feedback from colleagues on how they heard the archetypal elements within the story. Then continue to the next person until everyone has had a turn.

The instruction to mentally set aside the archetypes is important and has some fascinating results. Frequently (though not always) the teller will tell a story that

Teller 1 tells her story. The listeners consider the archetypes she identified earlier, and then provide feedback on how they heard archetypal elements in her story. The teller may find that she told a story about her archetype whether she intended to or not!

160

perfectly illustrates the three archetypes he or she chose. There's a bit of *power of suggestion* happening here, sometimes at a subconscious level. Some tellers will even say that they actively tried to *avoid* any archetypal elements in their story, and they were astounded at the ways the audience drew out the archetypes anyway. "I didn't think my story was about being a seeker, but you convinced me that's *exactly* what my story was about!" One debrief point here is that your identity is woven into your stories in very deep ways, whether you are aware of it or not, and it can be fascinating to have colleagues say, "Yep, that story is so uniquely *you!*"

How to Apply Archetypes to Your Stories

Slash Coleman is an award-wining storyteller, author, and producer whose stories have been produced as PBS Specials and archived in the Smithsonian Institution. He says he relies on archetypes to craft his unforgettable narratives.

"Stories that incorporate archetypes are more effective than stories that don't," Slash says. "I've seen it again and again in my workshops. Archetypes are like magic. They have the ability to turn a simple anecdote into a world-class Hollywood blockbuster."

The reason? Archetypes make extremely strong characters who make bold choices, and those are irresistible story elements.

He suggests that one simple way to make your stories more effective is to use portions of the archetype descriptions in this chapter.

"There's no need to fear copyright infringement when it comes to archetypes," he added. "It's part of our birthright. If you're telling a story about the time you volunteered at a soup kitchen, then use some of the verbiage from David Hutchens' description of the caregiver directly within your story."

As an illustration, Slash reviewed the *caregiver* card and spontaneously told this story. Note how he borrowed text from the description (italicized) and incorporated it into this telling:

Every month I volunteer at Meals on Wheels. We travel to Monroe Park and deliver meals to the homeless. I think in some ways I do it because I want *to alleviate suffering in others* and volunteering allows me *to feel a great wholeness.* I've been that way since I was a kid. Once, I found a frog that had injured its leg and I brought it home, made a splint out of a popsicle stick and let it hang around in an empty lunch box until it was better. I'm like the *Mother Teresa* of amphibians. I guess I've always been *about finding the source of pain and bringing attention to it.* Helping others is one of my more important missions in life.

Where Do I Go Next?

Archetypal language is a rich foundation for marketing and branding. Your thoughts about the deep archetypes of your offering will be especially valuable to your marketing and branding partners. Share the outcomes of your dialogue with them. (Even better, invite them along to be a part of this experience!)

Use the archetypes as a prompt for mining the team's stories. So, for example, write the three top archetypes your group identified on a whiteboard, and prompt team members to tell stories about them. ("So, we think of ourselves as a caregiver/jester type. Tell me about a time that we operated at our very best as a caregiver/jester. What happened?")

If there is consensus, you may wish to adopt an archetypal identity for your offering. This may be especially valuable in a marketing and branding context. ("Our next national developers' meeting is going to shock people from their complacency by having a rebel/king identity!")

Review your current key communications—especially those that brand your offering. (These may include the "About" page of the website or key presentations). Where do you see archetypal language? What archetypes do you see being communicated? Where have you missed opportunities to reinforce your brand? Do you agree that the correct personality has been applied?

Chapter 15 introduces a "strategy storyboarding" exercise that can be brought to life even more using these 16 archetypal characters.

Use this for feedback and team building. Have team members present their three cards for their personal archetypes to one another; then give team members an opportunity to respond. "You see yourself as a jester/companion/prophet? That's funny, because I would have said you are a jester/prophet/seeker, and here's why . . ."

If you do choose to do this exercise with your kids like I did, please be mindful. Archetypal identities connect to us deeply. Be certain that any conversations that you have with your kids using archetypes are *only* positive, supportive, and appreciative. There must be no shame of any kind associated with this exercise. Identity and self-perception are tender, tender things for children. Please proceed on this sacred ground with dignity and love.

This exercise works even better with cards! Go to www.DavidHutchens.com to order a set of 9 Muse Archetype Cards. It is a deck of cards that contains the 16 archetypes along with all of the descriptive text featured in this chapter. Instead of using sticky notes, participants can take turns drawing from the decks and laying their cards.

Use this exercise when you want the team to explore future events that may disrupt the work—and then generate plans to be ready for those scenarios.

FUTURE
★ STORY SPINE ★

For this exercise you will need:

- Pencil and paper

- A slide or handout that shows team members the story spine structure

Stories are simulators. When we hear stories, we see—and feel—ourselves in the story, and it becomes a valuable way to test our reactions and mental models without those pesky real-world consequences.

At a primal level, story is a survival technique. In the classic *The Uses of Enchantment*, Holocaust survivor Bruno Bettelheim says that some children showed high levels of resilience in concentration camps because of the fairy tales they had been told over and over, which had equipped their young psyches with rehearsal in chaos, fear, vulnerability, and survival. They had already met the wolf at the door.

In this exercise, you will similarly use stories to simulate possible future events and increase your team's capacity for agile responsiveness.

With connections to Pixar and Hollywood screenwriting, the classic story spine structure is a template delivered with a twist: You are using it to tell the story of a plausible event that hasn't happened yet, but *could*. This innovation of using the story spine for a future story comes from Kat Koppett, master of bringing improvisation-inspired learning to leadership development. You can find her version of the offering in her book, *Training to Imagine*.[1]

What is going to happen in the future? What might go wrong? What might go right? And—most important—*will you and your organization or team be ready for it?* This is the realm of a discipline known as *scenario planning*, and this simplified framework is a simple way to introduce teams to the discipline. In this process, you will use the story spine template to define possible futures that your team or organization may face and then construct possible stories, events, and management strategies leading up to those futures.

An important feature of this story is that even though it describes a possible future, it is told in the past tense. Because the story begins with "Once upon a time," you will tell the story as if the events had already passed. This may seem odd for a story that is about an event that hasn't happened yet, but the effect is powerful. By telling the future story as if it had already happened and been resolved, this invokes the reality in the mind. People can visualize themselves as taking action as protagonists in the story. It becomes real and as a result intimidating future events are rendered toothless. You won't truly feel the effect until people start telling their future story—and you will feel a buzz of energy start to creep into the room.

1. Kat Koppett, *Training to Imagine: Practical Improvisational Theatre Techniques for Trainers and Managers to Enhance Creativity, Teamwork, Leadership, and Learning*, 2nd ed. (Stylus Publishing, 2012).

Where Did the Story Spine Come From?

The story spine is a classic story structure. It has been linked to story development at Pixar,[2] and to the Hollywood screenwriting guru Brian McDonald in his much-praised book *Invisible Ink*. But its genesis is traced back to Kenn Adams, a playwright and actor who developed the spine as an exercise for improvisational (*improv*) theatre.

Just take a quick read through the story spine structure. As you do, notice how easily a story starts to formulate in your head—even before you've defined any of the details!

Here is the story spine, which is so simple it can be presented on a cocktail napkin:

This is us, today, right now
{ Once upon a time . . .
Every day . . .

Catalyst event
{ But one day . . .

Actions and consequences (repeat as needed)
Because of that . . .
And because of that . . .
And because of that . . .

Climax/Moment of change
{ Until finally . . .

A different world . . . and Key learnings
{ And ever since then . . .
And that's why . . .

----

2. "Pixar's 22 Rules of Storytelling" was a popular Internet meme developed by Pixar storyboard artist Emma Coats, and featured the story spine as rule 4. You can find it with a quick Google search.

Get Ready for This Exercise

The story spine can work with one person as an individual activity, or it can be scaled to large groups, with members broken into subgroups of around five people.

You'll need about 1 hour for the exercise as it is presented here.

Give each participant a page that lays out the story spine. You are welcome to create one using the text that is presented in the napkin image.

Introduce the Story Spine

Start by explaining the story spine, similar to how I explained it at the beginning of this chapter. (Sharing its Hollywood bona fides is a great way to start. People are engaged by the idea that they may be tapping into Pixar magic when they craft their stories!) Walk participants through each of the stages. You might even ask someone to think of a favorite movie and describe how it follows this structure.

Share the purpose of the exercise: "Using the story spine, we are going to imagine possible scenarios that could affect [you/the team/the organization] in the future, and we are going to weave stories about how we will survive those scenarios."

Start with the Climactic Event: "Until Finally . . ."

Every great story has a transformational moment when everything changes. So what are some possible events that could affect or disrupt business in the future?

Participants may notice that this is actually close to the end of the story spine. We are not starting at the beginning, and this is intentional. Instead, we wish to identify the disruptive action first—the "until finally"—and then in a few minutes we will come back and build the story around it.

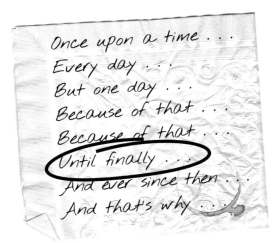

Give participants a few minutes to think individually about events that could disrupt the business (or team) in the future. These aren't necessarily negative events! (For example, your organization acquires another company.) Tell them to think in terms of:

- A significant change to a customer or key account

- Changes in leadership

- Changes to the structure of the team or organization

- A legal event

- A competitor makes a big change

- Disruption to relationships or trust levels

- Marketplace disruption

- Disruptive technologies

- Health and safety disruptors (I worked with one logistics organization at a safety summit, and many wrote variations of agonizingly plausible scenarios, such as ". . . Until finally someone was crushed by a shipping container.")

- *Black swans*—events that are extraordinary, but plausible

Write down at least four or five possible disruptors on a page. Give the group 5 minutes to do this individual work.

Identify a Single Event That the Group Will Focus On

Each member of the small group will take turns sharing his or her events with the others.

At the end of this conversation, there will be a lot of possible disruptors—probably too many to build stories around. The team should identify the items that they deem most urgent or most important to build a story around. Multiple team members may choose the same item (but be aware that they will each construct their own separate story about that item), or each member may choose a different item.

At the end of this discussion, each team member will have a single event that he or she will build a story around.

Complete the Story Spine!

Working individually, give each participant 10 minutes to write a story around his or her event.

Participants will want some information on each of the story spine elements. Again, you are welcome to reproduce the text below. (If you do, please include the statement "Copyright 2015 David Hutchens.")

Once upon a time . . .
Every day . . .
But one day . . .
Because of that . . .
Because of that . . .
Until finally . . .
And ever since then . . .
And that's why . . .

Describe the hero of this story, which is you, the team, or the organization. This is a short articulation of the normal state of affairs. *Remind participants that even though this is a story about something that may happen in the future, they will write it in the past tense—as if it has already happened and been resolved.*

Describe how [you/the team/the organization] create value. This is the work that will be disrupted in the next part of the story.

Describe a plausible catalyst event that will ultimately lead to the *until finally*. This is the teller's choice! This is their story, and they get to tell it however they wish.

Write the consequences of the catalyst. This may be the meatiest part of the story, as you describe the ripple effects and multiple consequences of the catalyst. Use "because of that" statements as many times as you think is necessary. Participants might want to focus equally on *thoughts* and *behaviors*.

This is the disruptor—positive or negative—that you identified at the beginning.

How is your world different because of the disruptor? What were the consequences—positive or negative? How did this affect the work? The marketplace? The team?

This is the moral of the story. Be explicit in letting others know what they should take away from the story. How should they think or act differently?

Allow participants 10 minutes to write the story. (Give them alerts when there are 5 minutes, then 3 minutes, and then 1 minute left.)

As a final step, each person should think of a title for his or her story and write it at the top of the page.

Here is a story one person captured using the story spine:

> **Once upon a time** there was a logistics organization that had built a reputation for flawless, on-time service. **Every day**, the dedicated people worked hard to maintain their own high standards, even though regulatory pressures and management demands were making it harder and harder to keep up. **One day**, when our system was operating at capacity, one floor manager—who had just worked a double shift and had not slept—began berating his team and telling them they were behind schedule. **Because of that**, everyone was on edge, blaming one another, and focused on their own part of the process. **Because of that**, they started pushing the sorter to capacity, **until finally** one of our workers climbed up on the sorter to clear out some jammed items, and severed a tendon in his thumb and lost partial use of his hand. **And since then** his quality of life was compromised. And the company was hit with a huge settlement and ever since then team members have been aware why it is so important to collaborate and ALL assume accountability for the entire line. **And that's why** we need to maintain dignity and trust even as the pressure on us increases.

This story suggested a connection between organizational capacity and the management culture. This was a new idea to the team, and the beginning of a long-overdue conversation.

Next, the participants can take turns telling their stories using the Story Circle structure (Chapter 2). If you have a lot of team members, you can use Twice-Told Stories (Chapter 5) to bring the most powerful stories to the larger group.

Where Do I Go from Here?

You might discuss: What is the likelihood of each of the events happening? What would need to be in place for our company to respond, based on the actions you proposed in your stories? What wisdom can we draw from the "And that's why . . ." lessons learned?

You might also wish to discuss the variety of stories. Were there common themes? Did some people address similar challenges with radically different stories?

Based on the experience you just shared, and the disruptors you identified, what needs to happen next?

Be sure to capture the stories so that they are not lost.

Use this when you want a fast, energizing, and visual method for quickly reconstructing your memory of a big story that has happened in the past, or use it to surface compelling stories from your history that you might otherwise never have thought of.

VISUAL TIMELINE

For this exercise you will need:

- Blank copier or printer paper so that each participant has at least one sheet. Legal-sized paper (8.5 × 14) works best, but if that is not available, then standard letter-sized (8.5 × 11) will work, too.

- If you have plenty of table space, flip chart pages are even better. If space is an issue, some participants may be willing to take off their shoes and get down on the floor to work.

- Markers or pens for each participant. Multiple colors are good.

172

This process is, possibly, the easiest to facilitate in *Circle of the 9 Muses*. It brings together a very basic exercise in visual thinking that will help people reconstruct their memories of events in the past in a way that is intuitive and meaningful. Additionally, it works as a story-mining process because the timeline reveals many substories that are worthy of closer exploration.

Identify the Story You Want to Tell

A *Visual Timeline* is a classic storytelling device in which you or your team will reconstruct the story of a past event by drawing a dynamic line that depicts the ups and downs of the event.

You'll begin by identifying the event that you wish to depict for your timeline. Here are some examples:

- Create my individual leadership or vocation story

- Reconstruct more than eight years of our company's institutional memory since the day we were founded, with key decisions from our major stakeholder groups

- Capture the broad story of a one-year design project with our team

- Tell the story of our weekend at the beach last summer (with Mom, Dad, and the kids all having an opportunity to tell their version).

- Recall my changing emotional state since just this morning, for creating a mindfulness diary.

- Working with my partner to take turns telling the story of our marriage

As you can see, this is an infinitely scalable activity, in that you can depict very brief and recent events just as easily as you can render complex, multiyear epics.

Here's how to conduct the exercise.

Establish the Start and End Dates

Have team members turn their blank page sideways (landscape). This horizontal space is the canvas for their timeline.

Have them draw a line near the bottom of the page, leaving plenty of room above it.

Because this is *your* story, you get to decide when it starts and when it ends. (For example, perhaps you want to make the case that "the story of our health-care project" actually began in the year when James Watson and Francis

Crick conceptualized DNA, or maybe your timeline begins "two years ago, when I joined this team.")

Draw a Line that Tells the Story!

Think broadly of everything that happened from the beginning to the end. Good events are *up*; negative events are *down*.

Don't plan what you will draw in advance. This is an intuitive process. Just grab the pen, start remembering, and let the line reflect the memories. Because we store our histories as emotional information, you will probably have no trouble recalling the main ups and downs along your timeline. While some people choose to move slowly and thoughtfully, I have seen others produce a dynamic line in 30 seconds.

You'll also notice that the examples I've shown aren't particularly polished. As always, this is not an exercise in

On a large sheet of flip chart paper, define the beginning and end of your timeline. Leave plenty of space at the top and some beneath.

174

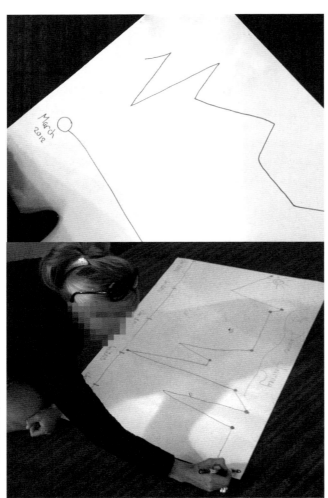

Don't plan your line. Just start drawing, and adjust as you recall events and their highs and lows. As your hand follows your emotions, it is fascinating to watch how the line emerges with an intelligence of its own.

art but in communication. For this exercise your rough, shaky line is just as effective (or more effective) than the beautifully rendered output from that one coworker who went to art school.

Reflect for a Moment

Look at what was just created in the space of less than 2 minutes! Your simple line is loaded with meaning, feelings, and memories. When you look at your line, it will bring your history and the accompanying memories vividly to life.

In fact, your line is also loaded with meaning for others. Although we don't know the details (yet), we can make some inferences about your story. In the top-left image we can see that things were going *awesome* in the period after March 2013—and that something really dramatic happened soon after that good run. We are already making a connection to this story at a purely abstract, emotional level.

But that's not a great way to tell a story. Let's bring it to life by populating the line with more meaning.

Fill in the Story Details

Imagine someone might later review the line that you drew. You can imagine the questions they will want to ask. "Why does it start at that low point?" "What is that turbulent area that looks like white-water rapids at the end?" "Why does it swing up and then down so dramatically at that point?"

Enhance your timeline with text, titles, and simple icons and stick figures to bring a little more meaning to the presentation.

To build participants' confidence in their own visual competency, I often provide an Icon Cheat Sheet to demonstrate how simple stick figures, arrows, and icons can communicate a great deal of meaning. You can find a reproducible copy in the Appendix.

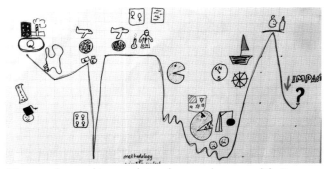

Use metaphors and icons to bring the story elements to life. For many people, this bird's-eye view of their own story is a revelation. They've never stepped out of themselves to view it quite like this.

Draw out the Meaning

In *Circle of the 9 Muses*, the telling of the story or presentation of the timeline is never the end of the conversation. It is always the beginning. The purpose of these exercises is always to draw out some deeper meaning, reveal our mental models, and then turn that awareness into something valuable that can move the organization.

My colleague David Sibbet is the world's most influential pioneer in the use of visual-thinking techniques for organizational meaning making. In his conception of the visual timeline, he has participants leave a horizontal space near the bottom where they can capture *key learnings* at each of the major inflection points. This prompts the storyteller to start illuminating some of his or her own mental models, and act purposefully in using the image as a tool for knowledge sharing.[1] I did this at one organization where young professionals remained in job rotations for about 18 months before moving to the next job, and none was being deliberate about capturing what he or she learned and sharing it with the organization. The value delivered by this exercise—with the key learnings called out—was quite dramatic.

1. David Sibbet has a series of large, beautifully produced visual-thinking templates available for purchase at his website, www.Grove.com. The Grove's program *The Personal Compass* is a visual-planning workbook that includes the Visual Timeline and other activities that allow you to "review your past, take stock of your present, and imagine and plan your future." The work is exciting, innovative, and deserving of your attention. Learn more at www.Grove.com or http://store.grove.com/product_details.html?productid=48.

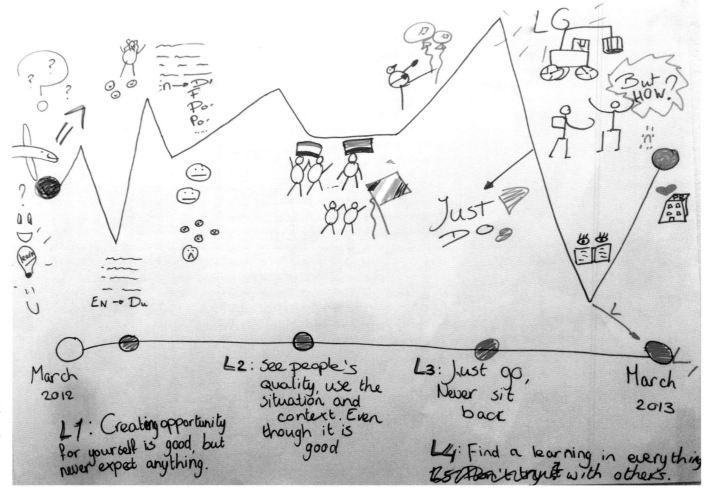

Here you can see all of the elements come together: The expressive up-and-down narrative line; visual icons to bring the story to life, and key learnings at the bottom. This fun and simple exercise delivers a lot of insight.

March 2012

March 2013

L1: Creating opportunity for yourself is good, but never expect anything.

L2: See people's quality, use the situation and context. Even though it is good

L3: Just go, Never sit back

L4: Find a learning in everything L5 Don't try with others.

Finally, write the title of your story beneath the line.

People sometimes express surprise at how engaged they become in the process. It is a reflective process and one in which the teller becomes deeply absorbed. Even when exceedingly rough in style, the final image holds a great deal of value. It becomes a knowledge artifact in which people have invested a great deal of meaning and attention. Expect to see many participants take out their cell phones to capture a picture of their drawing. Most people will roll their drawings up carefully to take with them. I've never seen anyone throw his or her drawing into the trash.

The final step, of course, is to take turns telling the stories. In small groups, present your visual timeline and answer questions. Then be ready to receive with full attention the fascinating stories that your friends and teammates are waiting to share with you.

Applications

There are a lot of ways you can draw value from those squiggly lines and smiling stick figures.

There are three primary ways that I use this.

The first is as a pure storytelling exercise, as described above. Bring your team together, give everyone a piece of paper and markers, have the team work individually to draw their timelines (usually around some shared experience, such as "our journey ever since the merger"), and then take turns presenting their stories to one another.

Take turns sharing your timelines with one another.

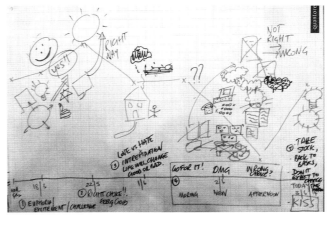

I'll never stop emphasizing: This isn't an art contest. The goal is to communicate and create meaning. The messiest drawings often communicate the most.

Make note of the interesting differences, similarities, and overarching themes as your team members tell fascinatingly different versions of the same shared story.

Second, you can use it as a mining exercise. I discussed earlier how sensitive the environment is to storytelling and how sometimes it's difficult for stories to show up. But the visual timeline is very effective in forcing stories to emerge. Change is a potent generator of stories, and therefore *stories live in the many inflection points* of the timeline. Every time the character of the line takes a sharp upturn or downturn, you can bet a story is lurking there. If you have a group of people who say they can't think of stories, pull out a sheet of paper, and have them start drawing the line. Tell them that the resulting line is a gold mine of stories, just waiting to be harvested and told. "Pick any inflection point on your line, and then tell that story!"

The third way I have used this is collectively. If your group is tasked with creating the institutional memory of your work, project, or organization, it can begin with the horizontal timeline with the start and end dates and then begin telling stories along the line. (See how this is described in more detail in "Fractal Narratives.") After they have identified the stories together and posted them on sticky notes, they can move the sticky notes up and down on a flip chart or whiteboard and then draw the line that connects them. In this group version of the exercise, participants draw the line *after* identifying the stories and not before.

Those are just three possible applications. As you pull your team into this fast, fun exercise, be sure to reach out to share the innovative uses you have discovered.

Other Options and Ideas

The Visual Timeline is an incredibly flexible tool, and there is no end to the variations.

Go big. I saw one group create a large visual timeline across the long, felt-covered wall of a hotel ballroom by sticking push pins into the wall and connecting them with yarn. Over the course of a three-day conference, they pinned corresponding knowledge documents and photos to the wall along the line.

My colleague Susan Gabriel is a leadership development consultant at Goodwill Industries International, and I loved her innovative use of the timeline. Before a program, she draws the entire history of Goodwill on a whiteboard along a timeline—and then over the course of the program invites participants to post their stories to the timeline. It may be "I joined the company at this date," but Goodwill is an old organization! The best stories are the ones where participants connect their personal stories of healing and rehabilitation to historical events that happened over its history of more than 110 years!

Make it fractal. On a flip chart or whiteboard, create a line that represents your perspective of the team or project—and then assign each team member to tell the story of the line between two inflection points by rendering that segment line on a separate piece of paper. Thus, the visual timeline becomes a container for lots of smaller timelines. A true fractal storytelling structure.

Take it into the future. The ending date of the timeline doesn't have to be in the past or today. If you wish, project your ending into some point in the future! Once you cross over today with your marker, keep going! Your timeline becomes speculative and you or your team can use it to forecast possible future scenarios with all of their predicted ups and downs.

Break the rules. Some participants will want to break the rules by drawing multiple divergent lines on their page—or by adding extra character by furiously scribbling tangled, untraceable lines. Let them! This exercise encourages creativity and ingenuity. Because it is an exercise in *assigned meaning*, let participants bring their own spin to it. The lines mean what they say it means.

Where Do I Go from Here?

As you can see, the Visual Timeline is highly flexible. It can be used for future visioning work, for institutional memory work, for individual or collective story mining, for team building, or even as a team energizer. For that reason, it connects in one way or another to most of the other ideas in this book.

A next step may be to be more disciplined about constructing institutional memory through Fractal Narratives (Chapter 11), or to organize in Story Circles (Chapter 2), so that team members can begin sharing the specific stories at the inflection points within their timelines.

You may have participants respond to their colleagues' stories using a listening construct, such as harvester/witness (as described in "Summoning the Muse," Chapter 6). The timelines also provide a large enough pool of stories that you may wish to begin drawing out the meaning through Story Element Extraction (Chapter 13).

Use these frameworks when you wish to exercise leadership by defining the bigger story that your people are living, and bringing their individual stories together into a greater whole, or *metanarrative*.

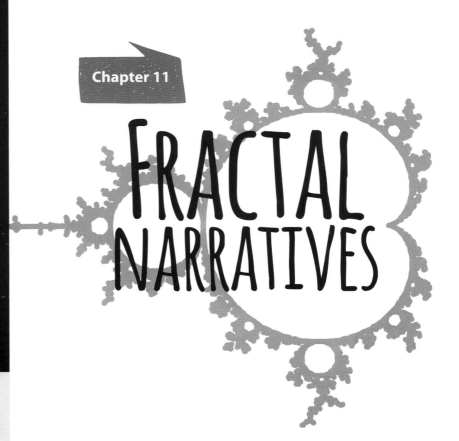

Chapter 11

FRACTAL NARRATIVES

For this exercise you will need:

- A space for story circles (as described in Chapter 2)

- A large whiteboard or wall with butcher paper

- Multiple stacks of sticky notes with markers

A fractal is any structure that shows similarity at different levels of scale. In this fractal image you can see how smaller branches are structured with the same pattern as the larger ones. A healthy culture is one where the stories have a fractal structure.

The exercise Twice-Told Stories (as described in Chapter 5) makes an impactful and important point: The stories that people in organizations tell do not exist in isolation. They are always part of a bigger, shared story.

Fractal Narratives builds on that idea and takes it one important step further: It is the role of you, the leader, to shape and define what that bigger story is. This is a significant act of leadership. A role of the leader is *maker of meaning*, which means defining and narrating the larger story that we are all experiencing and living into.

Fractal narratives is my term for describing stories that are purposefully nested within bigger stories, or metanarratives. A *fractal* is any structure that shows similarities at different levels of scale. In nature, the branching of a tree is an example of a fractal. If you were to take a picture of a large branch, then zoom in for a photo of the smaller branches emerging from it, and then compare those photos side by side, you will see that the branching patterns are quite similar. Or, you may have seen fractal screen savers on your computer: hypnotic, pulsing, often beautiful shapes in which it appears you are zooming into the screen infinitely—and yet the overall pattern stays consistent despite the scale.

Biologically speaking, fractal structures are signs of health and adaptability. For example, the more fractal your bronchial tubes are, the healthier your lungs are. Fractals create infinitely complex systems in highly efficient ways.

An adaptive and healthy organization is one where the individual stories reflect themes and truths that also define the organization's bigger story. That is, to the extent that the smaller stories align to and reinforce the organization's larger metanarrative, meaning has become fractal. Imagine the power and adaptability of an organization in which everyone is creating aligned—though wonderfully varied—stories.

As a leader, then, one of your opportunities is to generate fractal story alignment. It works by first defining the broader story that you as a leader wish to lead people into—and then using that as a structure for harvesting stories from your team members.

If all of this sounds abstract, it's really quite practical. Let's look at some examples to bring this idea to life.

Let's Start with an Example: Values Stories

To give an example of how this looks, let's focus specifically on values stories—which, you may recall, are one of the four core categories of leadership storytelling described in Chapter 1. Say you have identified that as a leader, you wish to create a culture in which the organization's shared values are a real differentiator, and a prime opportunity to define *how* people will do the work. (And for most leaders, this is surely a worthy pursuit.)

Now let's say you've brought together a cross functional group of four managers. Because of the small size of the group in this example, you'll create a single story circle. (You can, of course, scale this exercise up with multiple story circles.)

Write the company values on a flip chart or on a whiteboard. For the sake of this example, let's say the company values are *openness*, *quality*, *people*, and, oh why not, *rock and roll*. Create a space for each of those four values. The space will need to be big enough to hold a series of yellow sticky notes.

Prepare your people to begin telling stories around the four values. (See Chapter 2, "Host a Story Circle," for more details.) Anyone can start, and he or she can choose any one of the four values to begin with. Let's say Mary Alice begins with a story about *openness*. She tells her story.

Together, she and the group give her story a title, and they write that title on a yellow sticky note and place it in the area under *Openness*.

Use a whiteboard or flip charts to capture the broader structure for the storytelling session. As team members capture their story titles on sticky notes, they will add them to the framework.

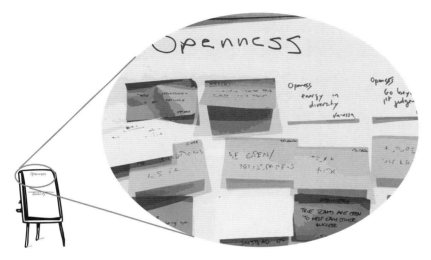

Over a period of an hour, your team of four may tell seven or eight stories. As described in "Twice-Told Stories," it is an impactful moment when at the end you point out that all of these individual stories are like chapters in the larger story that you are all living together: in this case, the story of your company's values in action.

Let's back up now and look at this from a high level. *This exercise is an act of leadership.* By choosing to frame the story circles around the organization's values, you have made a dramatic statement: "Our values are important, and they define who we are, and we will be intentional stewards of the organization's values so that they are true differentiators for our business." By creating a purposeful

occasion to come together to uncover and tell these stories, you just gave urgency, vitality, and life to the metanarrative of your organization as a values-driven system. In a very real sense, you just gave shape to the identity of the organization.

You can draw from other metanarratives for fractal storytelling. Let's look at some.

Storytelling and Institutional Memory

I wrote portions of this chapter on a long, round-trip flight to Saudi Arabia, where I worked with an energy company that was instituting story work. After five years of working on a massively complex project, the company realized that it had failed to capture any of its experiences and decisions so that others in the organization's future might learn from them. (Do you think five years is much too long to arrive at this conclusion? Most organizations I know *never* come to this insight.)

This is a case of *historical* storytelling and reconstructing the past for knowledge management. The organization's data systems for making these institutional memory stories accessible to future members of the organization are complex. But at its heart this is a challenge of storytelling. And the process is elegant enough for you to use with your team today.

Capture the stories from your past experience — your institutional memory—using a timeline to frame the story session.

Draw a single horizontal line on a whiteboard, flip chart, or long strip of butcher paper.

Tell your storytellers to define the beginning and end of the timeline. In most cases, the end will be today, but leave that to the creativity of your participants. (Maybe they will choose to place the ending in the future and tell a future story!)

Likewise, have them define when the story begins. There may be an obvious beginning, such as the date when the project or event was commissioned—but again, leave that up to the tellers. (Who knows? Maybe they will place the beginning hundreds of years ago with some discovery that affects the work today.)

Now have participants begin to identify stories on the timeline. In their work at IBM, Cynthia Kurtz and Dave Snowden found that it is more fruitful if your storytellers begin at the recent ending of the timeline. I, too, have found that it can be productive for participants to start with the most recent and fresh memories and then work

backward to rebuild the memory. "What happened before that? And what happened before that?"

If you have already explored story circles in Chapter 2, you should be well familiar with the process. Have members tell the stories, representing each with a title on sticky notes.

In the case of a large group, you may break the story teams up so that you are producing multiple perspectives of the same timeline. This exercise can be quite fascinating as each team recreates the past, tells the stories, and builds the timeline in its own way. The differences between the timelines may be more informative than the similarities.

Yet another possibility is to begin this exercise using a variation of the Visual Timeline process described in Chapter 10. After the team has captured a series of sticky notes on the timeline, have participants reposition the notes and draw a line that renders the highs (good events) and lows (challenging events).

Combine this exercise with the visual timeline (from Chapter 10) to create another level of meaning and narrative data.

The resulting presentation is especially expressive and easily decoded by anyone who wasn't part of the original story session. "Wow, something really awful happened here soon after the *Launch Date*. Tell me about that!"

Other Fractal Story Frameworks

Cynthia Kurtz points out that there is a nearly endless supply of constructs for collecting stories. It's just a matter of identifying the larger story you want to tell.

You may use the archetypes that you identify for your team or offering, as described in Chapter 8, "Leadership Story Archetypes." For example, if you identified that your team (or product) has the identity of a prophet/rebel/king (see descriptions in Chapter 8), write those three words on a whiteboard, and collect stories about times that

the team or offering displayed any of those characteristics in remarkable ways.

Have you brought the members of your organization along on a shared path of *innovation*? Collect the individual stories of innovation using a framework such as Everett Rogers' classic *Diffusion of Innovation*.

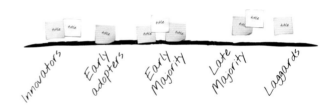

Show the framework on a whiteboard, flip chart, or long sheet of butcher paper—and bring your members together in a story circle to identify and tell stories about each stage of the model, capturing the titles of each of their stories on sticky notes.

Are you a member of a high-performing team? You can capture the stories of your history together using Bruce Tuckman's classic team stages model.

John Kotter's eight steps of change model is another great framework for capturing stories:

It is an act of leadership to name and frame the bigger story that the team is living . . . And then to capture individual stories within that frame.

I know one leader whose team was struggling after a part of the organization had been sold off and downsized. She said, "You know what? I think we are going through a grief process." She brought the team together, talked them through Elisabeth Kübler-Ross's classic stages of grief framework, and had them share their stories of shock, denial, anger, bargaining, depression, and acceptance. (In this case, the team was still angry and bargaining, so it was a powerful orienting moment to validate where they were in the process and to envision what the pending acceptance and healing might look like.)

The leader observed her team's experience, provided a framework and language to name what was happening, and gave them opportunities to be heard and make sense of their individual experiences and ultimately move forward.

This is one of the highest applications of leadership storytelling: *the leader as framer of meaning for the collective experience.*

Where Do I Go Next?

Fractal storytelling involves a crucial decision on your part. Your role is to answer the questions *What is the broader story I want to define or call attention to? What is the story that we are living right now?* This chapter suggests a few constructs that can give shape to those metanarratives. (This section continues in the next chapter with an especially powerful metanarrative, the Hero's Journey.)

As a leader, simply define the larger story, put it up on a whiteboard or flip chart, and then host a story circle to identify the stories within that narrative.

You should also explore all the exercises in Part I, "Fundamentals" (Chapters 1 through 6). These processes will enable you to share and draw meaning from the stories that you identity.

Use these ideas when you wish to define the team's or the organization's experiences in ways that connect with timeless and universally appealing patterns of meaning.

Chapter 12

FRACTAL NARRATIVES AND THE HERO'S JOURNEY

For this exercise, you will need:

*   A whiteboard or flip chart with the Hero's Journey framework drawn on it in advance

*   Sticky notes and markers

This is a continuation of the previous tool, Fractal Narratives. It is called out separately here because of the significance of this robust construct. To fully appreciate this process, you should review that previous chapter first.

Joseph Campbell was an anthropologist who studied the narratives that have defined cultures across the ages, and he identified the elements that were common to all of them. His resulting construct, *the Hero's Journey* (also known as the *monomyth*) represents the grand story that humanity keeps telling and living, over and over. It is a tremendous intellectual contribution to our understanding of what it means to be alive in this world. It is the underpinning of the world's great narratives, from religions to cultural touchstones, such as the Greek myths, that have defined civilizations.

But it's also a supremely intimate story. It is the journey each of us takes through this brief life as we struggle to become self-actualized beings.

Campbell wrote his classic book *The Hero with a Thousand Faces*[1] in the 1950s, but it became a cultural sensation in the 1970s, when one of his young protégés—a filmmaker by the name of George Lucas—lifted the construct verbatim to become the outline for a science fiction film that he called *Star Wars*.

Today, Campbell's construct is massively influential, and is a staple of Hollywood screenwriting programs. (And, some criticize, it is responsible for the strong sense of sameness that plagues the plot lines of so many Hollywood blockbusters.)[2]

As the interest around organizational storytelling has grown, it has been only natural for people to look to the Hero's Journey or monomyth as a template for leaders to follow. Surely a model so timeless and so universally irresistible should be a model for leaders to emulate in their storytelling, right?

But as some leadership story practitioners have found, it doesn't work. Not quite.

The reason is that the Hero's Journey is the very definition of an *epic*. It is a massive story, and—unless you are compiling a detailed business history (as in the classic book *Barbarians at the Gate: The Fall of RJR Nabisco*)—in practical leadership contexts it is not normally appropriate for stories to be scaled to such an all-inclusive arc. My experience of leadership storytelling is that it is often brief: short bursts of narrative that are contextually situated around a certain outcome, often just a few minutes in length. Most leadership stories have time for only a single pass through Freytag's dramatic arc of setup, action,

---

1. Campbell, Joseph. *The Hero with a Thousand Faces*, 3rd ed., New World Library, 2008.

2. That's not the only criticism. Another is that the framework is overly male and imbued with metaphors of violence and domination.

climax, and conclusion. (See the description of Freytag's structure in Chapter 4, "Capturing Fire.")

But it takes *Star Wars*, for example, more than 2 hours to cover all the chapters of Campbell's model. (If you're counting all three films of the original trilogy, 6, and more than 12 hours if you add in the prequels.)

As a result, some story practitioners have struggled with the big, unruly Hero's Journey for leadership applications.

But there is tremendous value here, and the Hero's Journey is an ideal framework for story mining. Here's how you can use it.

The Manager of a Thousand Faces

First, let's take a look at the Hero's Journey, and then we will come back to the leadership implications. I'm going to make my description exceedingly brief; furthermore, I am going to use the truncated version Christopher Vogler advocates in his classic Hollywood tome to screenwriting, *The Writer's Journey*.[3] You will likely wish to go deeper, and

many resources are available for you to plumb the depths of Campbell's vital work.[4]

As we walk through the steps of the journey, you may notice how quickly your mind is able to string the elements together and visualize them as a dramatic narrative, with easily recalled images from *Harry Potter*, *Star Wars*, *The Lord of the Rings*, and more. (Even better, notice how these archetypal story elements have recurred in your own life and leadership.)

Broadly speaking, the Hero's Journey follows the adventures of a protagonist—who may be Luke Skywalker, Frodo Baggins, or *you* as a leader—as he or she moves through a sequence of experiences that begins in an *ordinary world* and pulls him or her into an *extraordinary world* (also referred to as the *underworld*) that will be full of trials and tests that will require the hero to do exceedingly difficult things. Ultimately the hero prevails and returns to the *ordinary world*—but the hero is forever transformed by the experiences.

3. Vogler, Christopher. *The Writer's Journey: Mythic Structures for Storytellers and Screenwriters*, Michael Wiese Productions, 1992.

4. Campbell's classics *The Hero with a Thousand Faces* and *The Power of Myth* are essential reading. Emmy-winning journalist Bill Moyers conducted a famous series of interviews before Campbell's death, which comprise the endlessly fascinating PBS series *The Power of Myth with Bill Moyers*. The DVDs can likely be found at your local library or for purchase online.

An Introduction to The Hero's Journey

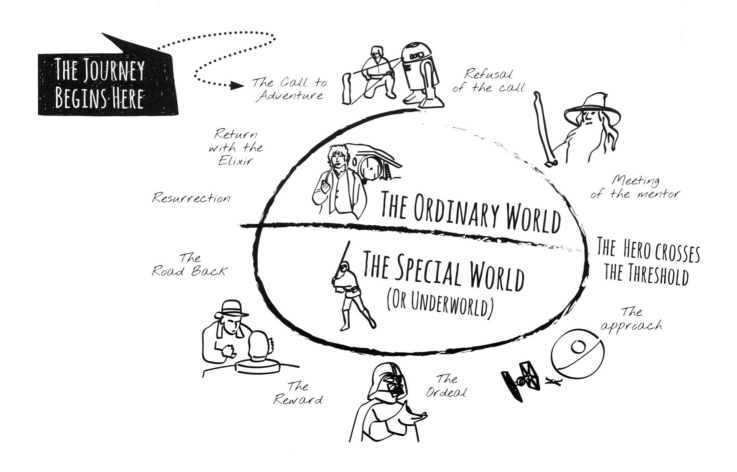

The Call to Adventure

It starts with a message. A recorded hologram of a beautiful princess saying, "Help me, Obi-Wan Kenobi. You're my only hope," or a magical owl carrying a special invitation to a young Harry Potter, who is locked under the stairs of a townhouse on Privet Drive. The call comes from an unfamiliar world, shakes us from our comfortable reality, and impels us to action and change.

Refusal of the Call

As the implications of the call start to dawn upon us—"We could die out there!"—we may hesitate or even experience fear. As the stakes become more evident, we may find ourselves clinging to comfort, like Bilbo Baggins looking for excuses to ignore Gandalf's invitation and hunker down in his hobbit hole in Bag End: "We [hobbits] are plain quiet folk and have no use for adventures. Nasty disturbing uncomfortable things! Make you late for dinner!"

Meeting of the Mentor

The hero won't be alone. He or she will have support. He or she will be accompanied by a wise mentor (think Gandalf, Obi-Wan Kenobi, Dumbledore . . .) who can lead the hero to greater self-awareness, and provide resources and knowledge needed for the journey. But, ultimately, the mentor cannot take our place; we are ultimately destined to face our trials alone.

Here the Hero Crosses the Threshold and Enters the Special World (or Underworld).

As the hero finds his or her way about this very different world, he or she must learn new rules and adopt new ways of thinking. He or she will also encounter new personalities and will have to make tough judgments about their allegiances and agendas.

Approach

It becomes increasingly clear to the hero that he or she will have to ultimately face a difficult test: a Darth Vader, a Voldemort, or another force that will require the hero to summon enormous inner strength and courage. There must be a period of preparation for the coming ordeal. (Recall Luke Skywalker in training with Yoda.)

The Ordeal

Ultimately the hero will have to come face-to-face with his or her greatest nemesis, putting all of his or her deepest vulnerabilities to the test. There may be dark moments where it appears that all is lost.

The Reward

Just as Indiana Jones grabbed that golden idol from the Mayan temple, the successful navigation of the ordeal will lead to treasure, or something precious and valuable that the hero will take with him or her.

The Road Back

The story isn't over. There is a long path that leads back to the ordinary world, and the hero must traverse this road—often with the demons in hot pursuit.

Resurrection

Right on the precipice of home, the hero will encounter one last severe test—one that will purify him or her of any remaining weaknesses and liabilities. This may require a sacrifice, a moment of devastating loss that will be necessary so that the hero may experience rebirth and salvation.

Return with the Elixir

The hero returns home, but he or she is fundamentally changed. Nothing can ever be the same again. However, the hero now occupies his or her ordinary world with an elixir, a potion, a treasure, or perhaps a deeper truth or heightened awareness that will elevate the quality of existence for his or her community.

As you reviewed the steps of the Hero's Journey, did you find it easy to connect it to movies you've seen? Did you also recognize how those elements have been recurring themes in your own life and leadership?

The Hero's Journey is the story of you, your team, your future, and the difficult things that you are trying to create together. As such, it is a powerful construct for making sense of your experiences.

And it is a powerful construct for mining stories. Similar to the fractal constructs suggested in the previous chapter, it provides a framework for helping your team members or colleagues identify the most compelling stories that they should be telling. Similar to the process described there, we will use the Hero's Journey as a metanarrative to shape your team's experience.

Here's how to do it.

Introduce the Hero's Journey

Before the session begins, draw the Hero's Journey on a flip chart or whiteboard. You may use my image on the next page for inspiration.

After you have brought the team together, begin the process by describing the Hero's Journey. For many people this is a new set of ideas, and it requires some explanation (much like I just presented above). This is actually a benefit of the process. The Hero's Journey is unique in its power to fascinate, and when I describe the different steps, I find that it effortlessly draws people in. It's easy to understand, and it's fun. And people love the idea that their story of leadership may borrow from Hollywood's secret recipe for stories.

> Just think about everything that has happened since we started Project Epsilon 18 months ago!

> Things have been challenging since the layoffs in January. Today we're going to talk honestly about what has happened since then.

> Two days ago I brought you to this mountain retreat to talk about the future of our team. Tomorrow we return to our ordinary world. What a journey it has been!

> We created this organization eight years ago with a big vision. Today we are preparing for our initial public offering (IPO). A lot has happened to lead us here!

Connect Stories to the Stages of the Journey

Now it is time to begin the story mining. As always, you will need to frame how you ask the question. What is the bigger story or journey that you want to capture a series of smaller stories around? In framing the dialogue, you should provide a *theme* and a *timeline*.

Here are some examples of things that you might say to frame the dialogue. Notice how each of the following statements frames the specific journey and timeline:

Have participants first work individually and brainstorm stories for each of the steps. Working quietly and individually, they will think of a story or two to go with each step and then write a compelling title for that story on a sticky note.

Tell participants that they probably won't think of stories to go with every stage, and that's okay. Certain stages will jump out at them and they will recall important stories. Those are the best stories to capture.

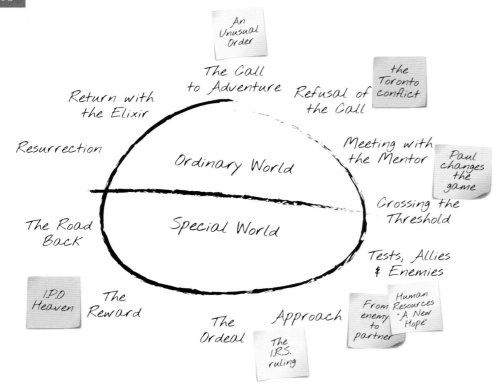

As team members share their stories, they will gain a strong appreciation for the greater journey they are on . . . especially the future "chapters" that haven't happened yet.

Then bring them together, and have them place all of their sticky notes on the appropriate part of the model.

You'll probably have clusters of stories. Some stages may have no stories, and others will have a lot. That's not a problem. Your purpose here is not to bring every step of the monomyth to life but to recall the stories from your experience that matter most.

Depending on the time and the amount of sticky notes, you may choose certain titles—perhaps based on how compelling the title is, or how much urgency the teller feels to tell that particular story.

It is possible that participants will identify stories that are not directly related to one another. That's okay. The stories are not going to line up in a perfect series of chapters that build on one another. Within the timeline that you defined, there were multiple story lines, multiple mentors, and multiple ordeals, and they happened on different timelines. On the old TV westerns, they used to cut away from the main hero and say, "Meanwhile, back at the ranch . . ." to show some parallel action or secondary story line. Narrative is a flexible container that can accommodate all of these concurrent story threads.

As the facilitator of the storytelling, you can call out the similarities between these stories. "Wow, so there wasn't just that one big ordeal with the lawsuit. We were actually being tested from the very beginning!"

Option: Ordeal Storytelling and Prophesying Your Ending

The Hero's Journey construct can serve to reorient the team and create awareness of their bigger story. This can be an especially powerful exercise if the team is in the middle of the *ordeal*, if the work is becoming so challenging that you fear the team may be losing hope. In that case, the ending of the team's story hasn't happened yet. So, make the story session reflect that!

Before the team begin brainstorming individually, say to them: "We are in the middle of our story. We are in the ordeal. So only brainstorm stories for these first six stages—starting with the call to adventure up through the ordeal." (Or you may choose later stages if you would like to include stories up through, say, the resurrection. You decide. You're the narrator, remember?)

The power of this is that it orients and changes the meaning of the current challenges, and gives the team a prophetic look into its future. Where does our story go next? We won't stay in the ordeal forever! We may survive this, or we may emerge battered and barely standing—but we will at some point return to our ordinary world with the elixir!

Where Do I Go from Here?

The Hero's Journey is a powerful construct for articulating your organization's strategy. Turn to Chapter 15, "Strategy Is a Story" for ideas on aligning your people to action within the Hero's Journey.

If you have prophesied the ending as described in the option above, you may choose to begin telling some future stories. So, what *do* that reward and return with the elixir look like? Spend some time defining this future using Future Story Spine (Chapter 9) or Creative Tension Pictures (Chapter 14).

Use this exercise to find the buried patterns and recurring themes that are threaded across the many stories in your team or organization.

Chapter 13

STORY ELEMENT EXTRACTION

For this exercise you will need:

- A group of stories to analyze

- Large-sized sticky notes of differing colors

- A lot of wall space for posting and rearranging the stickies. This may be a large whiteboard, multiple flip charts, or a very long sheet of butcher paper taped to a wall.

Every story you hear is packed with meaning. They're like those clown suitcases, where the clown pops it open and starts pulling out a ridiculous amount of content: Clothing! A vase! An extension ladder! Another clown!

Amazing how so much meaning can be packed into such an efficient, little package that is a single story.

And that's just one story! When you have a bunch of story suitcases, they collectively hold deep wisdom about the team and the organization. With a little bit of thought and an elegant process, your team can begin to mine those stories for gold.

As we explored in Chapter 6, "Summoning the Muse," the great opportunity of story work is to build your and your team's capacity for meaning making. Here is a simple process for hearing the deep wisdom that your organization's stories is waiting to release to you.

First we will look at a simple version, and then a more robust process that can dig even deeper into a large pool of stories.

The Classic Version: Working with a Few Stories

The harvester/witness model described in Chapter 6 allows individual team members to immediately respond to a story as makers of meaning. Here, harvesting is a group analysis as team members begin to surface the meaning not just *within* stories but *across* stories.

Let's say you host a single story circle with five members in the group. They will generate five stories. There's a lot of information buried in those stories!

The team will identify some of those themes with a classic sticky note "affinity grouping" exercise.

At the conclusion of the story circle, provide a question that frames what you would like for them to draw from the story. An open-ended question usually works best:

Each participant writes a single big insight they got from one story on a sticky note. If I was in a story circle with four stories (including my own) I will create four stickies.

"What new truth or big insight do you take from that story?" You may also tailor the question to your unique context: "What do these stories reveal to us about *innovation*?"

Let's say the team starts with Karen's story. On a sticky note, each of the five team members will write down the "one big insight" that they took from Karen's story. (Yes, Karen also identifies an insight from her own story.) Now there are five sticky notes with insights from Karen's story.

They will do this with each member of the story circle. At the end, the team will have 25 sticky notes, each with its own big idea.

Next, have team members place their stickies on a flip chart or wall. Instruct them to group similar items togeth-

er, and then identify the theme or category of that grouping. They may write the theme on a larger sticky note, or directly on the flip chart.

If you have multiple story circles, each team will create its own separate flip chart.

At the close of the activity, simply discuss: *What were the big themes? What did you hear that was expected? What did you hear that surprised you? What does this tell us about US? What needs to happen next with these insights?*

 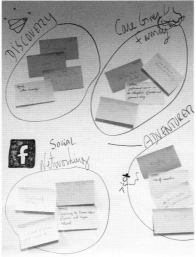 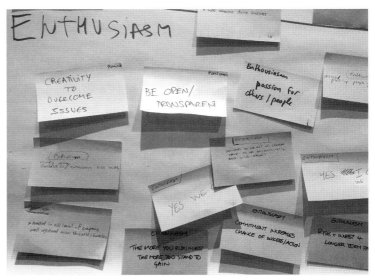

It requires thoughtful analysis to discover what the disparate group of stories have in common. Participants may be surprised as the themes begin to emerge.

Going Deeper with Story Element Extraction

When you have a *lot* of stories, the pool of meaning is quite dense. To extract meaning, the process needs to be a little more robust. This innovative variation of the process was developed by knowledge management pioneers Dave Snowden and Cynthia Kurtz.[1] With generosity and enthusiasm, Cynthia has agreed to share it with you.

For this exercise you will need approximately 20 stories for each group to work with.

The stories should be written down so that they can be distributed and reviewed by people who did not originally hear them. Thus, when you host a story circle (or any of

the "fractal" mining frameworks described in Chapter 11), build in some extra time for each teller to write down their story for you to collect.

You will also need large sticky notes in three different colors. Be forewarned the group will consume a lot of these sticky notes.

This process takes at least 90 minutes to complete. But you could easily continue over drinks and late into the evening.

---

1. Cynthia lays out a comprehensive guide for story element extraction in her book, *Working with Stories in Your Community or Organization: Participatory Narrative Inquiry*, available for download at www.workingwithstories.org.

With roots in the field of knowledge management, this process draws deep wisdom from the many stories that exist in the organization.

Distribute the Stories

Get into groups of three to six people. (If you have more people, then create multiple groups and have them all do this exercise at the same time.)

This works best with a lot of stories. To get the clusters of meaning we need for the analysis, you should have at least 20 stories to work with. More is better.

Ask the group, "What is this story about?" Yes, keep the question that simple and that broad.

What is this story about?

Distribute the stories to the groups. The format of these stories will depend on how you have previously collected the stories. So, for example, if you previously did the timeline exercise as described in Chapter 11, "Fractal Narratives," you'll have all the story titles on sticky notes. If you have the entire stories captured in a written format, that's even better.

If you only have around 20 stories, then you may give every group the same bundle of stories. If you have a *lot* of stories, each group may have a totally different group of stories. This exercise will work either way.

The group should review the stories. If members are unfamiliar with the stories, then they will need to read them or otherwise review them. They can do this out loud, but if you are constrained by time or if the stories contain sensitive information you should review them silently.

Collect Ideas

Participants should write their answer to the question "What is this story about?" on sticky notes. One brief idea per sticky note—only a few words per note.

So for example, let's say we're in a group together shuffling through our stack of stories, and for some reason the Coca-Cola story that I shared earlier in "Four Core Stories" is in there. If you recall, that story went like this:

> Back in the 1980s before we introduced New Coke, we tested it endlessly with focus groups. Consumers were unanimous: New Coke tasted better. So why did it fail in the marketplace? Because we never asked the crucial question: *What if we got rid of Coca-Cola and replaced it with New Coke?* That would have revealed the deep, emotional connection people have about our brand. We thought they wanted better flavor. We discovered they want to maintain their emotional connection to our brand!

So, let's say our team spends a few minutes talking about that story, and members create sticky notes (all the same color) to answer the question "What is it about?"

Perhaps the team captures these ideas about the Coke story:

Notice that these are perceptions, and some are emotional and maybe even debatable. This is fine! Perception and emotion are welcome in this exercise. This process is meant to reveal those mental models.

The team does this for *all* the stories it has been given. At the end, the team will have around 30 to 100 sticky notes.

Cluster the Answers

The group should have anywhere from 30 to 100+ sticky notes with ideas on them. (If it started with 20 stories, this assumes it came up with around three to five ideas for most of the stories.)

Kurtz makes a fascinating recommendation here: Have participants turn the sticky notes 45 degrees so that they are diamond shaped rather than square. "I find that squares cause people to start the process of categorizing their notes as they write them," she explains. "Something as simple as getting them to turn them 45 degrees breaks their categorization thinking."

Now stick all the notes up on a wall, whiteboard, or series of flip charts. Tell participants that whenever they see ideas that are similar, place them close together. When they see ideas that are dissimilar, place them farther apart.

A series of clustered ideas will emerge. The group should try to come up with six to eight clusters of similar items.

Note that at this point, we are no longer talking about the specific stories! We have left the stories behind, and will spend the remainder of the exercise talking only about the meaning that we have extracted from the stories.

Name the Clusters

Now get the sticky notes of a second color. Give each cluster a descriptive name.

After the team groups the insights, they will give each cluster a descriptive name on a different colored note.

Describe the Attributes of the Clusters

Now get sticky notes of a third color. The team will discuss:

- What is *positive* about each cluster element you identified?

- What is *challenging* about the attribute?

The team will capture from two to four ideas on the third color of sticky notes.

Let's pause and reflect on what we have now. There will be several large groupings that might look something like the one below.

On the left we can see our original ideas grouped by the similarity which the group decided all had to do with "brand" (including one that you may recognize from the New Coke story). The name of the cluster is up at the top, and the *positive* and *challenging* attributes are in a third color on the right.

Again, you'll notice that some of these attributes are opinions; some are principles; some are specific to the

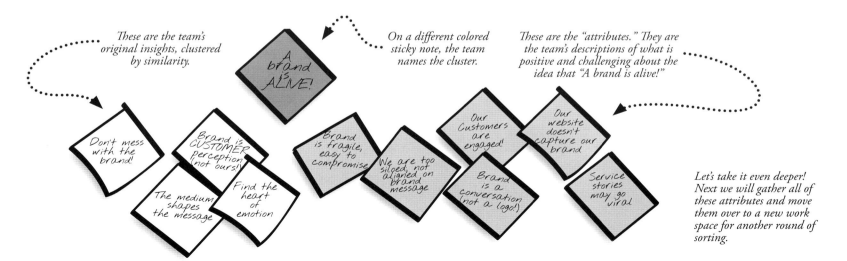

These are the team's original insights, clustered by similarity.

On a different colored sticky note, the team names the cluster.

These are the "attributes." They are the team's descriptions of what is positive and challenging about the idea that "A brand is alive!"

A brand is ALIVE!

Don't mess with the brand!

Brand is CUSTOMER perception (not ours!)

The medium shapes the message

Find the heart of emotion

Brand is fragile, easy to compromise

We are too siloed, not aligned on brand message

Our Customers are engaged!

Our website doesn't capture our brand

Brand is a conversation (not a logo!)

Service stories may go viral

Let's take it even deeper! Next we will gather all of these attributes and move them over to a new work space for another round of sorting.

company and others aren't. But some important themes and truths about the team's work are starting to emerge. It's all good.

Transfer, Group, and Name All the Positive and Challenging Attributes

But we're not done yet! As Dave and Cynthia discovered in their work at IBM, one more round of sorting and affinity grouping can help distill the extracted meaning down to its purest essence.

Grab all of those attributes on the third color of sticky notes, and bring them over to a new space for one more round of sorting and clustering.

Cluster them by similarity, exactly like you did before. This should move a little faster than it did before, because the team will be familiar with the process.

And, exactly like before, come up with descriptive names for the clusters.

The team is now having conversations that may be quite far removed from the stories they originally told, but which hold urgent relevance for the organization.

Assess and Reflect

Do you see what we just did? We extracted story meaning like boiling down a solution so that all the extra stuff vaporizes and only the core elements remain. Cynthia calls these "story elements"; Dave refers to them as "archetypes."

If multiple groups were working simultaneously, teams can take turns sharing their final story elements with one another.

Discuss the final story elements. What deeper truths do these reveal to you about your organization (or the original bank of stories that you started with)? How would you describe the meaning of these elements to someone who just came in?

How might these elements inform what you will do next (whether the context is marketing, knowledge management, change management, strategic communications, etc.)?

Use this exercise when you want to tap into the core structure of leadership storytelling or to engage your team in creating a shared story of your future.

CREATIVE TENSION PICTURES

For this exercise you will need:

- Two blank sheets of flip chart paper for each participant

- Plenty of colored markers

- Because flip chart paper is large, a lot of space to spread out. (Some people will take off their shoes and sit on the floor for this exercise.)

- Tape or another method of hanging the paper on the wall

You can't expect anyone to execute something they weren't part of creating.

—Meg Wheatley

Think about how much of your messaging as a leader is saying to your teams, "We are *here*, and we need to be *there*." Every day, in ways mundane and significant, leaders move people forward.

What if instead of dictating direction to your team, you invited them to help you articulate it?

That's the idea behind creative tension pictures, which is one of the easiest exercises in *Circle of the 9 Muses* to execute. (It rivals Visual Timeline for ease of implementation.) You can also scale it very easily. That is, it works with a small team of three people, and I have used it in a conference ballroom with more than 100 people.

In this visual exercise, members of your teams will create metaphorical depictions of the current state and then the desired future state of the team (or project, function, organization, or any other frame that you choose). It's a pure form of Storyboarding (which is described in Chapter 16), and it works for many of the same reasons. It is deliberately slow and reflective, and metaphorical thinking triggers the mind to access its network of thoughts, memories, emotions, and concepts. This simple exercise always yields a meaningful experience.

In his classic book *Images of Organization*, Gareth Morgan shows how he uses this exercise in high-conflict scenarios, such as in bitter disputes between labor and management.

The instructions are simple. Draw a picture of your current reality; and then another of your desired future. Use as many images and as few words as possible. Take turns presenting your images and ideas. That's all there is to it.

The exercise has the curious effect of diffusing the tension in the conversation. Because storytellers from both sides of the dispute are all focused on the rough stick figures in their collages, this has the effect of externalizing the discomforting feelings. When I tell the story of my two images, I'm no longer pointing at *you* or even at *me* but at the metaphorical representation that represents how I perceive the story. Conversations that have been mired in stalemate for years suddenly find traction and movement without defensiveness.

The instructions are exceedingly simple.

1. Give each of your team members two sheets of flip chart paper and some markers.

2. Ask them to draw two pictures for you: an image of *where we (as a team, function, project, or organization) are today* and then *where we need to be in the future* (20 minutes).

3. Instruct them to make their depictions visual, using as few words as possible.

Have them take turns sharing their images with one another.

That's it! It is basic, even remedial. But as is often the case with the simplest things, there are deep currents moving here.

What's Going On Here

Robert Fritz says his model of *creative tension* is the core structure of all leadership. It is also the most basic unit—the atomic structure—of all leadership storytelling.[1]

Creative tension is enabled every time a leader articulates two states: where we are today (our current reality) and where we want to be (our desired future state). When you articulate those two states, you create a tension that generates movement and change. *We are here. We should be there.*

Fritz depicts the dynamic with a memorable metaphor. Imagine a rubber band stretched between your hands. One side is current reality and the other is the desired future state.

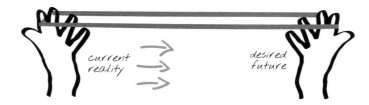

1. My own understanding of creative tension is driven by my work in the organizational learning community, and the influential work of Peter Senge and Robert Fritz. It's a concept I explore in my Learning Fable entitled *The Lemming Dilemma*. My personal exercising of creative tension has been greatly informed by mentor and friend Teresa Hogan of Refreshing Perspectives in Atlanta, Georgia.

210

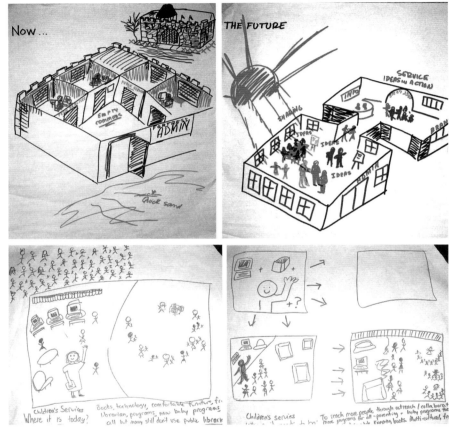

*An international group of librarians came together to discuss the existential crisis of their industry ("What does it mean to be a librarian in the age of the Google search bar?"). Hundreds of librarians began defining new visions for their future with Creative Tension Pictures. One of the insights that emerged was that libraries need to embrace a **customer service and user experience** mental model.*

It is the nature of tension to resolve. Furthermore, it resolves in the direction of stability. In creative tension, the clear, compelling, consistent vision is the stable structure, like a stake in the ground. The current reality is unstable and always changing. So enabling creative tension creates movement that draws people toward the vision. Leaders who create and innovate consistently are masters at enabling this creative tension in their own lives and among the people they lead.

Simply articulating the two states creates tension and movement. In a very real way, this exercise is a potent act of leadership. This is not an exercise in preparing for change; the change is already happening in the room as participants sketch and engage one another.

By inviting your team members to articulate the current reality and desired future, you help them exercise their own cores of leadership; you also unleash their creativity to generate new insights with the potential to move the organization.

Options for Creative Tension Pictures

This is one of those basic exercises that is endlessly configurable, and sure to benefit from the creative adaptations you make to fit your team and context. Here are a few options.

- *Go kindergarten.* I once arrived for a program where I was intending to start with this exercise, and was surprised that the host of the event had placed a box full of glue, pom-poms, pipe cleaners, stickers, glitter, and googly eyes at each table. For a brief moment I thought about objecting, but what the heck? We went with it. It added a level of playfulness that served the group well, and members were ingenious in using the materials at hand (especially the pipe cleaners) to physically link the posters to one another, creating an impromptu, self-organizing network of desired future states.

- *Mind the gap.* The power of creative tension is that space between today and the future. It implies an urgent question: *What will get us from here to there?* Most often, when people share the narrative of their two images, this is exactly the conversation that emerges naturally. However, you can be even more prescriptive and add another round in which you ask participants to create a *third* picture—one that goes in the middle and depicts the journey (including the new behaviors, new tools, new processes, and new beliefs) that will take us to where we need to be.

- *Sculpt it.* Instead of flip chart paper and markers, give participants several blocks of modeling clay or kids' Play-Doh sculpting dough. Instruct them to create three-dimensional models of the current reality and the desired future state.

The Fast Version: Visuals Speak

Using outside resources, you can reduce this exercise to a fraction of the time. Christine Martell is president of VisualsSpeak, and she has produced a beautifully packaged set of hundreds of images that you can use for this exercise. Rather than draw the current reality and desired future state, invite the team to instead select a series of images to depict those two states. If I have a big enough space, I like to lay out the images on the ground so that participants can physically move about the room, looking at the metaphorical images and deciding what they mean.

The dynamic of this approach is a little bit different. Rather than draw meaning out from their own imaginations, the visuals will speak to participants with surprising connections that they would not have thought of otherwise. People are always intrigued by the approach, which is very fast, very easy, and able to draw them into a deep dialogue very quickly. For these reasons, I often use this flexible tool to begin my meetings. Check out VisualsSpeak at *www.visualsspeak.com.*

212

Build it, via the *Think with Your Hands* Methodology

One of my very favorite activities to bring to groups is the LEGO SERIOUS PLAY (LSP) method, which originated from the LEGO company in Denmark around 2000. The brilliant methodology uses actual LEGO bricks to build a spatial, dimensional representation of the current and future organizational system.

Two people instrumental in the early development of LSP have influenced my application of this resource.

Per Kristiansen, partner at Trivium Consulting in Copenhagen, certifies facilitators around the globe (along with key LEGO innovator Robert Rasmussen) to use the LSP methodology in comprehensive strategic interventions that can be many days in length and result in incredibly detailed LEGO models of the organizational system (including suppliers, partners, channels, markets, and more). It's a beautiful thing.

My friend Jody Lentz, who is right here in Nashville, Tennessee, developed a half-day workshop based on LSP principles and materials called "Think With Your Hands," which he and I both bring to groups all around the world, and it can generate big insights into a creative tension story in just a couple of hours. Both LSP and "Think With Your Hands" use specially designed LEGO sets and a defined methodology—but at their heart, they are variations of Creative Tension Pictures.

You can facilitate your own simplified versions of these processes. Use your imagination! For example, you can distribute Play-Doh or other modeling clay and ask your team members to sculpt their current reality and desired future.

"We need to connect the innovation pipeline to market needs."

"We have self awareness! Need to get better at facing outward."

"Decentralization good; isolation bad!"

"Can suppliers keep up with our carousel of offerings?"

Learn more at Per Kristiansen's website: www.Trivium.dk

or at Jody Lentz's website: www.JodyLentz.com

- *Provide a cheat sheet.* When you tell your team that you want them to draw pictures, expect to see a look of panic in their eyes. Emphasize that this isn't an art contest, and that rough is better. The idea is not to dazzle with beauty but to communicate something that matters. I usually will take it a step further and provide an Icon Cheat Sheet that I developed for these exercises to spark people's imaginations and reinforce that crude stick figures are a powerful tool for communication. You are welcome to photocopy mine to use for this exercise.

- *Tell the story.* The responses to the pictures will be a series of descriptive statements. These will be quite revealing . . . but the conversation becomes even more robust if you connect it to stories. This can be done with simple story prompts:

  Tell me about a time (you, the team, etc.) embodied that current reality.

  Tell me about a time we/they displayed characteristics of the future state.

  When have you seen another person or team display the characteristics and capabilities that you desire for the future?

Where Do I Go from Here?

A next step may be to be organize in Story Circles (Chapter 2), so that team members can begin sharing the specific stories that are triggered by this exercise. You can also use the harvester/witness framework (as described in "Summoning the Muse," Chapter 6) as a way of teasing additional meaning out of the images and stories.

See? It's just stick figures! An Icon Cheat Sheet is provided in the Appendix. Share it with your team members before starting this exercise to build their confidence in visual thinking.

Use this framework when you want to communicate your strategy message in a way that creates high engagement and participation.

Chapter 15

STRATEGY IS A STORY

For this exercise you will need:

- Awareness of a strategic message you wish to communicate with impact; or one in which you would like to engage the best thinking of the team to help define and develop.

In the previous chapter, we explored how leaders move people forward with creative tension. Here, we will add some additional levels of meaning to the story. Between the *current reality* and the *desired future state* is the strategy—the journey that will get us from here to there.

Think about the next critical strategy message that you need to share with your team, one that will require everyone to rally and align to make the work happen. How do you intend to share that message?

Many leaders are tactical, make-it-happen kinds of folks, so it is very likely that your message will include the key metrics, goals, and accountabilities that people need to meet. That's a great start.

What if you communicated that message as a narrative?

I have spent much of my career helping organizations position their strategic imperatives in a way that generates high engagement, and I'm about to share one of my secret recipes with you. Strategy is a story, and it is defined by aspiration, goals, heroes, and monsters (which, more often than not, are our own ways of thinking). Articulating strategic messages as a story extends an opportunity to your people to step into the story in a way that can be deeply meaningful and energizing.

It's a lot better than telling them they'd better hit their sales goals *or else.*

There are two ways to use *Strategy Is a Story*. The first is as a communications platform: a way of becoming clear on the message, and its many supporting message points, which you will reinforce with consistency on numerous occasions to your team or organization.

The second is as an ideation tool using storyboarding. This is a process that invites you (or a team) to think critically about the strategy in creative ways that will generate new possibilities for taking action.

First, let's look at the template for the strategy story.

A Journey of Heroes

In Chapter 12 of *Circle of the 9 Muses*, we explored Joseph Campbell's classic construct, the Hero's Journey, as a framework for sense making in the organization. Here, that archetypal template appears again as a framework for the strategy story you are presenting to your people. When I develop strategy communications for my clients, I often use this shortened, simplified version of the Hero's Journey as a sort of checklist for defining critical message elements in a strategy story. First, let's look at language and images from the Hero's Journey to define the steps, and then we will look at an example.

Think of a strategy that you need to communicate to your team, and then reflect on how you might connect each of the following movements to your message.

The Call to Adventure

Don't bury it. Let people know you are going on a journey together. Your strategy story starts with the invitation, right up front. In *Star Wars*, Luke Skywalker was called to action when R2-D2 played a hologram from Princess Leia: "Help me, Obi-Wan Kenobi. You're my only hope!" Note that I've seen many strategy messages begin and end with the call. ("Okay, people. Here are the new goals. Time to get on board.") But we're weaving a narrative, and our strategy story is only warming up.

The Ordinary World

The call doesn't exist in a vacuum. You are asking people to step away from the comfort of the hobbit hole in The Shire because of a darkness that is lurking. There are tough realities in your world or marketplace that people need to understand. So tell them. (In the language of Creative Tension, this would be our *current reality*.)

The Hero

You've presented a big goal, and a tough world. So who is going to save us in this dire circumstance? The answer is us! We are the heroes we've been waiting for. We must summon our greatest powers—and courageously face our weaknesses—in order to move forward.

The Dragon

There are dragons (or Darth Vaders, or Lord Voldemorts) standing between us and our goal. These may be competitors or marketplace difficulties. Just as often, these antagonists are our own beliefs and mental models, which must be confronted.

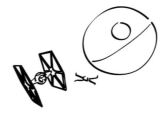

The Journey

Like Frodo Baggins on the path to Mordor, you should expect many trials and challenges along the way. We will have to make hard choices, and we will experience discomfort (or worse). There may be times when the journey becomes so difficult that we may feel like giving up hope.

The Outcome or Elixir

But we've been to the mountaintop, and we've seen a glimpse of how good things can be. When we accomplish our mission, a better world awaits us! There will be rewards, both internal and external, that we all can share and that will have made the hard journey worth it.

Of course, when you communicate your most critical leadership imperatives, you probably won't be literally quoting Yoda or evoking the descent of the Death Eaters over Hogwarts. (Although who's to say you couldn't?) Your message will consist of your real-world equivalents.

Here is a typical strategy story that I might develop for a client. (This one is an example I just made up and is an aggregate of multiple messages that I typically encounter.)

Call to adventure

We are inviting you on a journey! We have set a challenging goal: to achieve metric X and to be recognized as a leader in Y.

Ordinary world / current reality

We've been successful in the past, but we can't count on that success to carry us into the future. Our context today is *[more complex/more competitive/more regulated]* than ever before.

The Hero

But we are the people of Company Z! Our legacy of *[innovation/ resilience/whatever]* has been a part of who we are since our earliest days. Today that spirit is alive in your work.

The Dragon

However, we are often the victims of *[our own success/our own ways of thinking/our deeply siloed organization/etc.].*

The Journey

That's why today we must adopt new mental models about our work, new tools and processes, new ways of working together. This will feel uncomfortable to us. It will be hard. But this is how we will achieve our mission.

Outcome or Elixir

When we do, the result will be *[new opportunities/new markets/ new innovation/a better place to work/etc.]*

As you might have already sensed, each of the statements in this message demands detail. Stories are fractal, and every element maps to a network of additional stories and supporting points.

One of my colleagues was the director of communications for a Fortune 100 company, and she showed me how to create a *message house* that organizes these cascading messages and subpoints in visual form. (Once again, I'm making this one up for the sake of example and tossing in everything but the kitchen sink.)

Example: A Strategy Narrative "Message House"

Journey to "Synergy 3000"

We are calling on our people to achieve metric [X] and be recognized as a leader in [Y].	Our work is tougher than ever. We've been successful in the past, but can't count on that success to carry us in the future!	But we are the people of [company Z]! The legacy/spirit that defines us is more alive than ever!	However, we must overcome some challenges. Some are external; many are internal.	Today we must adopt new tools, new processes, and new mental models. This is how we will achieve our mission.	When we arrive, we will enjoy new opportunities, new markets, new innovation, a better place to work.
–Individual measures –Organizational measures –Financial measures	–More regulation –Loss of our patent –Disruptive innovation from startups –Customer has more choices	–Must display resilience –Act upon our capacity for innovation –Be willing to talk straight –Etc.	–Our siloed culture –Outdated or conflicting systems –Lack of trust across functions	–Supply chain automation –Agile/Lean processes –New acquisitions –Decentralized functions –Etc.	–A sustainability leader –Forbes' 100 Best Places to Work –Top 25 for shareholder returns

An example of a strategy story "message house." In the top row you can see the six "chapters" of the message which correspond to the Hero's Journey elements described on the previous pages. On the bottom you can see supporting points. Note that this is an example with a mashup of messages that I encounter frequently. One developed from your reality would surely tell a more coherent and specific story.

Share the Story

This *Strategy Is a Story* chapter is a framework (and not a process.) That is, it is a way of clarifying your thinking around how to articulate an important strategy message. For next steps, you have many choices.

- *Align the leaders.* Share the framework (perhaps in the message house format) with other leaders who share responsibility for implementing the strategy. This will ensure the leadership team is reinforcing a consistent message.

- *Say it.* You can certainly share the strategy story verbally when you communicate with your team. Do the supporting points belong as part of this verbal presentation? You decide, based on the audience and context. Often, the main narrative works best as a standalone, high-level orientation, and will elicit questions, which you are then prepared to respond to using the supporting points.

- *Visualize it.* Hire an artist to create an image, info-graphic, or storyboard of your strategy story. I have a team of artists I reach out to for capturing strategy stories as infographics, *learning maps*, storyboards, and more. Illustration is an incredibly engaging way to draw your people even deeper into your strategy with a high level of engagement, retention, and emotion.

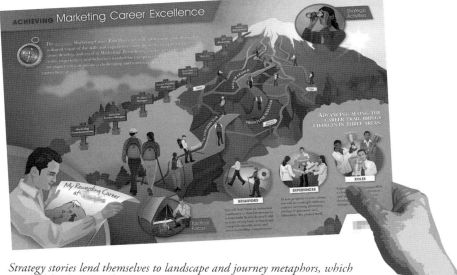

*Strategy stories lend themselves to landscape and journey metaphors, which are ideal for depicting **from** and **to** states—as well as the gap between them. For the most polished presentation, I engage my design partners to render the story with beautiful artwork.*

222

Sometimes I find it just as effective to use my limited art skills and draw it myself. Here is an example I developed for an organization that was centralizing its HR function and needed to engage team members in a conversation about the intent and implications.

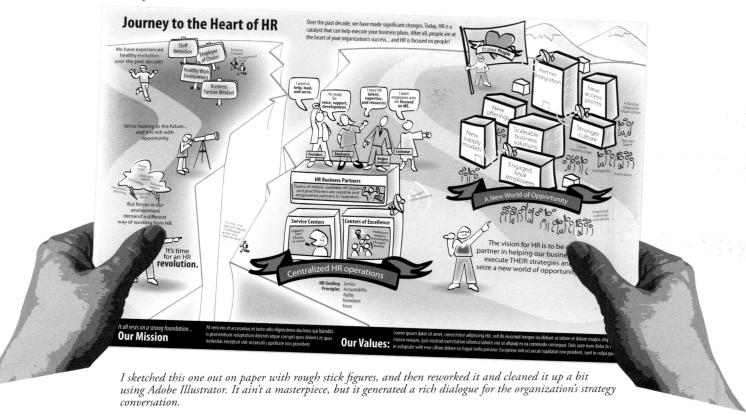

I sketched this one out on paper with rough stick figures, and then reworked it and cleaned it up a bit using Adobe Illustrator. It ain't a masterpiece, but it generated a rich dialogue for the organization's strategy conversation.

With the help of a learning partner, this can be presented as a detailed *learning map*—a table-sized graphic that invites your people into a deep exploration of the strategy narrative over a 2-hour to 4-hour learning experience.

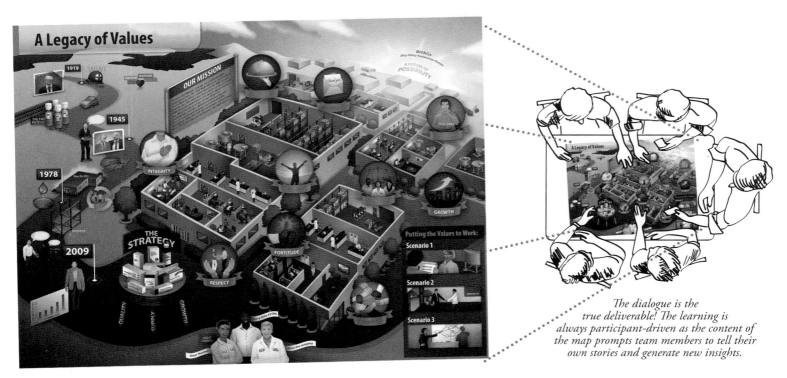

The dialogue is the true deliverable! The learning is always participant-driven as the content of the map prompts team members to tell their own stories and generate new insights.

The ultimate visual expression of a strategy message is a learning map—a table-sized visual that is used in an organizational learning context. Members of the organization gather around the image and analyze the stories, metaphors, and quantitative data. Complex strategic messages are presented with compelling simplicity in a way that invites all members of the organization to participate.

Strategy Is a Storyboard

For this exercise, you will need:

- Flip chart paper

- An assortment of colored markers

- About 3 hours (to explain, create, and present the storyboards)

- A room with a large wall where the team can display and present its storyboard

Let's get the whole team involved! After all, they are the heroes of this story, so they should have a hand in defining the narrative.

This is another storyboarding exercise, very much like those presented in the Creative Tension Pictures, Innovation Storyboarding, and Storyboarding Frameworks chapters. That means it is a generative exercise that will produce new ideas. It should not be thought of as the final word on your approach to strategy, but as a mind-stretching exercise that can be used in the process of defining the strategy. You can conduct this with the leadership team that is responsible for defining the strategy or with the team that will be responsible for executing the strategy. Either way, the team will come away from the exercise with a deeper, archetypal awareness of its strategy.

Explain the Hero's Journey to your teammates, similar to how this chapter explains it. You should spend a few

minutes on this and on drawing your team into the Hero's Journey. They need to understand this context so that they can create the storyboard. Don't worry—if you spend just a few minutes with the Hero's Journey, they will get it quickly.

Tell the team that its task is to create a storyboard of its strategy and that it should follow the steps of the Strategy Is a Story template (The Call, The Context, The Hero, The Journey, The Dragon, and The Outcome or Elixir). Members will illustrate each chapter of the story with colored markers over a series of flip chart pages. At the conclusion of the exercise, they will tell their story to an audience of your choosing. Thus, they should think about how they will present their dramatic strategy epic.

There are a few important principles to reinforce, some of which I always say whenever inviting a team into a visual-thinking exercise.

- *Rough is good*. People are almost always anxious about visual-thinking exercises. It is good to keep reinforcing that this is a *communication* exercise, not an art contest. And, in fact, rough images are often more effective at communicating than finely rendered ones. Stick figures, boxes, and arrows will go far. (In the Appendix, you will find an Icon Cheat Sheet with ideas for images that participants can easily copy.)

- *Think by drawing*. Tell the team *not* to spend an hour planning every detail members will draw. That defeats

The call

Ordinary world

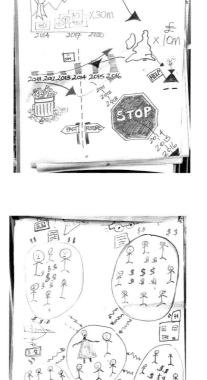

Dragon

Hero

Journey

Return with the Elixir

For one team of leaders from a global retail products company, envisioning their strategy in a storyboard resulted in a paradigm-shifting conversation. They imagined themselves as Peter Pan, overcoming threats in a sea full of competition and marketplace pressure.

the exercise. They should spend around 5 minutes talking about their general message and approach—but it is important to put pen to paper as quickly as possible. The process of drawing will trigger new ideas. They will discover what they want to say *after* they start drawing, not before.

- *Use as few words as possible*. Words can be used for titles, labels, and quotations. Participants should not fill the page with lists or dense blocks of text.

- *Use at least four flip chart pages*. More is okay. This is to prevent participants from thinking too narrowly and squeezing multiple chapters onto a single page (with a resulting loss of message detail).

After you have explained the Hero's Journey and gone over the simple ground rules, the team is ready to get to work! I find that 2 hours is about the right amount of time for teams to complete and rehearse their presentation.

The previous pages shows a strategy storyboard developed by a leadership team at a global luxury brand company. The team presented its marketplace challenges as a sea filled with sharks and pirates preventing it from gaining market share. And who is the ideal hero for defeating a bunch of sharks and pirates? Peter Pan, of course!

Like many teams do, this team became especially invested in the presentation of its story. Using a digital music player, members downloaded a bunch of MP3 songs to

Option: Cast the *9 Muse Archetypes* in Your Storyboard!

The Hero's Journey is an archetypal story. Why don't we bring in some archetypal characters? This exercise becomes even richer if you populate the storyboard with the 16 archetypes presented in Chapter 8.

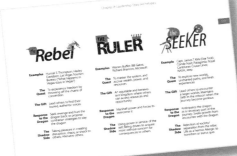

As team members plan their strategy storyboard, have them review the 16 archetypal identities and use them to illustrate the protagonists and antagonists of the story. These may include **themselves**; their **customers**; their **brand**; other **constituents** or groups in their value chain; and more. In each case they may wish to depict the *current* and *future* archetype. (How must the identity change? What aspects of the identity must we lose?)

Because the archetypes are metaphorical, they are easy and fun to capture visually. And they add yet another level of engagement in the way that archetypes are uniquely able to do.

serve as the cinematic soundtrack to the presentation. It's hard to communicate just how effective this was. When the team revealed that the hero (*us*) was Peter Pan, the audience erupted in delirious applause.

The strategy story presentation often generates a rather profound insight that, if it emerges, you should certainly call out. The team or organization often shows up *twice* in the story: once as the dragon and again as the hero. We are both antagonist and protagonist in our own story. We are part of the problem, and we are the solution.

The idea that *the problem is us* can be a touchy one to discuss in organizations, even though it is almost always true at some level. Presenting this tough truth in a metaphorically driven story has the fascinating effect of neutralizing defensiveness. When we see it rendered in the story, it feels removed from us, less personal, and even entertaining.

Even better, this hero story redeems us. Sure, we are the problem and helped perpetuate our dilemma, but we are also the people who are going to save the day. Indeed, the most beloved heroes are flawed, such as Indiana Jones and his fear of snakes. Overcoming the flaw makes the victory so much sweeter.

Where Do I Go Next?

Note that this exercise can also work individually. However, it can take quite a long time for one person to fill four or more flip chart pages with detailed drawings. If you choose to work individually, simply create the storyboards on several sheets of standard 8.5 × 11 printer paper. This will scale the exercise to more manageable dimensions and speed the process.

After defining the strategy or creating the strategy storyboard, the next step is to invite others into the conversation. Remember—a story is always the beginning of a dialogue and not the end. Now is an opportunity to invite your people into a conversation about how they personally connect to the strategy narrative you have presented.

One possibility is to have other teams create their own strategy storyboards to illustrate what their piece of this journey looks like. After all, they will have to take action to deliver the strategy, which will send them on their own Hero's Journey with its own set of dragons.

Creative Tension Pictures (Chapter 14) are another way to invite people into the conversation by defining the current reality and desired future states for the change.

Use this exercise when you wish to define new processes or new customer experiences—especially in an innovation context.

Use the other frameworks to engage your team in generating new insight into any process.

INNOVATION STORYBOARDING

+ STORYBOARDING FRAMEWORKS

For this exercise you will need:

- A stack of index cards for each participant. (Get a lot! It's very possible a participant might use as many as 20 cards.)

- A set of colored felt-tip pens, such as Sharpies, for each participant

230

The beginning of motion picture technology brought with it new insights into our ability to make meaning. In 1918, the Russian director Lev Kuleshov conducted a famous experiment that had huge implications for the developing language of cinema, and how audiences interact with the images they see projected on a screen.

In his experiment, Kuleshov filmed an actor staring into the camera with no expression. Later he filmed individual subjects, such as a bowl of soup, a child in a coffin, and a pretty woman reclining on a lounger. Then he edited those shots so that each was followed by a so-called reaction from the man. However, the reaction in all three cases was the same identical footage he had captured earlier. For early film audiences—many of whom had never seen a motion picture— the effect was powerful. They described the man's hunger, sadness, and lust (respectively) and even marveled at his acting.

Of course, today we experience this all the time in our media-saturated world, so this capacity of the mind to construct a story may not strike us as extraordinary. When given two pieces of information that are

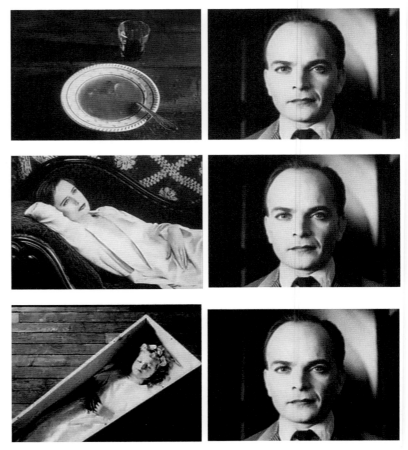

The famous Kuleshov experiment, 1918. Identical film footage of an actor with no expression were intercut with images of a bowl of soup; a pretty woman; and a child in a coffin. Early audiences were amazed at the "acting" as the man seemingly "responded" to each image with hunger, sadness, or lust respectively. Audiences were confused when they were told it was the same footage.

not correlated (visually or otherwise), the mind will work pretty quickly to fill in the gap between the two items by filling it in with a story. It's remarkable, really, how effortlessly this happens.

This is why comic books and graphic novels are such a vital art form. In his brilliant work *Understanding Comics*, artist Scott McCloud demonstrates vividly how when you put two pictures side by side, you have created—in a very real sense—*movement*. The audience supplies the meaning that strings the pictures together.

Storyboarding is powerful for this reason. It makes your story visible, and invites a unique kind of cocreative participation from both the maker of the storyboard and the audience. By rendering only a few frames of your story, your mind (and your audience's minds) fills in the spaces in between with robust narrative meaning. The engagement this creates is strong. I have seen teams present storyboards that generated cheers, laughter, groans, or even shouts of anguish.

Furthermore, storyboarding differs from verbal storytelling in that it works beautifully as a pure *ideation* process. A certainly spontaneous improvisation goes into verbal storytelling, but storyboarding is different. For one thing, it is slower and that means the creator is forced to reflect more deeply on the meaning he or she is creating on the

Even very young children are able to grasp the narrative movement that is created when images are placed side by side. Source: George Herriman, Krazy Kat 1918 *[Comic Anthology].*

232

paper. Also, the use of your hands and the kinesthetic feel of markers on the paper activates expansive, nonjudgmental thinking. Per Kristiansen, one of the innovators behind the LEGO SERIOUS PLAY methodology, calls the hands "the leading edge of the mind." The act of moving your hands actually generates (or *constructs*, for our constructionist theorists) new connections and new knowledge in the mind.

There are many scenarios where storyboarding is a powerful exercise. You can use it to generate new insights into *current reality* by having participants generate a series of story frames that depict *what is*.

It is also used to generate big insights into *desired future states* by having participants draw the story frames of *what could be*. It is especially useful in innovation work, and legendary design firms, such as IDEO, rely on it to pioneer new products and processes.

First we will focus on a classic storyboarding exercise—an *innovation* story. Then we will explore how to extend storyboarding to your other work challenges.

Classic Innovation Storyboarding

In this exercise, you or your team will create a new, innovative offering. This may be a new product for your customers, a new process to improve work flow in the organization, the addition of a new feature to an existing product or service, or the application of a current offering to a new customer group. Or it may be a redesign of a current offering that you think could be better. You will gain tremendous insight into this offering by rendering it as a story.

Working in pairs or trios, you will create a storyboard with three "chapters" that you will recognize from your Marketing 101 class:

Each of these three chapters will be illustrated with three subsections:

The innovation storyboard should have at least nine cards, but it may have many more. For example, you will likely wish to create multiple cards depicting the "steps of the hero using your solution." This can be a rich exercise in user experience design.

Introduce the storyboard elements above.

Team members should generate at least one card for each subsection. That means the final storyboard will have at least nine cards. (If they create title cards for Problem, Solution, and Benefit as shown in my example above, that will put them at 12 cards.) They will probably generate even more than that, since the "steps of the user encountering your solution" often ends up being multiple cards.

Split the group up into teams of two or three. I always like the energy of multiple groups working simultaneously at different tables, so if you have only four people, then create two pairs working separately.

Emphasize that rough is better and that their storyboard will be very effective with stick figures, smiley faces, squares that represent buildings, arrows, and so on. (In the Appendix you will find an Icon Cheat Sheet with simple ideas for images that team members can easily copy.)

Also emphasize that they will think by drawing. They should not spend an hour planning in detail what they will draw! It's important to put pens to cards as quickly as possible. They should just start making a line, even if they're not sure yet what they are creating! Because the hand is the leading edge of the mind, insights emerge after they start drawing, not before.

Give them 90 minutes to work, and tell them to start creating the cards.

As you circulate and see how they are doing, point out a couple of advantages of the card-based approach:

• They can quickly change their minds about the content simply by adding or removing cards.

• Even more powerfully, they can switch the sequence of cards around. This is one of the main advantages of the storyboarding methodology. As participants move deeper into the work, they may have flashes of brilliant insight: "Wait a minute! What if the last step in our process would work better as the first step?"

At the end of the work, if there are multiple teams, they can take turns presenting their innovation storyboards to one another.

If the teams are both working on the same problem, they may even wish to combine cards from the two presentations for even greater flashes of brilliance.

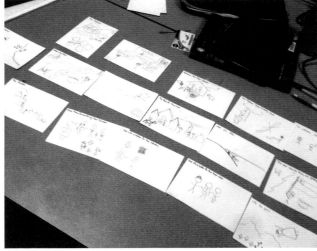

The index cards beg for experiments in sequencing. "What would happen to our process if we switched these two cards?" "How does our offering look different if we reverse the entire sequence?" "What if we got rid of the third step?" Encourage participants to play.

Stick the cards up on a cork wall, or tape them to a whiteboard; you can use them as visual organizers as you begin capturing further resources or action plans for each story element.

The Fast Version

If you want to generate faster insights that perhaps don't go as deep into the problem solving, you can shorten the work cycle. Also, this works well if you are working alone and would like to move faster.

Instead of using multiple index cards, use three sheets of standard copier paper turned lengthwise in landscape orientation; or use a single large flip chart page.

Use the same outline, but combine the three chapters so that each is rendered on a single page. Note also that in this version of the exercise, you lose the ability to resequence steps. Nonetheless, even in this compressed cycle of work the visual thinking will generate fresh and surprising ideas while giving you a more detailed vision and mental map of what you wish to create.

Other Storyboarding Frameworks

We just explored the power of storyboarding in an innovation context. But you might have already sensed that storyboarding is a powerful tool with applications far beyond innovation. It is an endlessly configurable tool that you can use anytime you want to render visually *what is*—and it is even more powerful for showing *what could be*.

"All things are created twice: first in the mind, then in reality." Stephen R. Covey popularized this quote in his classic *7 Habits of Highly Effective People*, and it is a perfect positioning of storyboarding process. Storyboarding exists as an additional step between imagination and reality, between vision and execution. It is a powerful opportunity to reflect and think expansively and critically before creating.

Storyboarding works for *any* future process that requires human engagement. For example, if your team is planning next year's big sales summit, you might storyboard the entire event from the participants' point of view (from checking in to the hotel, to the keynote address, to the cocktail social, to the awards ceremony, and so on). The visualization may reveal challenges to the design or opportunities to vary the energy with different kinds of activities.

As another example, you might storyboard the user interface for a new piece of software or smartphone app. What

does the user see upon launch? Where will he or she click? What happens next?

An Example: *My Creative Process* Storyboard

Michelle James is an expert in applied creativity, and she designed a whole-brain, story-based methodology and workshop called "Create Your Own Creativity Model." So much of Michelle's work captures my own imagination.[1]

I was invited to speak to a group of artists and musicians here in the rich creative community of Nashville, Tennessee, on the topic of creativity. What a great opportunity to do some self-awareness work! Inspired by Michelle, I developed a storyboarding exercise to help people enhance their awareness of their own creative processes.

I offer this here both as an exercise that you are welcome to modify or repeat exactly as described, and a case study on the process of connecting a storyboarding exercise to a specific challenge.

---

1. If you are intrigued by the conversation that creativity storyboarding introduces, you should certainly look at Michelle's offerings, which provide a robust menu of programs that can take you and your team quite deep into an exploration of your own capacity for creating. This includes Michelle's methodology and program for leading students to create their own creativity model. Learn more at http://www.creativeemergence.com.

The *My Creative Process* storyboard exercise has been a hit here in my home of Nashville, where there is a strong creative population in music, book publishing, and entrepreneurship. But it is powerful in any context where you are focusing on innovation or environments that depend on creativity. (Which would be all environments, right?) Organizations depend on regular output, and yet creative product is notorious for being cyclical and irregular. It's a classic challenge for managers in creative environments. In my career as an advertising copywriter, I don't recall ever having strategic conversations about *how* each of us created—and I can imagine now how helpful those conversations would have been for a manager trying to align a crazy team of unpredictable creatives.

I find that this exercise is especially meaningful at an individual level. Everyone I know—my friends, my colleagues, my kids, and myself—is at some level a frustrated creative. I bet that you feel the need to create and that you also know how it feels to be stuck—whether it is a case of writer's block or a lifelong frustration that you're not generating the work you know you're capable of. People are often deeply moved by this exercise because it leads

This is the product of My Creative Process storyboards for a group of artists and musicians in Nashville. In this case, we had limited time, and instead of index cards, each person used a single flip chart page divided into three "chapters."

238

to self-awareness around the most sacred parts of their identity.

I almost forgot to mention that, like all storyboarding, this exercise is a lot of fun! There is nothing more energizing than being in a room where people are telling the story of their own creative process. I learn a lot every time I do this.

I'll never forget the artist who told me that a big part of her creative routine was to walk around her house and yard backward.

"Backward?" I asked her.

"Yes, I go out the front door, walk around the entire property backward, and end back at the front door. When I get back to my desk I have lots of ideas."

"Why does that work?" I asked her.

"I don't know why," she said, "but it does."[2]

Michelle James explains the unique power of this exercise in self-awareness:

> "While there are patterns and themes true to all creative process, there are as many ways to create as there

are people, no one's creative process fits neatly into an externally designed set of steps. Rather than impose linear sequential steps to a nonlinear, individually unique creative process, I use storytelling as the entry point to the Create Your Creativity Model process I developed. Using story, along with Socratic dialogue and visual-thinking exercises, participants extract meaning and relevance, from within themselves, before getting into the design and development of their unique creativity model. Then they form what they had "mined" into a model. After it is created, there is a sense of pride and celebration participants experience in clearly seeing how they indeed *are* creative, and in a unique way. It gives them the courage to put themselves out there."

Building the Exercise

Let's look at the process of making this happen. We've decided to build a storyboarding exercise on the subject of the creative process. What needs to happen next?

We need to begin with a structure. When you ask people to create a storyboard, they are going to look to you for guidance, a framework, an outline, and a series of chapters to give them direction.

---

2. Why do you think this works? I have some theories! I think it has something to do with the forced change of perspective from a physical and motor point of view translating to a mental mind-set.

If you recall, the innovation storyboard in the previous chapter was built on the classic problem/solution/benefit structure.

So what are the chapters for our personal creative process storyboard?

I always begin at the simplest level of before/during/after. Remember, we are rendering a story here, and before/during/after puts us on a timeline of change, which is where stories live.

In terms of the creative process, I might further define these chapters as:

- *Visioning* (All the actions you take *before* you start creating)

- *Executing* (The actions *during* the creative process)

- *Making it live* (The actions *after* the act of creating)

To further define how this might work, I developed a page of prompts or things to think about during each of those

Visioning Prompts
- How I get ideas

- When and where I get ideas

- Activities that spur new connections

- What *incubation* looks like

- Validating the vision (research and talking)

- Who I involve in the process

- Introversion vs. extroversion

- Dealing with feelings of vulnerability

Executing Prompts
- Getting started

- Cycles of activity

- Routines and rituals

- Introversion vs. extroversion

- Bringing in resources (people, tools, and materials)

- Getting stuck and unstuck

- Individual vs. collaborative

Making It Live Prompts
- Testing it externally

- Responding to feedback and critical judgment

- Cultivating my market

- Getting the word out

- Increasing exposure

- Selling it and making money

- Extending its life cycle

three phases. You can see those prompts in the previous box, which I also placed in a handout and distributed to my audience.

Now Begin the Activity

Introduce the storyboarding activity and the structure you defined (in this case the stages of my personal creative process).

Distribute materials, including the Icon Cheat Sheet to build confidence.

Allow participants 45 to 60 minutes to create their storyboards.

Have them take turns sharing their storyboards with one another.

A group of artists deepens their self awareness of their own creative processes, from the Vision stage to the Execution stage to Making It Live in the marketplace.

Where Do I Go Next?

You can probably see how to extend this exercise to other topics besides creativity, and that's the beauty of storyboarding. It is very easy to adapt. To do so, simply:

- *Name the story that you want participants to storyboard.*

- *Provide a high-level structure to guide them.* This might be a "before/during/after" framework. Other possibilities include the innovation processes described in the previous chapter (Problem/Solution/Benefit) or even the Hero's Journey (as described in Chapter 15, "Strategy Is a Story").

Or you could use a classic change journey, which is *Current reality/New behaviors and mind-sets/Desired future state*. (See Chapter 14, "Creative Tension Pictures.")

- Then give them a series of index cards (which allow you to define steps at a more micro level and thus takes longer), flip chart pages, or copier paper (which are for broader steps and moves faster)—and put them to work!

Storyboard Your Offering Using Presentation Software

Every time I develop a new learning program with my partners, I begin with a simple storyboard. It gives me a vivid overview of the program, allowing me to assess issues of energy and flow while triggering a lot of new ideas. It also invites my partners and clients into the dialogue in a way that gets them excited about the offering.

It's easy to do. Using PowerPoint (or Keynote on the Mac) I simply create the experience by dropping images in sequence. In some cases, I will take a picture of what I need using my phone camera, or I find images with a free or Creative Commons license using websites such as www.Compfight.com to bring to life almost any action or idea that I can imagine. (My colleagues sometimes make jokes about me. "This is a Hutchens presentation. It's going to have stories and pictures." But the truth is they love it!)

Are you planning a regional meeting? A wedding reception? A party? An off-site retreat? Open up a blank slide, go search for some images, and drop them into place to show the story. As always, stay open to being surprised by what emerges as you select and place the images!

When I develop new learning programs, I like to begin with a storyboard to bring the experience to life and engage my partners in the dialogue. This can be done quickly using presentation software, such as PowerPoint or Apple Keynote.

Use this exercise when you want to immerse your team in a world very different from your own so that you can encounter new and innovative ideas for your work.

Chapter 17

STEP INTO A STORY

STORY FIELD TRIPS

For this exercise you will need:

- A learning need for your team

- Physical access to a compelling story site

- Time and resources to manage an immersive event

I'm standing in the middle of the campus at the U.S. Olympic Training Center in Colorado Springs, Colorado, with the executive team of one of the most successful software innovators in Silicon Valley.

"Over the next two days," I tell the team, "I want you to make a note of anything you see that you think helps to create a *culture of high performance.*" Some of the executives are already happily distracted as they raise their camera phones to capture pictures of passing Olympic and Paralympic athletes. "Capture notes of anything that grabs your interest," I tell them. "It might be a technology you see. It might be a conversation with an athlete. It might be a symbol, a color, or a feeling. It might be the architecture. Anything is fair game. At this point, you don't have to know *why* it is important. Later, we will explore your observations to tease out something that will be valuable to your work."

This has become a familiar refrain in the immersive leadership experiences presented with my friends and colleagues at The Conference Board. With my friend and longtime mentor, Dick Richardson, we invite teams of leaders to step into some of the most compelling stories in the world—be it through the stories of the Apollo program at the National Aeronautics and Space Administration's (NASA) Johnson Space Center in Houston; the Battle of Gettysburg at Gettysburg National Military Park in Pennsylvania; D-day at Normandy, France; and more.

These experiences are fascinating because they manifest physically the dynamic that takes place every time we hear a story. After all, neuroscience shows us that when we listen to a story, our minds process it as if it were a real experience. So what happens when we bodily step into a fantastic, compelling story? Our belief at The Conference Board was that it would lead to even higher levels of engagement in learning that can be lasting and transformative. We found that to be true.

Creativity theorist Edward de Bono coined the term *lateral leaps* to describe the mental process of connecting two previously unlinked ideas in the mind. This is the unique power of story field trips. They are data-rich environments that continue to generate value-producing lateral leaps of insight even after the event is long over.

As an act of learning design, this is serious work. My team, including Dick Richardson and Jeff Jackson, invested enormous resources into creating compelling story experiences that could lead to strategic dialogue and business transformation.

But you don't have to be a learning designer to create powerful story field trips. You are surrounded by accessible opportunities to step into a story with your team for powerful learning.

How to Step into a Story

To create an immersive story learning experience with your team, we will once again draw from Joseph Campbell's Hero's Journey, or monomyth (which is explored in Chapter 12.) From a design point of view, this makes sense because you are, after all, inviting your team into a dramatic journey of learning!

Your steps are to:

- Identify the *special world* (finding the context for learning).

- Issue the call to adventure (framing the conversation).

- Cross the threshold (immersing in the story).

- Bring back the elixir (drawing out the connections).

1. IDENTIFY THE "SPECIAL WORLD"

2. ISSUE THE CALL TO ADVENTURE

3. CROSS THE THRESHOLD

4. BRING BACK THE ELIXIR

Identify the Special World

Let's begin with the most obvious question: Where will you take your team for the learning experience?

The best story field trips are in *story-rich environments.* That is, they are filled with history, dramatic tensions, and identifiable protagonists who experience clear arcs of change.

Additionally, they should feature some *story delivery mechanism.* Don't make the mistake of assuming that your team will naturally pick up the story simply by being present and walking through a site. There must be some vehicle for actually relaying the story to your team. This could be a person, such as a tour guide, historian, or docent like you might find at a museum or historic site, or an employee or leader at an organization you wish to visit. It could be printed materials, such as the signage and placards at a well-designed museum exhibit. Or it could be an audio or digital presentation, such as an audio tour available for rent at a museum or special smartphone tour guide applications that are becoming increasingly popular at historical sites.

Possibilities for story field trips may include:

- *Different organizations or centers of expertise*
  Tour an organization or facility that is renowned for excellence in some area. Is there a manufacturing fa-

cility with a reputation for *efficiency*? Is there a locally owned luxury hotel with a legacy of *customer service*? How about a new restaurant that is the latest offering of a local chef with a reputation for *innovating*? Is there a social enterprise in your town that is doing inspiring things through highly impassioned and *values-driven* leaders?

My partners at INSEAD and CEDEP in Fontainebleau, France, are situated in a campus right next to horse stables on the edge of the Forest of Fontainebleau, and they have seized the opportunity. The stables are a short walk from the campus, and my colleague Loic Sadoulet frequently pauses his executive development programs to walk over to hear stories from a "horse whisperer" and meet the stubborn horses who are transformed by his coaching. It is a powerful experience, Loic says. "The horse whisperer teaches the horse to relax when its world looks difficult and when instinct tells it to flee. The parallels between the effectiveness of the horse trainer and the effectiveness of leaders are wonderful."

- *Military sites or military museums*
  Many people aren't crazy about war metaphors, but I nonetheless find these sites tend to be rich in high-stakes stories with great implications for strategy, planning, resource management, vision, and much, much more. Often, you can find historians for local

battlefields who can tell you the fascinating details as you walk the hallowed grounds.

- *Sites of historical significance*
  You may have access to designated sites of political, civic, or cultural importance. These may include American Indian burial grounds, the state Capitol building, well-preserved plantation homes, monuments, architectural wonders, or other sites where something of historical or newsworthy significance happened.

Lighting the Olympic Cauldron at the Olympic Training Center in Colorado Springs. Metaphors, symbols, emotion, and story are your building blocks for transformative learning.

Executives at one of Silicon Valley's top innovators are discovering messages about organizational resilience through the sport of Olympic curling. These guys now have a knowledge advantage that their competitors don't have.

- *Cultural touchstones*
  Museums, symphony orchestras, legendary performance venues, old churches, and more tend to be drenched in story. One story practitioner I know invites her teams to sit among the musicians of the 300-year-old Slovene Philharmonic Orchestra in Slovenia, where they have a uniquely immersive expe-

rience of the performance as well as an opportunity to hear stories about the institution's rich history directly from the conductor and musicians.

- *Sport experiences*
  These can be tricky. I've seen groups attempt to build a learning experience simply out of attending a

A team of executives at Gettysburg. "Business as war" may be an outdated mental model. But Gettysburg and other battlefields offer deep learning into strategy, and decision making in a complex or chaotic environment.

Looking for lessons in innovation? You should check out the second stage of the mighty Saturn V rocket at Johnson Space Center. That's our friend, NASA historian (and retired HR leader) Harv Hartman weaving his storytelling magic.

hockey or football game, and come away disappointed. Yes, a baseball game is technically a self-contained story (with its own antagonist, protagonist, conflict, and so on) but it is a superficial one. Sport experiences work best when coupled with a behind-the-scenes view that is built on more robust stories. For example, you might access a coach, a team member, or even

"Houston, we have a problem." This is where it all went down. That's me at historic Mission Control in Houston. It's okay to act like a fanboy geek. The emotional rush signals the brain to store the learning.

someone in the organization's leadership to serve as a storyteller who can provide a more complete narrative perspective on the people or events. At The Conference Board Team USA Leadership Development Experience, Olympic and Paralympic athletes, coaches, and leaders are the compelling storytellers who bring the experiences to life so that the program is about so much more than just sports.

Issue the Call to Adventure

How will you frame the experience to your people? What is this story experience *about*? Stories contain their own wisdom, so to an extent you should frame the journey as something that the story can deliver.

This requires a bit of listening. When Dick Richardson and I develop immersive experiences for The Conference Board, we begin with an extended period of *story listening* in which we look for the narrative wisdom that is already threaded through the story.

For example, we might have a difficult time making our program at the Olympic Training Center into a dialogue about, oh, say marketing and branding.[1] On the

1. Sure, it's possible. But it would require a bit of conceptual acrobatics; or perhaps bringing in the Olympic Committee's public relations expert to serve as our primary storyteller.

250

other hand, you might sense how the Olympic Training Center is perfect for hosting a dialogue around creating a high-performance organization.

Similarly, the Apollo Leadership Development Experience (at Johnson Space Center or Kennedy Space Center) is an ideal place to host a dialogue on leading teams for innovation.

With my partners at learning company Blueline Simulations, we sent a team of medical sales representatives to Disney World's Magic Kingdom for a program on exceptional customer experiences.

The idea is to frame the experience broadly in a way that draws out the natural wisdom of the story, while being relevant to the strategic conversation that is urgent for your team to have.

On the other hand, it may be that you are comfortable encountering the story experience with no agenda at all and minds wide open to emergent meaning. When my colleague first approached the Slovenian orchestra, she said, "We didn't know what the outcomes would be. We practiced presence and waited for the questions to emerge from the story." When participants surrender themselves to the process of listening and learning, that itself becomes a part of the learning.

Note that when Dick and I have developed these immersive story experiences, they are often two and a half

days and sometimes up to five days long. But that's in the service of a robust and carefully engineered set of learning objectives. For your team, we're seeking spontaneous and useful insights. A 2-hour to 4-hour immersion will be ample. For example, you might meet your team at the site in the morning for a 3-hour or 4-hour experience, go to lunch together afterward, and be back at work by 1 PM.

Let's quickly check off our to-do items:

- Find a story-rich environment to host your team.

- Identify a person or vehicle for telling the story to your team.

- Identify the broad theme that you are looking to explore from the site.

Of course, make any other plans (such as travel, lunch, and other expenses) for this to be a fun event!

You're ready to step into the story!

Cross the Threshold

Once you and your team cross the threshold into the special world of the story, it is important to foster two sets of awareness: one around the story you are encountering (listening "in the text") and the other around value-producing insights (connecting "in front of the text").

In Chapter 6, "Summoning the Muse," we explored the value of giving audiences a special task or role to focus their attention as they receive the story. Remember, stories are incredibly rich containers of information, and audiences will find themselves adrift if you don't provide a frame to direct their attention.

This isn't hard to do. At the beginning of the experience, simply remind your team of the theme of the event. "We are here today to explore the topic of *collaboration*."

Then, invite participants to think expansively, and capture details. "As you look around the facility, and as Mrs. Summers tells us the stories about how this company was built, make a note of anything you find interesting. It can be any part of the story—a detail, a quote, or something that just strikes you as unusual. At this point, you don't have to know why it is important. If it catches your interest, that's enough."

That last sentence is important. Team members are only *noticing*, not *connecting*, at this point.

My colleague Terrence Gargiulo has success in having his participants be a little more exclusive in what they notice. He calls his events "Study Tours," and he instructs his participants to observe just two or three interactions or pieces of data, and come back prepared to talk about them.

For The Conference Board experiences, we distribute Moleskine notebooks to each participant for note capture. The books are compact, and the beautiful design just seems to invite people to populate the pages with notes. They are ideal companions for these experiences.

We also hosted an *innovation tour* of Silicon Valley organizations in which we distributed iPads to each participant (on loan) and used a note-taking app that allowed participants to capture both handwritten notes and spontaneously captured photos on the same page.

At different points in the tour, it may be helpful to remind people to capture ideas. Sometimes, they become so immersed in the fascinating stories they forget to capture their notes.

But otherwise, stay immersed in the story! Avoid the temptation to interrupt with frequent connections to your business. Instead, capture the thought quietly so that you can come back to it later.

Bring Back the Elixir

Recall that the denouement of Campbell's Hero's Journey features a return with the elixir—the hard-won knowledge, insight, or item of value that has the power to transform the ordinary world. This is the goal of every learning journey.

As we have explored elsewhere in *Circle of the 9 Muses*, after you hear a story the conversation isn't over. It's just beginning! As a leader, you host additional conversations to begin drawing the meaning out of the story, making its value explicit and actionable.

Although the assistance of a trained facilitator can greatly enhance this conversation, you can exercise your leadership role as weaver of meaning simply by asking some basic questions:

- *Draw out the data.*

    What did you notice?

    What were some of the notes you captured in your Moleskine notebook or iPad?

    What jumped out at you as being significant or interesting?

- *Connect it to the frame.*

    We are here today to talk about the theme of [*collaboration, or whatever*]. How do you think that connects to our theme?

(Note that some details may not be directly connected to the theme. That's okay. Allow for a broader interpretation. "Why else do you think that detail is important? What does it say to you about collaboration in general?")

- *Bridge it to your world.*

    How might that idea/behavior/dynamic show up in our organization?

    Have you ever seen it in our work? Why or why not?

    How might that idea/behavior/dynamic be used to benefit us in our work?

- *Ask for stories.*

> Tell me about a time you saw something similar in our work. What happened?

> How was that different than what we saw today? How was it the same?

- *Make plans for action.*

> Based on what we just discussed, what needs to happen?

> What should we do differently? (Who should do it? By when?)

If you wish, capture ideas on flip chart paper as you host this conversation. Be sure to capture and follow up on any insights and actions that this conversation generates.

The Stories Keep Working on You!

One of the curious effects of these immersive story experiences is that they keep working on you. The more compelling the story is, the more likely it is to continue percolating in your subconscious and generating invisible ripples of helpful disruption to your thought processes.

I keep thinking about the stories I've heard at the Olympic Training Center, and they return to my consciousness at the most interesting moments. I may be in the middle of a challenging piece of work, and something that a Paralympic swimmer said, or an encounter in the athlete dining hall, will suddenly flash in my mind.

Really great stories get inside of you, where they keep communicating and delivering their gifts.

Special thanks to my wonderful team at The Conference Board, including Jeff Jackson and Dick Richardson, as well as our partners James Sayno at the Olympic Training Center and Harv Hartman (retired), from NASA's Johnson Space Center in Houston.

Use this when you want to bring your storyboards or story ideas to life in fun, creative, and dramatic ways with professional-looking books, movies, and more through easy-to-use technology.

Chapter 18

DIGITAL STORY TELLING

FILM IT
SHOOT IT
POST IT

For this exercise, you will need:

- A computer (desktop, laptop, or notebook or iPad)

- Resources that you either create (a series of pictures or videos you intend to capture) or download (images and artwork with appropriate licensing)

- Software that makes the work easy and fun

People get excited when they see your story delivered with a semiprofessional level of polish. It's almost embarrassing how just a little bit of effort can turn your organizational audience into gushing fans who are convinced of your genius.

You can create digital stories individually or as a team activity. That is, you might simply choose to work alone to deliver an exciting presentation of a story you wish to present to the organization.

However, it is also a lot of fun to task your team with the challenge of rendering its story as a movie, comic book, or photo book. Imagine a training day or corporate retreat where you equip everyone with the technology and software tool (such as iPads loaded with Apple iMovie video creation software), and task them with using the software to create a story for an evening presentation. I have a colleague at a Silicon Valley software organization that had an "organizational movie night" in which teams created organizational movies using the iPad over a period of 24 hours. The theme was "The Power of Our Culture." It was incredibly fun, and the movies that the teams produced are still cherished as important cultural artifacts to this day.

There are a lot of ways to bring your story to life digitally. The choices are increasing all the time.

This short chapter will give you a few ideas of what is possible. Software is constantly in flux with new innovations coming out almost daily, making it difficult to compile a decisive list in a printed book. As a result, I have not attempted to list the options exhaustively or to capture the long URL addresses for your Web browser. Instead, we will look at a few ideas to spur your thinking. Then you can simply do a quick Web search for the type of solution or specifically for the examples that were popular at the time of this writing, which I have listed.

Note that many of the options shown on these pages are absolutely free, and none cost more than just a few dollars.

 ## Comic Book Applications

Comics aren't just kid stuff. They are a dynamic art form and (as we explored in Chapter 16: "Innovation Storyboarding"), unique in their ability to create a sense of narrative movement on a page. Simple software allows you to present very robust stories in a traditional comic or graphic novel format—quickly, and with vivid humor and style.

Using the software, you simply take a series of photos and drop them into the prepared templates, which are laid out as frames in a comic book. You can then easily add visual elements, such as dialogue balloons and thought bubbles, that show what the people in the pictures are thinking, and descriptive boxes, such as "Meanwhile, back in manufacturing . . ." You can even have fun with classic comic book tropes, such as action text items. You know, *bam* and *pow* stuff. This can be an extremely fun way to present any type of story. Just take some pictures on your smartphone, and drag them into the frames. Some software even applies a classic halftone newspaper printing filter to render a more authentic comic book feel.

One of my colleagues created a graphic novel manual for dealing with common scenarios in the customer service department. It was a great way to share information that would have otherwise been dreadfully dull. (It also made this undesirable development task a lot more energizing for my friend.) The comics were so funny and so successful they got distributed all around the organization, finding an audience well beyond the customer service team.

- *Search for:* Comic book maker software, such as ComicBook! or Halftone 2 on the iPad App Store

Even the dryest business processes take on nuance and a compelling urgency when placed in context with human emotion and conflict. And the comic book style injects the presentation with some fun. It took me 10 minutes to build this on my iPad, using an app that cost just $1.99.

▶ Movie-Making Applications

This is a now-ubiquitous category of consumer software, with new innovation emerging all the time. It's an exciting time to be doing video work, because the software makes it increasingly easy to shoot spontaneous video and then instantly add professional-looking transitions, title cards, and music. I've seen some apps that even give suggestions of what you should shoot and in what sequence for maximum narrative impact.

Go Hollywood! It has never been easier to capture your story in video using consumer-grade tools that are fun to learn and, in many cases, free. Try challenging your people to create movies as a teambuilding exercise. You won't believe the brilliance that emerges.

The Apple iPad, for example, has a popular app called iMovie, which includes templates for movie trailers that are fun and easy to use. In these apps, there is typically direction on the kinds of shots to capture, and automatic formatting with title cards and music. As my colleague discovered with his organizational movie night, the linear filming style is especially well suited for "*a day in the life*" themed stories.

Of course, the more straightforward use of a tablet or smartphone that is equipped with video is simply to set it on a tripod or other stable surface and film team members telling their stories. In some story programs, when the sponsors have determined that story collection and archiving is an important activity, we have a *story studio* set up in the corner of the room. This is just a well-lit area of the room with a pleasing background where members can stand, look right into the camera, and tell their stories. (This works best with an activity such as the Twice-Told Story, where the team has self-selected some of the stories as being particularly valuable and worth telling again.) Again, you can use the movie-making application to easily apply simple formatting title cards or banners that feature details, such as the name of the teller and the name of the story.

(For more polished applications, I work directly with my team of video production partners to produce beautiful corporate narratives.)

- *Search for*: Apple iMovie and Microsoft Windows Movie Maker. Note that tablet-based apps tend to be more user-friendly (and less fully featured) than desktop software. This can be an advantage if you have challenged teams to create a movie within a deadline.

Slide Applications

I heap a lot of grief upon PowerPoint. Because it deserves it. But the fact is that this tool, which has been such a blight on modern business communication, can also be a potent storytelling tool. The trick is to fill the screen with big, bold, expressive images with minimal text—and then to advance the narrative with your speaking and not by loading it with bullet point text.

I think it makes a difference to fill the slide space completely with the image. It's a subtle thing, but white margins—and image borders, drop shadow effects, page numbers, and footers—all remind people that they are looking at a PowerPoint slide. They break the spell. There has been something of a renaissance in the artful application of slide software with a growing community of thought leaders. Books such as Garr Reynolds' *Presentation Zen* and Nancy Duarte's *Resonate* are wise, paradigm-shifting resources that have redeemed this otherwise atrociously overworked tool.

Death to the bullet point! For your slides, think in terms of single, bold, metaphorical images that fill the frame, bringing to life each beat of your narrative.

- *Search for:* Apple Keynote, PowerPoint, and Prezi. Chances are that you already have this software on your computer, but new innovations are emerging all the time. It is worthwhile to conduct a periodic search to see what new innovations are available. Also search for the aforementioned books by Duarte and Reynolds.

Photo Book and Storybook Applications

There are many photo-sharing and photo-archiving sites on the Internet. Your desktop computer and notebook computer both probably have the software installed as part of their operating systems. Photo software allows you to capture images, drop them into predesigned book templates, add captions and text, and so on. Your layout is then transferred digitally to a production facility that specializes in this work. The results can be surprisingly professional, with glossy pages, cloth binding, and glossy, wraparound dust covers.

Photo books require that you use high-definition photos, which you will need to be purposeful about capturing. (For example, "the story of our project," "a day in the life in the Legal Department," or "the day the chief executive officer visited our site.") If you plan in advance, you can capture these images over a period to build your narrative, or you can challenge the team to build a photo story over just a few hours. This can be a lot of fun, with teams running around the office frantically trying to capture the perfect images of their work.

Note that photo books do not always have the virtue of immediacy. You can certainly distribute digital portable document format (PDF) copies of the book or print the pages on your color printer. But the luxury-printed, hard-copy version of the book will need to be ordered in advance, with time allowed for production and shipping. If you give each member of the team a surprise copy of the produced book at a celebration dinner, it is a guarantee there will be hugs and tears. And the team will treasure the book, featuring "the story of us," forever.

- *Search for:* Apps and Web-enabled services, such as Apple iPhoto, Shutterfly, and Picaboo

Image Resources

It is easier than ever to find images to support your many storytelling activities. I was recently creating a visual story in Apple's Keynote application, and I needed to illustrate the idea of *agility* metaphorically. I did some searching without really knowing what I wanted, and quickly found a great, copyright-free image of a guy playing Jenga. (You know, the stacked-tower game where you have to remove wooden blocks without the tower tumbling down.) It was a perfect solution to my communication challenge, and it took only 60 seconds to search, click, download, and drop into my presentation. Beautiful.

- *Search for:* Sights like www.TheNounProject.com (which is the source for the Creative Commons subhead icons I used in this chapter); or www.Compfight.com, which searches contextually for images across the social media photo site Flickr, indicating any licensing and usage limitations. (This is the source I described where I typed in "agility," and it suggested the lovely—and free—Jenga image.)

When using online images, it is important to be aware of different licensing requirements. Spend a few minutes educating yourself about Creative Commons images online, which often allow you use of images for a tiny fee, simply with a citation, or sometimes with no restrictions at all.

Pretty cool, right? Whether you film it, shoot it, or download it, technology makes it incredibly easy, inexpensive, and fun to gather resources to bring your story to life. With just a little investment of time, you can delight your audience, send your team off on a bonding creation experience, and look like a hero to your organization.

The "Icon Cheat Sheet for Left Brainers"

You may use this handout for exercises that require your team to capture insights visually, including "Visual Timeline," "Creative Tension Pictures," "Innovation Storyboarding," and more. This page provides a few ideas that will give team members confidence that they can communicate a great deal with a few simple stick figures and arrows, while also emphasizing that visual thinking is not an art contest.

You may photocopy this page for your use with your teams. Please keep the copyright statement on the page and don't use it for commercial purposes.

ICON CHEAT SHEET FOR LEFT BRAINERS

Relax. This isn't an art contest. Your challenge is to populate your messages with meaning by accessing both right- and left-brained thinking styles. Your images will include a combination of quantitative and text-based information, as well as qualitative, metaphorical, image-based information. A few ideas are provided below to stimulate your thinking.

People, relationships

Stick figure men, women, kids   A crowd

Feelings, emotions

Aspiration, rewards

Ideas, dreams, thoughts, quotes

Veni vedi veci!

This light bulb gives me an idea ...

Connect your ideas!

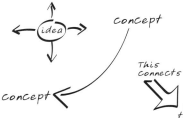

idea

Concept

Concept

This Connects

to that

Places

R&D   Legal   HR

Work   Home   Place of worship   Departments in your organization

The 10 Story Types, the Seven Basic Plots, and the 36 Dramatic Situations

Chapter 4, "Capturing Fire," presents several classic story templates that can inform your leadership storytelling. Here is a more inclusive list from the works referenced by Blake Snyder, Christopher Booker, and Georges Polti. What do you think? Do you envision a place for any of these in your leadership storytelling?

The 10 Story Types from Snyder's *Save the Cat!*

- Monster in the House: Stories of the thing that wants to invade your safe world, and eat you or destroy you (*Alien*, *Jaws*)

- Out of the Bottle: Stories of wish fulfillment or ironic comeuppances

- Whydunit: Solving mysteries and in the process uncovering dark truths about human nature (*Chinatown*, *Se7en*)

- Golden Fleece: Also known as "The Road Movie"—a series of unrelated encounters that lead the hero to self-discovery (*O Brother, Where Art Thou?*)

- Rites of Passage: Going through life transitions and challenges that everyone goes through. The process of life developing you into someone more fully human (*Rocky*)

- Institutionalized: People constrained by the system, until one breakout person tries to assert his or her individuality (*One Flew Over the Cuckoo's Nest*)

- Buddy Love: My life changed forever as a result of knowing you. This has three subcategories: love story, buddy story, and a boy and his dog. (*E.T.*)

- Superhero: An extraordinary person in an ordinary world. Great people dealing with little people (*Superman*)

- Dude with a Problem: An ordinary guy faces extraordinary circumstances (*Die Hard*)

- The Fool Triumphant: An underdog goes up against the institution and wins (*Forrest Gump*)

Booker's Seven Plots from *The Seven Basic Plots*

- Overcoming the Monster: The protagonist fights against an antagonistic force that seeks to overcome him or her. (*Beowulf*, *Jaws*, *Alien*)

- Rags to Riches: The protagonist acquires resources (such as fame or wealth) and then loses all of it so that he or she can learn a greater lesson. The protagonist becomes even richer at the end, which may come in the form of material wealth or wisdom. (*Aladdin*, Steve Martin's *The Jerk*)

- The Quest: The protagonist sets out to acquire something he or she desires and faces many trials, tests, and temptations along the way. (*Raiders of the Lost Ark*, *The Wizard of Oz*)

- Voyage and Return: The protagonist goes to a strange land, encounters a series of adventures, and returns forever changed. (*The Odyssey*, *Alice in Wonderland*, *The Matrix*)

- Comedy: A progression that leads the hero from confusion, to a stage of "it gets worse," to a happy denouement in which the confusion is lifted. (Shakespeare's *A Midsummer Night's Dream*)

- Tragedy: The protagonist is an *antihero* whose series of decisions lead to his or her fall from grace—and perhaps even to his or her death. (*Taxi Driver*)

- Rebirth: The protagonist starts out as an antihero but experiences transformation and redemption by the end of the story. (Ebenezer Scrooge in *A Christmas Carol*, Bill Murray's character in *Groundhog Day*)

Polti's 36 Dramatic Scenarios

Ready to roll up your sleeves? Here are all 36 of Polti's dramatic scenarios, which show up over and over in every good novel or movie you have encountered. These scenarios attract us at a purely human and emotional level. They make for great entertainment and even great gossip. (Notice how many of these show up as headlines on gossip magazines at the supermarket checkout.) Some of these make sense in a leadership context; others have a prurient element and are likely not to be generative in your organizational stories. What do you think? Do you see a creative opportunity to incorporate any of these scenes into your leadership stories?

- Supplication: "I'm begging for your help."

- Deliverance: "Save me!"

- Vengeance for a crime: "I'll make you pay for what you did."

- Vengeance taken for kindred upon kindred: "You hurt my sister, so I'm going to hurt you."

- Pursuit: "Run! They're after us!"

- Disaster: "It's the end of the world as we know it." (Aliens! Meteors! Big ants!)

- Falling prey to cruelty or misfortune: "We used to have it all. How far we've fallen."

- Revolt: "Fight the power!"

- Daring enterprise: "We're on a mission to do the impossible."

- Abduction: "They took her away!"

- Enigma: "All we have is this series of diabolical clues."

- Obtaining: "I won't give up until I get what I want."

- Enmity of kinsmen: "Brother rises up against brother."

- Rivalry of kinsmen: "Mom always loved you best."

- Murderous adultery: "I'll kill you for seducing my girl."

- Madness: "He's out of control, and no one knows what he will do next."

- Fatal imprudence: "I made a big mistake and now all is lost."

- Involuntary crimes of love: "I was blinded by love, and now look what I've done!"

- Slaying of a kinsman unrecognized: "I thought I slew my enemy, and then I discovered he was my brother."

- Self-sacrificing for an ideal: "I'm willing to sacrifice all for my beliefs."

- Self-sacrifice for kindred: "I'm willing to sacrifice all for you."

- All sacrificed for a passion: "I'm willing to sacrifice all for something that is valuable only to me."

- Necessity of sacrificing loved ones: "I'm willing for you to sacrifice all because of my beliefs."

- Rivalry of superior and inferior: "The little guy goes up against the big guy."

- Adultery: "You violated our vows!"

- Crimes of love: "I will love you even though I'm not supposed to."

- Discovery of the dishonor of a loved one: "You have brought shame on our house and family name."

- Obstacles to love: "I love her . . . but I can't be with her."

- An enemy loved: "I'm not supposed to love him, but I do."

- Ambition: "I will get what I want and nothing will stop me."

- Conflict with a god: "I will go head-to-head in a match I can't possibly win."

- Mistaken jealousy: "I thought you were cheating on me. It was all a misunderstanding!"

- Erroneous judgment: "Oops. I thought you were guilty. Sorry!"

- Remorse: "I am guilty. I admit it. I am sorry."

- Recovery of a lost one: "Our son was prodigal but now he is found!"

- Loss of loved ones: "There was nothing I could do to save him."

Note that there are many frameworks that attempt to compile archetypes. The most fascinating contemporary archive is the crowd-sourced wiki experiment at www .TVTropes.org in which story consumers all around the world are identifying and cataloguing archetypes in popular culture.

Bibliography

Books

- Bettelheim, Bruno. *The Uses of Enchantment: The Meaning and Importance of Fairy Tales.* United States: Vintage Books, 2010.

- Blair, Madelyn. *Essays in Two Voices.* Jefferson, MD: Pelerei, 2011.

- Booker, Christopher. *The Seven Basic Plots: Why We Tell Stories.* London, United Kingdom: Continuum, 2006.

- Buster, Bobette. *Do Story: How to Tell Your Story So the World Listens.* London, United Kingdom: Do Book, 2013.

- Campbell, Joseph. *The Hero with a Thousand Faces.* 3rd ed. Novato, CA: New World Library, 2008.

- Denning, Stephen. *The Leader's Guide to Storytelling: Mastering the Art and Discipline of Business Narrative.* San Francisco: Jossey-Bass, 2005.

- ———. *The Springboard: How Storytelling Ignites Action in Knowledge-Era Organizations.* Abingdon, Oxon, United Kingdom: Routledge, 2000.

- Dietz, Karen, and Lori L. Silverman. *Business Storytelling for Dummies.* Hoboken, NJ: John Wiley & Sons, 2014.

- Duarte, Nancy. *Resonate: Present Visual Stories That Transform Audiences.* Hoboken, NJ: John Wiley & Sons, 2010.

- Gargiulo, Terrence. *Once Upon a Time: Using Story-Based Activities to Develop Breakthrough Communication Skills.* San Francisco: Pfeiffer, 2007.

- Haven, Kendall. *Story Proof: The Science behind the Startling Power of Story.* Santa Barbara, CA: Libraries Unlimited, 2007.

- Hutchens, David. *The Lemming Dilemma: Living with Purpose, Leading with Vision.* Waltham, MA: Pegasus Communications, 1999.

- ———. *Listening to the Volcano: Conversations That Open Our Minds to New Possibilities.* Waltham, MA: Pegasus Communications, 2005.

- ———. *Outlearning the Wolves: Surviving and Thriving in a Learning Organization.* 2nd ed. Waltham, MA: Pegasus Communications, 2000.

- ———. *Shadows of the Neanderthal: Illuminating the Beliefs That Limit Our Organizations.* Waltham, MA: Pegasus Communications, 1998.

- Kahneman, Daniel. *Thinking, Fast and Slow.* New York: Farrar, Straus & Giroux, 2011.

- Koppett, Kat. *Training to Imagine: Practical Improvisational Theatre Techniques to Enhance Creativity, Teamwork, Leadership, and Learning.* 2nd ed. Sterling, VA: Stylus Publishing, 2012.

- Kurtz, Cynthia F. *Working with Stories in Your Community or Organization: Participatory Narrative Inquiry.* 3rd ed. New York: Kurtz-Fernhout Publishing, 2014.

- Mark, Margaret, and Carol S. Pearson. *The Hero and the Outlaw: Building Extraordinary Brands through the Power of Archetypes.* New York: McGraw-Hill Professional, 2001.

- McCloud, Scott. *Understanding Comics: The Invisible Art.* Reprint, New York: William Morrow Paperbacks, 1994.

- McDonald, Brian. *Invisible Ink: A Practical Guide to Building Stories That Resonate.* Seattle: Libertary, 2010.

- McKee, Robert. *Story: Substance, Structure, Style, and the Principles of Screenwriting.* New York: HarperCollins, 1997.

- Morgan, Gareth. *Imaginization: New Mindsets for Seeing, Organizing, and Managing.* San Francisco: Berrett-Koehler, 1997.

- Neal, Craig, and Patricia Neal. *The Art of Convening: Authentic Engagement in Meetings, Gatherings, and Conversations.* With Cynthia Wold. San Francisco: Berrett-Koehler, 2011.

- Reynolds, Garr. *Presentation Zen: Simple Ideas on Presentation Design and Delivery.* Voices That Matter. Berkeley, CA: New Riders, 2008.

- Sibbet, David. *Visual Leaders: New Tools for Visioning, Management, and Organization Change.* Hoboken, NJ: John Wiley & Sons, 2012.

- ———. *Visual Meetings: How Graphics, Sticky Notes and Idea Mapping Can Transform Group Productivity.* Hoboken, NJ: John Wiley & Sons, 2010.

- ———. *Visual Teams: Graphic Tools for Commitment, Innovation, and High Performance.* Hoboken, NJ: John Wiley & Sons, 2011.

- Signorelli, J. (2014). *StoryBranding 2.0: Creating Standout Brands Through the Purpose of Story.* United States: Greenleaf Book Group LLC.

- Silverman, L. L. (2008). *Wake Me Up When the Data Is Over: How Organizations Use Stories to Drive Results.* 1st ed. United Kingdom: John Wiley & Sons.

- Simmons, Annette. *The Story Factor: Inspiration, Influence and Persuasion through the Art of Storytelling.* 2nd ed. New York: Basic Books, 2006.

- ———. *Whoever Tells the Best Story Wins: How to Find, Develop, and Deliver Stories to Communicate with Power and Impact.* New York: AMACOM, 2007.

- Smith, Paul. *Lead with a Story: A Guide to Crafting Business Narratives That Captivate, Convince, and Inspire.* New York: AMACOM, 2012.

- Snyder, Blake. *Save the Cat! The Last Book on Screenwriting You'll Ever Need.* Studio City, CA: Michael Wiese Productions, 2005.

- Vogler, Christopher. *The Writer's Journey: Mythic Structure for Storytellers and Screenwriters.* Studio City, CA: Michael Wiese Productions, 1992.

- Zak, Paul J. *The Moral Molecule: The Source of Love and Prosperity.* New York: Dutton Adult, 2012.

Websites

- Callahan, Shawn. "Anecdote." Accessed June 20, 2014. http://www.anecdote.com.

- Center for Narrative Studies. "The Center for Narrative Studies." Accessed January 14, 2015. http://www.storywise.com.

- The Creativity Hub. "Rory's Story Cubes." Accessed December 31, 2014. https://www.storycubes.com.

- DinoIgnacio. "Pixar's 22 Rules of Storytelling." Imgur. September 15, 2013. Accessed June 20, 2014. http://imgur.com/a/fPLnM.

- Get Storied. "Change Your Story. Change Your World." Accessed January 14, 2015. http://www.getstoried.com.

- Internet Archive. "Full Text of 'The Thirty-Six Dramatic Situations.'" Accessed November 12, 2014. http://archive.org/stream/thirtysixdramati00poltuoft/thirtysixdramati00poltuoft_djvu.txt.

- Komond. (2008). "Kuleshov Effect / Efecto Kuleshov 'Amar el Cine.'" YouTube video, 00:45. January 14, 2008. https://www.youtube.com/watch?v=grCPqoFwp5k.

- New Story Leadership. "New Story Leadership." Accessed January 14, 2015. http://www.newstoryleadership.org.

- Snowden, Dave. "CognitiveEdge." Accessed June 20, 2014. http://cognitive-edge.com.

- Trivium. "LEGO® SERIOUS PLAY® method." Accessed January 1, 2015. http://www.trivium.dk/LEGO-SERIOUS-PLAY/LEGO-SERIOUS-PLAY-method.

- VisualsSpeak. "Want to Get New Insights?" Accessed January 14, 2015. http://visualsspeak.com.

Contributors, Partners, and Friends

Meet my friends and collaborators who contributed their wisdom to *Circle of the 9 Muses*. These are among the most influential and innovative thinkers in the organizational story community. I encourage you to check out their work, follow them on Twitter, subscribe to their blogs, ravenously chew into their books . . . and, in the instances where they have provided their contact information, reach out to them directly.

To the contributors who are featured here: Allow me to say once again, thank you for your generosity, your extraordinary spirit of collaboration, and your wisdom and laughter.

Emory!

Ollie!

276

Mary Alice Arthur • *Story Activist*

Mary Alice uses story in service of positive systemic shift and to create collective intelligence on critical issues. Her art is creating and hosting spaces for wise action, and narrative practice forms a key part of her work. Her powerful results from a telecommunications merger project were written up in the book *Wake Me Up When the Data Is Over: How Organizations Use Stories to Drive Results* (ed: Lori Silverman). She is a steward of the Art of Hosting and works with participatory practice all over the world.

Mary Alice's work demonstrates her belief that stories are the key to unleashing our knowledge, the wisdom is in the group, and that life is too short to have a boring meeting, an unchallenged imagination, or an uninspiring conversation. She is a powerful synthesizer and meaningmaker, valued for her ability to make the complex understandable, the simple profound, and the pathway clear.

• www.ArtOfHosting.org

• www.GetSoaring.com

Madelyn Blair, PhD • *Author, speaker, and consultant to management*

Madelyn Blair is a speaker, author, and senior consultant to management. Her specialty is unlocking personal resilience for individuals ready for a change and for teams needing to meet today's complex challenges with greater ease. Her background includes knowledge management and institutional analysis.

Dr. Blair is a regular visiting speaker at Columbia University and is a Taos Institute Associate and charter member of the Associates Council to the Board. She is on the Board of American Friends of Chartres. Dr. Blair received her doctorate in organizational psychology from the University of Tilburg, The Netherlands, and holds an MBA from The Wharton School.

She is the author of *Riding the Current* and *Essays in Two Voices*. She is a contributing author of *Lessons from the Field, Wake Me Up When the Data Is Over, Making it Real: Sustaining Knowledge Management*, and *Smarter Innovation*.

• www.MadelynBlair.com

• Twitter: @MadelynBlair

Bobette Buster • *Writer/Producer*

Bobette Buster, writer/producer of the feature documentary, MAKING WAVES: THE ART OF CINEMATIC SOUND, with Midge Costin (director) and Karen Johnson. A story consultant for Hollywood studios and major European production companies, Bobette is on the Guest Faculty of Pixar, Disney Animation, Sony Animation, Twentieth Century Fox, Catholic University of Milan, La Fémis (Paris), Screen Training Ireland, North By Northwest (Denmark).

She was a Creative Executive for Director Tony Scott (*Top Gun, Man on Fire*), Production Consultant with Larry Gelbart (HBO, Emmy Best Film, *Barbarians at the Gate*). She is author of *DO STORY: How to Tell Your Story So the World Listens* (Do Book Co., 2013), available on Amazon, iTunes, and favorite bookstores. A graduate and Adj. Professor of the University of Southern California's Peter Stark Producing Program, she created the first MFA curriculum for Feature Film, Television Story Development.

- www.BobetteBuster.com

- Email: info@bobettebuster.com

- Twitter: @BobetteBuster

- See her 20-minute DO LECTURE, "Can You Tell Your Story?" http://beta.thedolectures.co.uk/lectures/can-you-tell-your-story/

Shawn Callahan • *Founder of Anecdote*

Shawn is one of the world's leading business storytelling consultants.

He started his career in technology with companies such as Oracle and IBM but realized, at the end of the day, it was the human factors that determined the success of any enterprise.

In 2004 he founded Anecdote, a firm that helps leaders be better oral storytellers and corporations embed their strategies using stories.

Anecdote works with Global 1000 companies such as Shell, Danone, Microsoft, and Bayer all around the world.

Anecdote licenses its business storytelling programs to companies around the globe and currently has 28 partners in 19 countries.

Shawn is based in Melbourne, Australia, and can be contacted at www.anecdote.com

- www.Anecdote.com

- LinkedIn: au.linkedin.com/in/shawncallahan

- Twitter: @ShawnCallahan

Slash Coleman • *Professional Storyteller/Author*

NPR calls the award-winning storyteller who shares a name with a famous guitarist "extremely provocative and entertaining," and WGBH claims "Slash Coleman's storytelling performances have the power to change the way people think."

The NYC based author of *The Bohemian Love Diaries* and a personal perspectives blogger for *Psychology Today*, Slash is best known for his PBS Special *The Neon Man and Me* and is currently creating *The New American Storyteller* for PBS.

Slash's performances have been featured on stages nationwide including: TEDx, The International Storytelling Center, and Pete Seeger's Clearwater Festival and included in: *American Theatre Magazine, Backstage Magazine, The Washington Post*, and most recently on the NPR series, "How Artists Make Money."

• www.SlashColeman.com

• Email: info@slashcoleman.com

• Phone: 804-353-3799

• Twitter: @SlashColeman

Paul Andrew Costello • *Founder and President at New Story Leadership*

Paul Andrew Costello is an internationally recognized expert in narrative practice, having been a pioneer of the story revolution now revitalizing leadership and coaching in the corporate world. In 1995 he formed the National Center for Narrative Studies (www.storywise.com) where he developed the signature CNS methods of Living Stories and Narrative Room. These methods helped inaugurate the famous Golden Fleece group in Washington, and have been adapted in use by his many graduates. He has applied the power of narrative to diverse challenges, including a book on Obama's election strategy (*The Presidential Plot*) and to global peace by working with young leaders from Northern Ireland and Ireland (www.wiprogram.org), South Africa (www.sawip.org), and Israel and Palestine (www.newstoryeadership.org). Paul's new work embraces maps as a parallel tool to stories harnessing the power of narrative to help us navigate a world that seems to have lost its way.

• www.NewStoryLeadership.org

Karen Dietz • *Speaker, Author, Trainer, Coach and CEO of Just Story It*

Karen Dietz combines the science of storytelling with the art of performing to create stories that inspire, influence, and impact a company's bottom line. Her motto says it all: "If you want results, just story it!" Karen's clients: Disney, Princess Cruises, nonprofits, and entrepreneurs.

Wiley Publishers recruited Karen to write *Business Storytelling for Dummies* (2013). She is also the top global curator on business storytelling at www.scoop.it/t/just-story-it with 15,000+ followers. Witness her in action as she opens the San Diego 2014 TEDx conference with the power of story listening for changing lives. See https://www.youtube.com/watch?v=ahN_FDHFWmg

Her office is actually an art gallery of her hand-dyed silk panels of favorite story principles she uses with clients. Karen partners with JVA Art Group to bring amazing corporate stories to lobby and staff areas.

She received her MA and PhD in Folklore from the University of Pennsylvania.

• www.JustStoryIt.com

Terrence Gargiulo • *Organizational Development Consultant*

Terrence Gargiulo, MMHS is an organizational development consultant specializing in the use of stories. For his creative work with narrative, *INC* Magazine awarded him their Marketing Master Award. Terrence's story-based communication skills assessment earned him the 2008 HR Leadership Award from the Asia Pacific HRM Congress. He is a frequent speaker at international and national conferences.

Terrence wrote the libretto for his father's opera *Tryillias* which was accepted for a nomination for the 2004 Pulitzer Prize in music. In 2009, he co-founded the Occhiata Foundation to produce American operas and promote arts engagement in schools through the multi-discipline prism of opera.

Terrence enjoys scuba diving, cooking, singing, and fencing. He was a Junior National Champion, member of three US Junior World Championship teams, NCAA All American, and an alternate for the 1996 Olympics.

• www.MakingStories.net

• Email: terrence@makingstories.net

• Phone: 415-948-8087

Marcus Hummon • *Songwriter, recording artist, composer, playwright, author*

The songs of Grammy-winner Marcus Hummon have been recorded in genres diverse as pop, R&B, gospel and most notably in country music. His best known hits are "Bless the Broken Road" (Rascal Flatts), "Cowboy Take Me Away" and "Ready To Run" (The Dixie Chicks), "Born To Fly" (Sara Evans), "One Of These Days" (Tim McGraw), and "Only Love" (Wynonna). In 2005, "Bless the Broken Road" won the Grammy for Best Country Song. He has garnered numerous BMI awards, including five #1 awards from BMI.

In theatre, Hummon has written six musicals and an opera. Three of his musicals, "Warrior" and "The Piper," and the musical-dance-hybrid "Tut" were featured Off-Broadway as part of the New York New Musical Festival. "Warrior" and "American Duet" received invitations to be work-shopped at the prestigious Eugene O'Neill Summer Conference. His latest work for the theater exploring the life of Frederick Douglass will be premiered in 2015.

• www.MarcusHummonMusic.com

Robbie Hutchens • *Licensed Marriage and Family Therapist, President of Signet House*

Robbie Robinson Hutchens is a licensed marriage and family therapist and has been leveraging her clinical skills for 18 years. She is a clinical member of the American Association for Marriage and Family Therapists. Her systems training and creative mindset enable her to glean the complexities of relationships and equip her clients to manage their lives in a collaborative, refreshing manner.

Her practice also hosts a one-of-a-kind play therapy "clubhouse" that young children find engaging, safe, and fun. She supports the System of Care philosophy and is a volunteer member of the Coalition for Children's Mental Health for the State of Tennessee.

Robbie co-wrote a chapter, entitled "More Is Different: Understanding and Engaging the Exceptionally Gifted Child" in the *Handbook for Counselors Serving Students with Gifts and Talents: Development, Relationships, School Issues, and Counseling Needs/Interventions*, Prufrock Press, November 2011.

• www.SignetHouseLLC.com

Michelle James • *CEO, The Center for Creative Emergence*

Michelle James has been pioneering Applied Creativity, Storytelling, and Improvisation in business since the nineties. She founded the Capitol Creativity Network in DC and the Cville Creativity Network in Charlottesville, VA. Michelle is a business creativity consultant, facilitator, and coach who has designed and delivered hundreds of programs for entrepreneurs and organizations. Known for creating richly textured learning environments that weave together storytelling, improvisation, and other whole-brain approaches with creative solution finding methods and sound business practices, her work has been featured on television, the radio, and in several books. Michelle performed full-length improvised plays for 10 years and developed Quantum Leap Business Improv. She was recognized for Visionary Leadership in *Fast Company*'s blog, Leading Change; produced two Creativity in Business Conferences and a Creativity in Business Telesummit. She's writing a book, *Pattern Breaks: A Facilitator's Guide to Cultivating Creativity*, due out this year.

• www.CreativeEmergence.com

• www.CreativeEmergence.com/improv.html

Billy Kirsch • *President, Kidbilly Music, LLC*

Grammy and Emmy nominated, CMA and ACM award-winning songwriter Billy Kirsch has harnessed the power of creativity to lead a successful life as an entertainer and entrepreneur. His body of work includes award-winning songs and career songs for the artists who have recorded them. "Holes in the Floor of Heaven," recorded by Steve Wariner, won a Country Music Association song of the year award, was nominated for a Grammy award and was a number one hit. The list of artists who have recorded Billy's songs include Tim McGraw, Kenny Rogers, Englebert Humperdink, Alabama, Lee Greenwood, and Wynonna.

Billy's abilities as facilitator, leader, and performer are the foundation of his highly successful corporate event programs, Team Building Through Song® and Harnessing Your Creative Power. The presentations help people rediscover their creativity to become more innovative and engaged in their work.

• www.KidBillyMusic.com

• Email: events@kidbillymusic.com.

Kat Koppett • *Founder, Koppett + Company*

Kat Koppett, Eponymous Founder of Koppett + Company, holds a BFA from NYU, and an MA in Organizational Psychology from Columbia. She has lectured at Stanford, UC Berkeley, RPI, and Skidmore. Her book on the use of improvisational theater techniques for business development, *Training to Imagine*, has been called a seminal work in the field. In addition, Kat is a Certified Professional Co-active Coach, and the co-director of The Mop & Bucket Theatre Company.

Koppett & Company has designed and delivered programs for a diverse roster of organizations, large and small, including the Clinton Global Initiative, Apple, Facebook, Prezi, Chanel, Eli Lilly, AAA, JPMorgan Chase, Merck, Havas Health, and GE. Her most fulfilling improv gig to date is playing Mama to her daughter, Lia, who teaches her profound lessons daily.

•   www.Koppett.com

Per Kristiansen • *Partner, Trivium*

Per Kristiansen has been partner in Trivium since 2006. He spent a number of years working in the LEGO Group. First, as change agent in the Pre-School area, he then joined the LEGO SERIOUS PLAY activities, initially Executive Discovery, the start-up that developed and managed the method and later in the LEGO Company. Initially Per's role was two pronged: 1) Master Trainer and 2) Responsible for Europe and the Middle-East. When Executive Discovery was closed down and LEGO SERIOUS PLAY became part of LEGO, Per took on the role as global manager of LEGO SERIOUS PLAY.

Per has a masters degree in intercultural business, and has spent his career helping companies accelerate change and innovation, and in developing robust strategies. He has been based in Italy, Scandinavia, and in the UK. He now lives in Copenhagen with his partner Christina and their two sons.

•   per.kristiansen@trivium.dk

•   Twitter: @Per_LSP

Cynthia Kurtz • *Researcher and consultant*

Cynthia F. Kurtz is a researcher, software developer, consultant, and writer who has been helping communities and organizations work with their stories since 1999. Originally an ethologist, Cynthia discovered the field of organizational narrative at IBM Research, where she conducted research projects to help IBM develop internal and client services centered around organizational stories. She built on that work at IBM's Institute for Knowledge Management and at the consulting firm Cognitive Edge before launching her independent consultancy in 2009. She has consulted on over eighty narrative projects for a variety of clients in government, for-profit, and non-profit sectors. In 2008 she self-published the first edition of her textbook, *Working with Stories in Your Community or Organization*. Now in its third edition, the book is widely considered a vital resource for participatory story work. Cynthia lives in upstate New York with her husband and son.

• www.CFKurtz.com

• Email: cfkurtz@cfkurtz.com

Jody Lentz • *Facilitator*

Jody Lentz facilitates better teams, better meetings, and better decisions. His creative communication and innovative, visual approach help organizations think, plan and act strategically. His professional passion is engaging organizations to create high-performance, low-drama work cultures.

Since 2004, Jody's work has spanned the government, non-profit, and education sectors, as well as a wide range of established, entrepreneurial, and social business ventures.

Jody employs a deep and wide bag of tricks to transform planning meetings and workshops into lean-forward, hands-on learning experiences. One of these is "Think With Your Hands," a workshop powered by LEGO® SERIOUS PLAY™, which Jody introduced to David Hutchens, who now uses this workshop as one of his many story-telling tools.

Jody is a native of Nashville, TN, USA, where he lives with his wife of over 25 years; they have three sons and a grandson.

• www.ThinkWithYourHands.com

• Twitter: @Jody_Lentz

Michael Margolis • *CEO of Get Storied; Founder of StoryU*

Michael Margolis is a teacher, author, and entrepreneur. For 12 years, he's worked at the leading-edge of the storytelling movement. Michael helps lead the world's largest school for business storytelling. He also teaches "narrative intelligence" to companies like Bloomberg, SAP, and TATA. Michael is obsessed with how the Internet is evolving the way we approach innovation, marketing, and the humanization of business. The son of an inventor and artist, Michael has always been curious about the deepest mysteries. As a lifelong seeker, story is his yoga. Michael speaks frequently at venues including SXSW, TEDx, Google, Zappos, and UN Foundation. His work has been featured in *Fast Company, Wired*, and Mashable. He is also one of Twitter's leading voices on #storytelling. His most recent book is *Believe Me: A Storytelling Manifesto for Change-Makers and Innovators*. Michael is left-handed, color-blind, and eats more chocolate than the average human.

- www.GetStoried.com/redpill

- michaelm@getstoried.com

- Phone: 855-GO-STORY

- Twitter: @GetStoried

Christine Martell • *Principal Image Wrangler*

Christine is an artist, facilitator, and consultant specializing in using visuals to deepen conversations and uncover new stories. Her VisualsSpeak® tools are used by individuals and organizations around the world who want to improve their lives, teams, and performance through surfacing other ways of looking at the world. Communication deepens and we can more fully understand what each person means by what they are saying by using visuals.

She lives in Hillsboro Oregon where she serves on the leadership team of the local arts council and other community arts organizations.

- www.VisualsSpeak.com

Thaler Pekar • *CEO, Thaler Pekar & Partners*

Thaler Pekar is an internationally recognized pioneer in narrative and communication. Thaler guides smart leaders in finding, developing, and sharing stories that break through an increasingly complex marketplace and rally critical support. Her Heart, Head & Hand™ framework for persuasive communication is directing entrepreneurs and advocates throughout the world in increasing sales, visibility, income, and influence.

Thaler co-facilitated the opening plenary of the most recent Smithsonian Institution Conference on Organizational Storytelling. She often lectures at Syracuse University's S.I. Newhouse School of Public Communications and the Columbia University Graduate Program in Strategic Communications, and she is a contributor to the *Stanford Social Innovation Review*.

Thaler is a long-time resident of Hoboken, NJ, and a more recent resident of Unadilla, NY. She always crosses the street to walk on the sunny side, and she has a cat named Truthiness.

• www.ThalerPekar.com

• Email: tpekar@thalerpekar.com

• Twitter: @Thaler

Barry L. Rellaford • *President, Great Work Worldwide*

Barry Rellaford's great work is to help people discover, express, and fulfill their great work, which is not only what we do, but who we are.

Barry is the founder of Great Work Worldwide, a consultancy focused on inspiring individuals and organizations to perform meaningful and sustainable work. He is also a co-founder and master facilitator of FranklinCovey's Speed of Trust practice and co-authored the business fable, *A Slice of Trust* (Gibbs Smith, 2011). As an international speaker and consultant, he has shared transformational ideas about purpose, trust, and leadership with people from over one hundred countries. His clients include Procter & Gamble, Kroger, LEGO, G&J Pepsi Bottling, and Ford Motor Company.

Barry and his wife, Lorilee, live in the shadows of the Rocky Mountains with their family. Barry's interests outside of work include family activities, music, reading, people development, and the American West.

• Email: barryrellaford@mac.com

Dick Richardson • *Leadeership Development Expert*

Dick is a leadership development expert working with C-suite executives. Prior to owning his own consulting practice he was Director of Leadership Development for ITT, responsible for all executive and leadership development.

Prior to ITT, Dick held a variety of leadership positions in learning at IBM. His last position was IBM Director; Management Development, responsible for leadership curriculum for all IBM managers and executives. He was the founding Director of the IBM Center for Advanced Learning and holds two patents for innovations in organizational learning. Dick's international experience includes being the Manager of Management Development for IBM Asia based in Hong Kong, and numerous other overseas assignments. He has been recognized with numerous industry awards in leadership development and learning.

Limor Shiponi, Storyteller • *CEO, The Storytelling Company*

Limor Shiponi is a professional storyteller and CEO with The Storytelling Company Inc, Israel. She is involved in business practices concerning strategy, marketing, and organizational culture, and is the leading social media and content strategist for tech companies and corporations in Israel. She is highly involved in storytelling—the art and practice. Her English blog is well known among professionals, being an arena for debate and deep insights about the art.

Limor's heart's desire is with music, eventually becoming a practicing orchestra conductor. Her other fields of interest are numerous and she crossbreeds knowledge while performing her favorite sport—seeking and finding deep solutions to complex issues. Her latest storytelling program 'Honor Price' demonstrates less-known facets of her personal interests – the ability to balance the chalice and the blade, survival, women's doings in a man's world and sustainability.

Limor is the author of *Stories at Work* (Hebrew, 2006)

• www.LimorShiponi.com

David Sibbet • *Founder, Grove*

David Sibbett is President and founder of The Grove Consultants International. He is a master facilitator and considered a leader in the booming field of visual facilitation. The Grove is based in San Francisco and is hub to a global network of associates, partners, and other visual practitioners.

David is author of the best-selling Visual Leadership Series from John Wiley & Sons, including *Visual Meetings, Visual Teams*, and *Visual Leaders*. David is also designer of the Grove's Sustainable Organizations Model, the Drexler/Sibbet Team Performance System, the Grove's Visual Planning Systems, and author of The Grove's Facilitation Series.

He holds a Masters Degree in Journalism from Northwestern University, a BA in English from Occidental College, and a Coro Fellowship in Public Affairs. In 2013 he was awarded the Organizational Development Network's lifetime achievement award for creative contribution to the field of OD.

- www.Grove.com

- www.Davidsibbet.com

Lori L. Silverman • *Strategist, owner, Partners for Progress*®

Lori L. Silverman has authored *Stories Trainers Tell* (with Mary Wacker, Jossey-Bass/Pfeiffer, 2003), *Wake Me Up When the Data Is Over: How Organizations Use Stories to Drive Results* (Jossey-Bass, 2006), and *Business Storytelling for Dummies* (with Karen Dietz, PhD, Wiley, 2013). Bright House Networks, APHL, Lydig Construction, Homewatch Caregivers, and conference attendees have benefitted from her highly energized, practical, results-driven approach to the subject as a hands-on consultant and keynote and workshop presenter. Lori's also showcased tangible outcomes from workplace story use on more than 70 radio and TV shows.

As owner of Partners for Progress®, for 25 years she's facilitated enterprise-wide change and strategic planning initiatives for organizations such as American Family Insurance, the American Legion Auxiliary, Bechtel, Chevron, Duquesne University, Valmet, and the U.S. Air Force Reserves. Lori holds an M.S. degree in counseling and guidance from the University of Wisconsin, Madison and an MBA from Edgewood College.

- www.PartnersForProgress.com

- www.Business-Storytelling.com

- Phone: 800/253-6398

- Email: pfprogress@aol.com

Annette Simmons • *Author, Trainer, Speaker*

Annette helps organizations uncover their truth, and tell it. Her first two books focused on uncovering truth within organizations. *A Safe Place for Dangerous Truth* (1998), and *Territorial Games: Understanding and Ending Turf Wars at Work* (1997) showed how to reveal hidden agendas, unproductive internal "stories," and how to better manage group dynamics so teams thrive and flourish. This experience taught her the emotional clarity and power a story brings to messages of every kind. Her groundbreaking book *The Story Factor* (2001) was named by 1-800-CEO-Read as one of *The 100 Best Business Books of All Time* (2009, Penguin). Her books have been translated into 11 languages. The second edition of her how-to book, *Whoever Tells the Best Story Wins* (2007) comes out in May 2015.

Annette lives back in her hometown of Shreveport, Louisiana with Lucy, an Italian greyhound of substance and style.

• www.AnnetteSimmons.com

• Twitter: @TheStoryFactor

• Phone: 318-525-3012

Paul Smith • *Speaker, trainer, and author*

Paul is a popular keynote speaker, corporate trainer in leadership and storytelling techniques, and former executive and 20-year veteran of The Procter & Gamble Company. He is also the best-selling author of *Lead with a Story: A Guide to Crafting Business Narratives That Captivate, Convince, and Inspire* and *Parenting with a Story: Real-life Lessons in Character for Parents and Children to Share.*

As part of his research he has personally interviewed over 200 CEOs and executives in dozens of countries around the world. His work has been featured in *The Wall Street Journal, Inc.* magazine, *Time, Forbes, The Washington Post, Success Magazine*, and *Investors Business Daily* among others.

Paul holds a bachelors degree in economics, and an MBA from the Wharton School at the University of Pennsylvania. He lives with his wife and two sons in the Cincinnati suburb of Mason, Ohio.

• www.LeadWithAStory.com

• Email: paul@leadwithastory.com

Graham Williams • *Thought Provoker*

Capetonian Graham Williams is the author of six books. *The Virtuosa Organisation: The Importance of Virtues for a Successful Business* is to be published by Knowledge Resources early 2015.

The rationale for *The Halo and the Noose: The Power of Story Telling and Story Listening in Business Life* is that stories can free us or trap us. Like the two-edged sword, they can open us to new possibilities or choke and strangle us in existing paradigms and orientations. Writer Dan McKinnon advises, "A halo has to fall only a few inches to be a noose." The reverse is also true.

Graham's formal disciplines are psychology, economics, consumer behaviour, and business economics. He is a Certified Management Consultant and Executive Coach who brings loads of business experience and insight into the role and manner of using story to contribute to business life, and has worked in over 40 countries.

• www.HaloAndNoose.com

• Email: grahamwilliams@change.co.za

About the Author

David Hutchens is an author, business writer, and learning designer who creates communication and learning solutions for IBM, The Coca-Cola Company, Walmart, General Electric, Dannon, Nike, and many others.

A nationally recognized developer of innovative learning products, David's work has been recognized with distinctions such as *Training and Development*'s Training Product of the Year, the American Society for Training & Development's (now called the Association for Talent Development) prestigious Excellence in Practice Award, Brandon Hall Gold Award, and more.

He is creator of the Learning Fables—a book series that uses narratives and metaphors to illustrate principles of organizational learning. With titles that include *Outlearning the Wolves* and *Shadows of the Neanderthal*, the books have been translated into more than a dozen languages.

In partnership with The Conference Board, he is the creator and lead facilitator of the Team USA Leadership Development Experience, at the Olympic Training Center in Colorado Springs, and he is a facilitator of the Apollo Leadership Development Experience at the National Aeronautics and Space Administration's (NASA) Johnson Space Center in Houston and Kennedy Space Center in Cape Canaveral, Florida.

David is codeveloper of *GO Team: Powering Teams to Perform*, a just-in-time team-training resource. GO Team's library of 18 team-related topics allows you to build your own learning agenda tailored to your team's needs. Learn more at www.GoTeamResources.com.

He is developer of *The Speed of Trust: A Simulation*, a discovery learning program that is cobranded with Stephen M. R. Covey's best-seller *The Speed of Trust*.

He is the creator of learning maps for FranklinCovey, and for organizations in diverse industries, such as retail, pharmaceutical, financial, and manufacturing.

David led Storytelling in Organizations, a special interest group, and frequently speaks to organizations all around the world about the use of stories and metaphor as a way of creating shared meaning, preserving culture, disseminating learning, and speeding change in organizations.

David lives outside of Nashville, Tennessee, where he is coowner of Signet House LLC, a family therapy clinic he runs with his wife, Robbie (a marriage and family therapist). He has two teenaged children, Emory and Ollie.

Connect with David

- *Web*: www.DavidHutchens.com

- *Twitter*: @DavidBHutchens

- *LinkedIn*: www.linkedin.com/in/davidhutchens/

- *Public Facebook page*: www.facebook.com/DavidHutchens9Muse

- *Instagram*: http://instagram.com/davidbhutchens

- *About Me portal*: www.about.me/hutchens

- *GO Team™—Powering Team Performance*: www.GoTeamResources.com

- *Learning Fables*: www.leveragenetworks.com/store/learning-fables-set or www.Amazon.com

Explore 9 Muse Resources

Visit www.DavidHutchens.com today for facilitator materials, free downloads, information about 9 Muse Archetype Cards, and other resources that can help your bring the power of story to life in your team.

Index